THE AMERICAN IDEAL

THE AMERICAN IDEAL

Literary History as a Worldly Activity

PETER CARAFIOL

New York   Oxford
OXFORD UNIVERSITY PRESS
1991

Oxford University Press

Oxford   New York   Toronto
Delhi   Bombay   Calcutta   Madras   Karachi
Petaling Jaya   Singapore   Hong Kong   Tokyo
Nairobi   Dar es Salaam   Cape Town
Melbourne   Auckland

and associated companies in
Berlin   Ibadan

Published by Oxford University Press, Inc.,
200 Madison Avenue, New York, New York 10016

Oxford is a registered trademark of Oxford University Press

Library of Congress Cataloging-in-Publication Data
Carafiol, Peter C.
The American ideal : literary history as a worldly activity /
Peter Carafiol.
p.   cm.
Includes index.
ISBN 0-19-506765-7
1. American literature—History and criticism—Theory, etc.
2. National characteristics, American, in literature.
3. Criticism—United States—History.   I. Title.
PS25.C37   1991
810.9—dc20   90-45506   CIP

2 4 6 8 9 7 5 3 1
Printed in the United States of America
on acid-free paper

For
Mary Coulter Carafiol
and
Joseph Carafiol

Acknowledgments

During its long evolution, this book had the good luck to keep falling into the right hands. Friends and colleagues read part or all of the manuscript in its numberless versions, curbing its excesses and amending its deficiencies. In their sympathetic and constructive responses, they have been an ideal audience.

I am particularly grateful to my erstwhile colleague Bob Levine, who read draft after draft without complaint and with unerring good judgment. Johanna Smith disciplined my prose and clarified my thinking. Bill Spengemann repeatedly showed me, as he has for twenty years, how to mind my own argument. To Steve Mailloux my debts are more numerous and profound than I can account for here. Ours are the most productive disagreements I can imagine.

In its late stages, this book benefited from insightful readings by William Cain and Martha Banta. They retuned my sense of my audience and helped me see my own book in a clearer light. Finally, my friends Lisa Keppinger and Stan Beyer read the whole manuscript at the last moment with a care and intelligence that averted numerous false steps.

Much of this work was written or rewritten during a year of leisure made possible by an NEH Fellowship. I am grateful to the Endowment for making that work possible. Early versions of some portions of Parts I and III appeared in *The Centennial Review, American Literature,* and *College English.* I am grateful for permission to reprint that material here.

Contents

THE AMERICAN IDEAL

Introduction

Since 1980, when I began the work that has become this book, the field of American Literary Scholarship has come alive with self-criticism. After two centuries during which a belief in an idealized national identity sustained popular and scholarly discourse about American writing, and inspired the establishment of American Literary Scholarship as an academic institution, the ideal of "America" has become an easy target. The ascendancy of poststructuralist thinking in the profession over the past fifteen years has made it almost obligatory, even for Americanists, to dismiss as "myth" or repressive ideology what had hitherto been the unquestioned credo of their field. Like Scripture under the scrutiny of eighteenth-century German biblical criticism, "America" has lost its privileged status as a transcendent signifier and become an "other." It is no longer shocking for a scholar who has specialized for years in American literary history to say that "America" is, in several senses, passé—a thing of the past, a (long-term) fashion become old-fashioned, an object of scrutiny now firmly located *in* history, a product of historical motives subject to historical analysis and critique.

This trend might seem to support the claim that we are coming to the end of a particular way of talking about America, a way that depended on the assumption that to use the word *America* is to say something special, to do more than merely designate a political and geographical fact. That American Ideal has taken many forms during the past 200 years, but in American Literary Scholarship it found itself enshrined in a profession. And although American Literary Scholarship is not its only professional expression (there are others that depend on it still more heavily—like the military), academic scholars have been charged with enforcing its discipline over what is to be considered great writing in the United States.

This way of talking about America was an early strategy for adapting the model of Christian history to a post-theological, historical age, and it has provided its adherents with a way of telling a particular kind of story. Ever since Columbus conflated the New World with the Earthly Paradise, the American Ideal has been, like the Bible, a way of constraining particular interpretations by attaching them to something ostensibly solid and unchanging, at once real and ideal. As the focus of attention in Western culture has shifted from heaven to history, it has offered one of many strategies, a particularly powerful one, for containing historical uncertainty. It did not make sense of history by looking beyond history into a timeless world where the meaning was located. It found meaning in historical conditions themselves and imagined a historical progression leading not outside time into a new world of the spirit but into a New World of geography—the Promised Land.

For centuries, the word *America* has unified historical particulars and united oppositions, giving coherence to historical accounts. It provided a reason for beginning them and promised an organizing end. Dwelling in history, it continued to provide a model of ahistorical closure and totality that shaped the very narrative forms that have been marshaled to explain it. Now, 500 years later, even as we toy with interpretive "free play," the very persistence of American Literary Scholarship as a field implicates us in the rhetorical constraints of this all too familiar discourse. Even as we shake off the temptations of overarching theoretical strategies for explaining interpretation, we acquiesce in disciplinary conformity to essentially theological assumptions. In the starkest terms, as long as Americanists cling to this model despite the growing professional interest in developing alternatives to ahistorical historical accounts, the institution of American Literary Scholarship will enshrine a reactionary view of history, of explanatory narrative, and a reactionary and dangerous view of America itself.[1]

In this work, I want to suggest that despite revolutionary appearances and some real progress in the direction of a more historical critical practice, the ruling assumptions of American literary study sit more firmly on the throne than recent critical rhetoric would suggest. In the very midst of the energetic critique in the field over the past few years, its traditional practice abides more or less intact. That practice is shored up by its intricate and profound articulation with the ways Americanists generate histories and with the particular histories they have generated. Though the current critique of the field presents itself as having escaped these problems by dissenting from formalist methods and the canonical choices of the previous academic generation, actually it continues the larger tradition by adhering to characteristic forms of narrative coherence and to critical claims that oscillate between the cultural and aesthetic models of literary explanation that have always characterized American literary study.

Scholarly stories that do not correspond to this professional paradigm by reiterating in currently fashionable critical terms the coherence, or even the possible coherence, of a story about America are burdened, as far as reception within the field is concerned, with serious, perhaps fatal, disadvantages. Stories that would place American writing in English in the tradition of world writing in English, or direct students interested in the New World influence on writing to innumerable texts in numerous languages other than English, or even displace the Puritans as the founders of the American character and of American figurative strategies hint that we may not really know as much as we have thought about the subject we have been professing all these years. They suggest that in the very act of establishing a disciplinary field, we have unwittingly and with the best of intentions attained the appearance of mastery only by radically and (ultimately) self-destructively narrowing our inquiries. Even if such unwelcome observations could reverse the artificial (how could it be anything else?) isolation of our particular critical discourse from the larger critical conversation, who is glad to hear a story like that?

I first fronted this unpleasant fact at an earlier stage of this project, while it was still a book about Transcendentalism. As I read the history of scholarship in that field, I became convinced that, as a critical category, the word *Transcendentalism* was not only a fiction, like all organizing terms, but an obsolete fiction, one that had no purpose anymore. Worse still, even flushed as I was with the excitement of discovery, I saw that, by its own logic, my "revelation" could not have much of an audience. Because Transcendentalism was simply no longer part of any live debate, no one would much care whether it lived or died apart from the small group of specialists who had made it the focus of their professional lives and could not be expected to jump enthusiastically aboard my bandwagon. But, as I gradually came to see, the very fact that the fate of a belief so central to the larger field of American literature could be of so little general interest in the profession (much less in the culture) says something important (and depressing) about the institution of American Literary Scholarship as it is now constituted.

Thus my study of the critical institution of Transcendentalism led me outside that institution, as I believe the study of texts by Americans should dissolve the borders of what has been called American literature and lead beyond them to a reconsideration of literary history in general. American Literary Scholarship is a particularly useful case study in the larger problems that have inspired recent debate over the aims and methods of literary study in general. Those problems are grounded in the nineteenth-century origins of the discipline and bespeak the political and intellectual conditions that prevailed at the time. They have been preserved into our own time largely by disciplinary interests where they continue to shape practice, even as they inspire dissatisfaction, dissent, and the desire for revision. Therefore, my institutional critique leads to a consideration of the way the assumptions embodied in the American Ideal have also founded the sorts of historical narratives scholars conventionally produce.

Starting with a critique of the contemporary conversation about how to write an American literary history on historicist rather than ideal grounds, Part 1 argues that the revisionist trend is at once healthy in its skepticism about the tradition and too sanguine in its implicit claims to have left that tradition safely behind. It suggests that a foundational appeal to the American Ideal persists, though in altered form, even in those revisionist critics who want to make American literary studies more fully historical. Their revisionist attack on the American myth, for all its polemical point, has not thrust deeply enough, principally because critics have not sufficiently acknowledged either the profound influence of the American Ideal or the depth of their own complicity with it. Even among revisionists, I submit, that myth continues to legislate the kind of questions Americanists ask and the kind of claims they must make for their explanations, questions and claims that are inconsistent with the historicist assumptions of revisionist readings.

The rhetorical gestures of this tradition can be traced in the 100-year history of Transcendentalist scholarship, where their implications and consequences are fully elaborated. Part 2 offers a rhetorical history of that critical conversation from the "founding" of American Literary Scholarship at the beginning of the last quarter of the nineteenth century to the early 1970s, when the influence of Continental theory changed the direction of debate. While it adhered faithfully to this traditional rhetoric, Transcendentalist scholarship has always dwelled in an uneasy relationship with its own subject. On one hand, scholars have seen Transcendentalism as essential, both for their own professional self-definition and as the intellectual center of the larger field of American Literary Scholarship. On the other, Transcendentalism and particularly Transcendentalist texts never seemed to justify that centrality because they failed to meet established critical standards for either intellectual or logical coherence. My aim in this discussion is not to produce an institutional history that focuses on historical events and political motives but to trace the changes and the consistencies in the conversation about American writing as they appear in influential texts, texts that might be described as part of the canon of American literary criticism. I argue that these influential works and contemporary ones address analogous problems with analogous strategies and that the echo between them identifies the real problem, endemic in American literary history, as a more general one.

The subsequent chapters on Emerson and Thoreau in Part 3 propose that these writers, too, face the difficulties of writing explanatory narrative that recognizes its own place in history. But *their* prose suggests strategies for getting out of what I see as the current critical impasse. Viewed apart from the prevailing assumptions of American Literary Scholarship, their texts elicit another way of reading them, one that satisfies the impulse to make literature relevant, not by linking texts to the historical conditions of their production but by linking past texts to present interests.

If this choice of exemplars reveals my complicity in the traditional canon, it is not, at least, unwitting complicity. The point of these chapters is not so much to offer fresh readings of ''classic'' writers—an aim that would itself be suspect amidst professional debates about canonicity—as to illustrate, at least tentatively, an alternative to the most prominent current approaches to historical texts. Though revisionist discourse has focused, for the most part, on connections between text and context, I believe that the need to rationalize a relationship between the past and the present and to justify our interest in old books is at the heart of the desire for relevance that has motivated revisionist criticism. Rather than treating texts as windows into the past, indices of cultural conditions, I try to illustrate a way of making historical texts participate in contemporary conversations. Emerson and Thoreau are my texts here partly because they have been so much at the center of the critical conversation about American literature, but mostly because they have had the most profound influence on my work. It is they, rather than the numerous modern scholars from whom I have learned so much, who have taught me most of what I have to say in this book.

The final chapter elaborates on these points and reflects on the implications of Emerson's and Thoreau's prose strategies, and the posture toward the past they establish for American Literary Scholarship and for the aims and methods of literary history. By sandwiching a rhetorical history of Transcendentalist criticism and juxtaposed readings of texts by Emerson and Thoreau between accounts of the modern critical discourse, I hope to clarify the ways the literary practice of some nineteenth-century writers addresses the persistent problems posed by the critical tradition and points toward alternatives.

By calling attention to the lingering idealism inherent in the practice of American Literary Scholarship, my aim is to be both more rigorously historicist and more rhetorical. This book investigates some of the implications of assuming that American literature, like philosophy, does not describe a thing in the world, a territory for exploration, mapping, and development, but an institutionalized critical discourse, a structured conversation about selected texts.[2] While I do not believe that the institution of American Literary Scholarship could withstand the self-examination that its defense would require, given the intransigence of established institutions, the deepseatedness of our beliefs about America and its literature, I am not looking forward to rapid change. Debate about American Literary Scholarship, even in the context of the current revisionism, studiously avoids questions about its enabling critical choices. The risk is too great. Others, after all, have pointed out the logical limitations of the field and the incoherence of its assumptions. But Americanists' unwillingness to enter into substantial debate with voices of fundamental dissent from Yvor Winters to William Spengemann raises disturbing questions about what it takes to be heard in the critical conversation that constitutes American Literary Scholarship.[3] To entertain questions about those assumptions would be to acknowledge at least the theoretical possibility that they might be overturned and the field with them.

In my critique of that institution, I see myself less as a lone explorer plunging into uncharted territory than as a rabble-rouser clamoring, along with others, to get a hearing for unpopular views. The resulting soapbox tone of much of this book may seem to some occasionally intemperate. That tone, however, fairly reflects my share of the frustrations with many professional institutions and the assumptions, aims, and methods of professional scholarship that have fed the current fervor for disciplinary reform. Like many of my contemporaries, I believe we are not free from complicity in the trivialization of our work within our culture, and that the ways we pursue our study too often prevent the students we would like to reach from taking what we offer seriously. But unlike many of my colleagues, I do not believe that the solution to this problem will necessarily be found by thematizing contemporary political values in the texts we study or by subordinating the study of texts to the study of culture. The project of historicizing literary study in which so many scholars are engaged seems to me a more expansive and daunting one than that.

« 1 »

The Problem of American Literary Scholarship

Ah! The old questions, the old answers, there's nothing like them.

BECKETT

An abstract word is like a box with a false bottom; you may put in it what ideas you please and take them out again unobserved.

TOCQUEVILLE

I

After years of hostility, American Literary Scholarship appears to have taken critical theory into, if not its heart, at least its anthologies, proclaiming the virtues of its own diversity: We are large! We contain multitudes! But how trustworthy are appearances? As Terry Eagleton reminds us, "Critics who parade their pluralism are usually able to do so because the different methods they have in mind are not all that different in the end."[1] Like similar surprising reversals in Shakespearean comedies or Dickens novels, the long-deferred adoption of theory by American Literary Scholarship only discloses, somewhat belatedly, a concealed kinship. What is surprising is that Americanists have taken so long to acknowledge it. The explanations for both the long delay and the recent reconciliation can be discovered in the way changes in the prevailing theoretical discourse have meshed with the unchanging demands of American Literary Scholarship.

Stanley Fish describes theory as the effort to supply a set of rules that offer "some objective method of assessing" our claims to knowledge.[2]

10

So understood, theory is a relatively modern version of the more general foundationalist project. The belief in "America" is another, and older, variant formed on the Christian rather than the analytic model. Americanists initially distrusted theory because, as I argue in this book, American Literary Scholarship and the foundationalist version of theory that, until recently, dominated American critical discourse were mirror images of each other. Thus each saw the other as its opposite, despite their essential likeness. In the 200-year-old discourse about the nation and its literature, the belief in "America" has been, like the "theory" Fish describes, "an attempt to *guide* practice from a position above or outside it."[3] While theorists have labored to invent a perfect system above the troubled landscape of particular interpretations from which they could coolly order the critical tumult below, Americanists have started out from an assumed ideal order and imposed it on the facts. For generations of writers the word *America* has satisfied what Steven Mailloux calls the "theoretical urge."[4] They have believed in an overarching national identity without which they could not justify or organize their study.

The word *America* has been the *focus imaginarius* of a scholarly institution. "America," like divine providence, has been an assumption demanding illustration, not a thesis that required proof. Its *"whole point is not to be identifiable with the fulfillment of any set of conditions"* that might be subject to testing and thus to refutation.[5] An abstract ideal—the concept of "America" itself and of an "American" literary tradition—not only has endowed individual interpretations with coherence and validity but has determined canonical choices and, by prescribing the goal of their inquiry, given their field of study its reason for being.[6] Leo Marx tells the story of a young Americanist trying to explain his scholarly preoccupation with particularly "American" texts to an uncomprehending Britisher. In frustration, the young scholar falls back on the core of his interest. "I believe," he says, "in America."[7] That idealist faith and the need to preserve it in some form, including, when necessary, that of the disillusioned believer, have been, quite literally, the enabling essence of American literary studies for more than 100 years.

The erosion, in this century, of the nineteenth-century idealist historiography that engendered American Literary Scholarship has left Americanists clinging instinctively to old verities about the coherence of their field that they can no longer rationalize. Even those who want to associate themselves with a radical revision of the field continue to talk in terms that ring of an earlier era. When Frank Lentricchia laments "the failure of

American hope, the failure of ourselves," he takes on the persona of Vernon Parrington.[8] When Robert A. Ferguson condemns the Jeffersonian appeal to "self-evident truths," he mounts an attack on the historical nation of America that depends, as Van Wyck Brooks's similar attack did, on an imagined ideal of America as it ought to be.[9] And when Myra Jehlen cites the urge to transcendence in the literature of the "American Renaissance" as "arising from the exceptional situation of the new world," she not only assumes as fact what she ought to take as her problem but resurrects for twentieth-century scholarship a language and attendant assumptions that O. B. Frothingham or even Noah Webster would have been perfectly comfortable with.[10] I deliberately choose my examples from works by scholars who are active in efforts to "reconstruct" American Literary Scholarship because my point is that such claims are not peculiar to some reactionary wing of the field. They can be found any and everywhere in American Literary Scholarship because they are more than common, they constitute it.

Even as they continue to dwell within these old assumptions to preserve the rhetorical coherence and appeal of their field, revisionist scholars, having armed themselves from the theoretical arsenal, argue that American Literary Scholarship has lost its coherence. Yet, the myth of genesis that revisionist scholars in American literature invoke to legitimate their ostensibly revolutionary project mirrors the familiar drama of the rise and decline of the American Ideal that, seventy years ago, informed the writing of dissenters from the Genteel Tradition in American letters like Van Wyck Brooks. In the manner of those earlier writers, contemporary revisionists view the scholarly past as a period of interpretive harmony, a "Golden Day" of consensus predicated on the marriage of a nationalist faith in a unique American literary tradition with a formalist faith in the universal value of art. But in the past twenty years or so, they argue, that harmony has broken down under the pressure of (variously) the civil rights movement, the Vietnam War, the rise of feminism, increasing competition in the profession, and the influx of new theoretical approaches from Europe. As a result, the field is in confusion, these scholars assert with one voice. It is a "babble," wracked by "dissensus."[11]

Astonishingly enough, however, even as they stare chaos in the face, no one seems particularly worried. No sooner do they alert us to our dire critical straits than they reassure us that our fall was a fortunate one. The loss of our familiar perspective and its replacement by chaos may be distressing, they suggest, but it has also revealed to us how blind we were, in our earlier blissful harmony, to the dark side of American Literary Scholarship. Comfortable consensus, we are told, was purchased by an elitist ideology that repressed essential elements of America's diverse culture. Giving up that consensus, we have traded a pleasant lie for a troubling truth and so are ready, sadder perhaps but wiser, to work toward a better—if still cloudy—future.

What makes me uneasy about all this is the haste with which this revisionist history of the profession would carry American literary studies out of interpretive uncertainty into an ethically sanctioned new order. It seems especially peculiar that revisionary critiques of the tradition have appeared to nearly universal praise from many of the very traditional scholars whose work is, supposedly, being displaced. One might be forgiven for feeling that there is more going on here than meets the eye. Actually, though, there is less. Even as they take part in the general critique of the scholarly tradition that now seems to be in full swing in the profession at large, the debaters, despite their antiestablishment posture, are transacting business as usual. Even their dissent from the tradition of American Literary Scholarship reenacts the most traditional—even obligatory—gesture in American letters, one that the contemporary revisionist discourse has reconstituted as dissensus in order to dress up the chaos of incompatible opinions about American writing as a coherent trend or stage in the development of American Literary Scholarship. By doing so, revisionists imply that even the lack of any general agreement about what we are up to need not keep us from working away, if from different angles, at what we can continue to assume is the same project. Thus the apocryphal "dissensus" keeps the illusion of the traditional project alive by appropriating dissenting views into a new version of the old institutional order, allowing Americanists to continue dodging unanswerable questions. So formal a dissent can only seem doubly conservative when, even before the questions themselves are quite clear, official answers are getting the blessings of the Columbia and Cambridge University Presses. In such a context, one wonders whether revisionist questioning functions as inquiry or advertisement.

In either case, this premature flight to security exacts a heavy price of its own, distorting the past and constraining possible future orders. On one hand, the revisionists' myth of American Literary Scholarship can seem so neat only because it excludes more than half of the history it aims to describe and oversimplifies the critical debates that have enlivened scholarship in American literature over the past 100 years. On the other, revisionist criticism of American writing, has already produced a predictable critical rhetoric and canon. Ritual attacks on the fat target of aesthetic formalism, and on sexism and racism, and rueful acknowledgments of past ethnocentrism are the recurrent rhetorical gestures, the passwords, of what amounts to a New Orthodoxy in American Literary Scholarship.[12] This rhetoric goes virtually unquestioned because it comports so completely with the expectations—post 1960s white liberal turned academic professional—of its audience.

In revisionist rhetoric, political arguments over the canon too often displace attention from the impulses that prompted revision in the first place. Political earnestness represses an uncertainty about the relationship of literature to history that, while widespread these days in the profession as a whole, is particularly threatening to Americanists. Political commitment distracts from doubts about the integrity of the field that have arisen since scholars have lost confidence in the "National Character" that initially justified American Literary Scholarship. This ideal initially appealed as a strategy for overcoming contradictions inherent in an American Literary Scholarship. Its progressive demise over the past fifty years contributed to the questioning that has produced the widespread desire for changes in the practice of American Literary Scholarship.

Since the seventeenth century, "America" has had an ambivalent relation to the past. Just as revisionists cling to the traditional rhetoric of the American literary tradition they are critiquing, Americanists have always viewed the past as something to be both abandoned and revered. Plagued by this ambivalence, American Literary Scholarship has been consumed with the self-justifying task of connecting works of literary art to an exclusively *American* social context while largely ignoring the larger contextual field. They have danced around text and context in a typically Romantic oscillation that identifies the continuing entrapment of contemporary criticism in unresolved and unresolvable traditional terms. The question has been how to unite the disparate and fragmentary facts of experience in the New World into a coherent account about the national culture. Because of their allegiance to cultural values associated with the nation, Americanists have felt, even more acutely than literary historians in other fields, the need for persuasive answers to increasingly troubling questions about what connects particular cultural practices to culture at large. In that sense, an account of attempts to tell an American literary history speaks to attempts to produce historical narrative in general, that is, to explain the place of particular phenomena in a larger context and in relation to the present.

Poststructuralist discourse has placed those questions at the focus of scholarly debate, and more than anything else, it is because theory has finally taken up the question of how to connect text and context that American Literary Scholarship has taken up with theory. From an Americanist's point of view, literary studies seems belatedly to be learning what American Literary Scholarship has always known. In the past few years, historicist attacks on the foundationalist aspirations of literary theory by Walter Michaels and Steven Knapp, Richard Rorty, Stanley Fish, and others have moved literary and critical practice off the ideal high ground and place all interpretation, all human activity, in history.[13] The various critical approaches gathering under this historicist umbrella are united mostly by the general aim of explaining the relationship of texts to their historical contexts and by their antipathy to the formalist assumptions that have dominated modern criticism. Considering the fear endemic in the profession that literary studies has fatally alienated the society that supports it, this historicist argument can be seen as trying to do the profession a real service. It rejects the privileging of art that justified a distinct professional identity for literary studies after World War I. But sixty years later, that self-isolation seems self-destructive. In the face of more pragmatic concerns, historicism reminds us that criticism has worldly motives and practical consequences. By making art and criticism ''normal'' activities, historicism rebuts the all too common assumption that reading and writing are ivory tower pastimes that need not be taken seriously.

In this form, theory seems made to order for American Literary Scholarship. It reiterates, in intellectually fashionable terms, Americanists' own long-standing discomfort with formalism and their preoccupation with historical context. But because revisionists within American Literary Scholarship overlook this essential kinship, they misread the history of their own field, choose the wrong enemy, and so misdirect their own counterattack. Over the years, the consistent feature of critical discourse in the field has not been, as revisionists assert, the critical quest for a unique American *literary* tradition (a notion that comes up sporadically before Matthiessen). Nor has it been its reliance on aesthetic formalism, which was only one relatively recent strategy in a long series of attempts to identify what is ''American'' about American writing and has never held the unchallenged sway in American literary studies that its current detractors want to claim for it.

By so narrowly defining their professional past, revisionists enact a hopelessly ahistoricist impulse to abandon it. Repeated attacks on New Critical formalism by critics who would "reconstruct" American Literary Scholarship reflect a repudiation of the tradition rather than a productive relationship with it. It seems at best safely "academic" and at worst a sort of scholarly scapegoating to locate the problems that face the profession in such comparatively rarified, intellectual issues as the formalist appeal to universal values. Such contentions evade the fact that American literary studies has not, for the most part, taken its modern shape in the service of anything so broad and abstract as a modernist cultural ideology. In this century, American literary studies has fought its way to acknowledged status within the MLA and become an autonomous and self-justifying professional practice, serving the interests of a (by now) well-entrenched and successful academic establishment. It has been driven to this success at least since the twenties not by the nationalism or aestheticism the New Orthodoxy attacks in its mythic history but by the need to define itself as a distinct professional field. Ever since Moses Coit Tyler had to become a professor of American *history* in order to study American literature, American Literary Scholarship has used the word *America* to impose an automatic coherence on the writing Americans have produced and thus to justify the independent institutional identity of American literary studies. In contemporary scholarship, the word *America* continues to provide that locus of implicit coherence, that critical focal point about which American Literary Scholarship revolves and upon which it depends.

Consequently, despite the current *appearance* of enthusiasm for professional revolution, Americanists are not inclined to probe too deeply for the founding assumptions of their field. True, the recent redirection of theory toward a historicist practice enticed American Literary Scholarship to add theory to an already crowded interdisciplinary quiver, and as a result, Americanists no longer parade their idealist assumptions as they once did. New anthologies self-consciously eschew claims to presenting immutable portraits of America, content to represent themselves as embodying that fundamental tenet of the American myth, a diversity of views. But, behind that old critical bromide, the banished idealism lurks, active as ever. Even as American Literary Scholarship seems to open its arms to theory, the tradition is actually carrying out a strategy of containment to ensure the integrity of its project.

Old idealisms die hard. If the desire for a universally explanatory theory has conditioned use of the word *America* by scholars striving to present themselves as engaged in a vital debate, the idealization of "America" in criticism has, more recently, circumscribed the way historicist theory has been applied to American texts.[14] Theory has been admitted into the pages of the Cambridge and Columbia histories only after checking its teeth at their tables of contents. It enters not as a disruptive radical but as a good citizen dedicated to the communal project. Just as Freudian criticism found early acceptance within American Literary Scholarship by rationalizing the link between the text and the individual experience of life in America, theoretical discourse has gained acceptance among Americanists only as it has shown itself willing to lend a hand with the traditional critical chores.

II

Although much has been made of the "new direction" given American literary studies by the infusion of contemporary theory, a good deal of this enthusiasm is traceable simply to Americanists' congenital addiction to the new. American Literary Scholarship, like the town drunk, takes a new direction with each step, but theoretical studies of American literature are still under the influence of the idealist oppositions that have always intoxicated the field. In fact, far from breaking new theoretical ground, the most troubling implication of the way historicism has been adapted to the traditional project of American Literary Scholarship is that Americanists have been prevented by their allegiance to the imperatives of American Literary Scholarship—the dogmatic relationship between selected American texts and American culture, and the notion of a distinct American literary tradition—from enacting the more radical implications of contemporary theory.

In the hands of Americanists, the New Historicism has become a way of looking past the threatening question of whether there *is* an "American" "literature" attached to an "American" "culture," to a more fulfilling argument over *how* their relationship can best be described. In the work of recent revisionist critics, the imperatives of the American Ideal, the limitations on the kinds of accounts that are recognizable as

American Literary Scholarship, have overwhelmed historicist scruples. Armed with challenging theoretical tools, Americanists have still tried to construct narrative accounts of their subject that follow traditional forms.[15]

The historicist appeal to context has reconciled Americanists to theory by proposing a resolution to the key conflict in American Literary Scholarship between the concept of the "American" and that of the "literary."[16] While idealism provided cultural coherence, its literary corollary, aesthetic formalism, would deny literary status to most of the texts that might constitute an American literary history. The historicist focus on context has the advantage of accounting for both. It reinterprets the "American" as a larger social matrix against or within which texts are written, and broadens the notion of the literary into textuality so as to encompass not only nonliterary texts but nonlinguistic cultural acts. In this way, it more than meets the Americanist's need to fill out a national tradition congruent with the national history by including seventeenth- and eighteenth-century writing that does not fit into an idealist aesthetic.

Yet I would argue that, constrained by their perhaps unavoidable allegiance to the imperatives of their discipline and to the sort of historical narratives it has mandated, Americanists remain unable to produce coherent stories about their subject. Though some of the terms of that historical model have changed with the critical fashions, its most essential feature, its function in structuring our understandings, has remained intact. Scholars still carry on the debate about American writing in terms of oppositions—thought versus feeling, truth versus beauty, spirit versus form, knowledge versus interpretation, intrinsic versus historical meaning, art versus scholarship—that reflect their own continuing immersion in Romantic versions of idealist thinking. In their effort to preserve an ideal ground for their assumptions about America and its literature, twentieth-century scholars of American literature have been the last American Romantics. More pointedly, that persistent posture actually supports the division between art and life that marginalizes literary scholars even as they try to rationalize the relevance of their work. Professional imperatives have given artificial life to a defunct historiography—like a government subsidy that props up a dying industry.

Some of the most forceful of the recent historicist approaches to a new American literary history view history as constituted by the struggle for power. Powerful ideologies, they assert—the "relation [of texts] to centers of cultural domination''—determine not only how texts are written but, more importantly, what texts are read, and *how* they are read. This dramatic battle for literary supremacy has several advantages. It suits critics' aspirations to social influence. It makes criticism a champion of social justice rather than the self-absorbed preoccupation of isolated intellectuals, and it provides a nonformalist rationale for reading that justifies renewed attention to works that have been unfairly excluded by hegemonic forces.

Some of the most ambitious critiques of the tradition attack the established American literary canon from a feminist political perspective. Such critics as Annette Kolodny and Jane Tompkins argue that the interests of a cloistered elite have determined the works included there and have unjustly excluded numerous others. Thus the need for a new start that will, in Tompkins's words, ''move the study of American literature away from [a] small group of master texts . . . and into a more varied and fruitful area of investigation.'' A ''new historical criticism,'' she declares, is ''the only way of accounting for the enormous impact of works'' that have been ignored by traditional scholarship.[17]

Ironically, however, in their very desire to leave behind the errors of the past, Tompkins and Kolodny enact aspirations that are almost synonymous with the American literary tradition, and indeed with thinking about America since the discovery. The prospect of a new history to deal with the new facts raises an old problem.[18] Having repudiated the values that gave coherence to the old picture of American literature, Kolodny and Tompkins have to explain the coherence of a new one. In fact, they provide two explanations. The first is a ''weak'' inclusive argument for canonical diversity and the second a ''strong,'' exclusive argument for rejecting both the established canon and the traditional scholarship that enshrines it. These two approaches amount to alternate definitions of ''American'' writing, each of which embodies alternate but ultimately incompatible assumptions about how to justify reading noncanonical works. The ''weak'' argument contrasts the diversity of all the writing produced in America with the exclusivity of the tradition.[19] Kolodny asserts that the recent turn from ''commonality'' to ''difference'' as a ''central critical category'' makes it impossible for American literary studies to define itself by reference to works in the recognized canon without also considering an imposing array of previously neglected works in a variety of languages. "No longer," she says, "can we be so restrictive in what we choose to recognize as 'American.'"[20]

But Kolodny has the same problems managing this diversity that have met efforts to describe America and its literature from Webster to Whitman to Bercovitch. Despite her impulse to include everything, Kolodny still wants to be able to tell "a coherent, integrated story about our literary past" (p. 297). She has to imagine a narrative that organizes the American miscellany without leaving anything out. Somehow, the numberless parts must coalesce into a single whole. Her "insistence on difference and diversity" is essential to her purposes because it prevents intellectual repression—the "omissions and silences" that inspired Kolodny's arguments in the first place. It pledges, like a literary critical Statue of Liberty, to "accommodate," to "make room," to "embrace" all writing regardless of race, gender, or language (pp. 289–90). On the other hand, for Kolodny, as for previous jugglers of these terms, diversity mirrors itself as chaos. Historically, in the discourse of American literary studies, an appeal to diversity has represented not so much a triumph over restrictive orders as the inability to discover an acceptable one.

A coherent story has always been the object of pursuit in American literary studies. But Americanists cannot have it both ways. Coherence means exclusion; diversity means disorder. Even as she looks toward the possibility of new American literary histories, Kolodny warns against *any* order. "The zeal to assert common ground," she fears, "could have the impact of abbreviating the mapping of alternative landscapes" (p. 294). Any literary history, any coherent story about American writing (or about anything else for that matter) must exclude. And Kolodny is dead set against exclusion.

Unable to resolve this Romantic conflict in practical terms fitted to present conditions, Kolodny finds herself vacillating between an accommodating future and an idealized past. If the principles of a coherent American literary tradition remain obscure to us, she argues, future scholars, as they "reinvent" American literary history for themselves, may "see the interconnections that we cannot." And even if they cannot, "we will have given them so much more to work from" (p. 301). Kolodny's optimistic prophecies tease out the conflict between her politics and her theory. To keep her optimism afloat, Kolodny has to sink her historicism. While it is certainly true, as Kolodny suggests, that future scholars will see relationships among texts that we do not, there is no reason to think that they will do our job for us. They will not necessarily be interested in seeking out the particular "interconnections" that we cannot find. Nor can they be expected to want to "work from" the neglected texts that Kolodny and others have labored so hard to uncover for them (and us). We should not assume that future scholars will share our interests, not even our interest in continuing the quest for a "coherent story" about American writing. Such predictions erroneously imagine literary studies as a single project continuous through time.

Like many earlier American mythographers, Kolodny validates her ethical model for this better future by referring to the past. Like so many survivors of the sixties, including me, Kolodny would like to "keep faith with the spirit of those decades" (p. 306). She tries to do so, however, by imagining that the raging current of sixties political radicalism pours somehow unabated through the babbling brook of academic discourse. That radical spirit, Kolodny contends, incarnated in such resonant "moments" as Martin Luther King's declaration "I have a dream," "generated all the new scholarship" (p. 306). She portrays this new criticism as the revolutionary political "spirit" of the sixties reincarnated in academic (re)form, the latest hope for an America restored to its true self by its literature. Such jeremiad-like appeals to a neglected American spiritual heritage are all too familiar. They have been staples of our national self-portraiture since the Civil War. It is amazing, though, that they still retain so much of that old magic, having become the common stock-in-trade of State-of-the-Union rhetoric and beer commercials.

Perhaps these rhetorical postures remain popular, despite their bankruptcy, because they speak so strongly to the fugitive idealism of critics who grew up on Vietnam and Watergate and find themselves, in the Reagan era, repudiated by their culture and betrayed (not just disappointed as Brooks or Parrington had been) by the nation they would still idealize. At the heart of Kolodny's critical program broods a utopian fervor reminiscent of some versions of sixties radicalism, dreaming the end of the "System" and the advent of a new, and somehow system-free, world. These critics pursue an essentially Romantic quest in which the word *new* punctuates their prose like a ritual incantation. They want to "create something wholly new" (p. 301), to find "the key to the possibility of genuinely new, wholly reconceptualized literary histories" (p. 303). The adoption of this new critical faith amounts to an apocalyptic spiritual conversion to be won only through "struggle" and requiring an "initiatory baptism" (pp. 301–2). In appropriating this myth, Tompkins and Kolodny seem to imagine a sort of critical "New World" in which we will finally free ourselves of all the problems (sexism, a narrow canon, belletristic isolation, cultural myths) that plague the "Old World" of traditional scholarship.

In fact, of course, their "new" critic is as old as the European response to America, the direct (if more scrupulously gender-neutral) descendant of Crèvecoeur's "American," that "new man, who acts upon new principles [and] must therefore entertain new ideas, and form new opinions."[21] In American Literary Scholarship, each succeeding generation has made its professional way by defining itself as a "new criticism" opposed to a benighted or repressive established power—British literature, philological scholarship, the Genteel Tradition, historical scholarship, and, now, aesthetic formalism—standing in the way of the ostensibly "just" view of American literature and life that Kolodny calls "the integrity of memory." Getting to that view is for Kolodny, as it has been for others, a task of mythic proportions. It is "a heroic effort" in which she imagines "the creators of a new literary history" not just *struggling* against the tradition, "like Jacob wrestling with the angel," but, even more improbably, *winning* (p. 301).

It is no accident that Kolodny's rhetoric scales these mythic heights just where she elides the "weak" argument for diversity with the "strong" one rejecting both traditional criticism and the canonical works it has valued. Her assertion that we should read "the texts that were never taught in graduate school—*to the exclusion*" (p. 302) of canonical works would require just the exclusionary ordering principle that she has already rejected. Kolodny's mythic past and future stand in for that restrictive rationale.[22]

In any case, it is Tompkins's and Kolodny's strong attack on the existing canon and their promotion of an *alternate* one that has given their arguments prominence in the scholarly debate over the future of American literary studies. In *Sensational Designs*, which has been offered as an example of the possibilities of this critical line by scholars like Kolodny and William Cain, Jane Tompkins tries to rationalize the impulse to an alternate canon that Kolodny veils in myth. As a result, her conflicting arguments reflect the difficulties involved in revising the canon.

Tompkins goes after the canon by way of the critical tastes that have produced it. Despite the tremendous popularity in their own time of works like Susan Warner's *The Wide, Wide, World* or Harriet Beecher Stowe's *Uncle Tom's Cabin*, she asserts, traditional readers "cannot take sentimental fiction seriously" because they are imprisoned within "a way of seeing and evaluating literature which . . . is founded on modernist principles that were articulated in direct opposition to those which sentimental fiction stands for." And so, Tompkins argues, "we can and should set aside the modernist prejudices which have consigned these works to oblivion."[23] The "prejudice" that Tompkins sees in this process supplies the emotional impetus for displacing the canonical works that have been so unjustly promoted.[24]

But Tompkins's thrust cannot be merely negative; she has a canon of her own to justify. The ability to provide such justifications had been a strength of the formalist criticism she rejects. Formalism had the significant advantage, in its heyday, of offering an argument for the persistent interest of old books to modern readers. By positing a universal value for "art," formalist criticism could leap the historical gap between books and readers and put various readerly perspectives on an aesthetic common ground.[25] The need to find different but equally powerful terms to rationalize particular canonical choices confronts Tompkins with the same critical dilemma it posed for Kolodny. To rationalize both the connection between American texts and American culture and the continuing appeal of the nineteenth-century works she favors, Tompkins must make competing and incompatible claims.

Tompkins's fractured attempt to rationalize a particular canon and so give an altered coherence to American literature dramatizes the pitfalls of canonical revision, especially in American literature, where the canon and the field itself are mutually defining. Like the earliest proponents of an American literary canon, Tompkins attacks the prevalent aesthetic standards that will not sanction her choices and finds another rationale, not "Character" or "Democracy" or "Realism" now, but "Cultural Work" and typicality. And as usual, she has to stretch the rationale a bit to cover particular cases (Brown, after all, was not terribly popular, Cooper is already canonical, and *Uncle Tom's Cabin* or *The Wide, Wide, World*—an "absolutely unprecedented" phenomenon in American writing—could not, by any stretch of the imagination, be considered "typical"). She wants to justify her choices, not merely each for its own sake but as parts of the more ambitious project of recasting "the picture America draws of itself." To connect her texts to American culture, to offer a coherent view of America and its writing, she argues that we "can and should" free ourselves from our critical prejudices and read "sentimental" fictions from a nineteenth-century perspective. Those works are important, she argues, not because they are unique aesthetic objects but because they are typical of their culture, and their "force escapes the modern reader unless he or she makes the effort to recapture the world view they sprang from" (p. xiii).

On the other hand, to account for the modern appeal of these works, Tompkins asserts her own "interested" position. Like earlier critics who, Tompkins says, turned their personal "prejudices" into the restrictive canon that she wants to repudiate, Tompkins offers interpretations that "grow directly from the circumstances, interests, and aims that have constituted [her] as a critic" (p. xiii). She is "a woman in a field dominated by male scholars" (p. xiv), and Tompkins's book, like Kolodny's *The Land Before Her*, offers itself as a rereading of a major rhetorical tradition in light of feminist politics.

Considering the observation by Raymond Williams and others that a governing ideology is just that feature of critical work that most eludes the direct awareness of the critic, it is suggestive that the shapers of the New Orthodoxy so promptly confess their own ideological biases. Their formulae seem designed to demonstrate that these revisionists have not neglected to apply the standards of ideological scrutiny they direct at others to themselves as well. But one might distrust confessions so readily, even proudly, surrendered. Statements about ideology within a work, like Bercovitch's or Tompkins's or Kolodny's, are not descriptions of their ideology but instruments of it, not justifications for critical strategies but strategic moves in their own right. They serve the interests of those who make them. As Thoreau says, "A man's real faith is never contained in his creed, nor is his creed an article of his faith."[26]

Tompkins's attempt at a historicist revision of American literary studies falls into two halves. To justify the value of these works, Tompkins ties them to their cultural contexts. Sentimental fictions succeeded, she asserts, because they worked in "an idiom to which a contemporary [i.e., nineteenth-century] audience can respond" (p. xviii). But this historicist argument does not explain why modern readers would want "to understand what gave [sentimental] novels force for their initial readers" (p. xiii). It explains why modern critics have neglected sentimental fiction for seventy years but not why they should stop neglecting it. Like the *old* historicism, it leaves open the question of how scholarship establishes a relationship between the past and the present.[27] And an answer to that question is crucial to efforts to justify literary scholarship and rationalize literary history. On the other hand, her historicist admission of an "interested" position as a woman working in a profession dominated by white males does only the other half of the job. The readings she produces treat her texts as allegories of contemporary political values. They explain her own personal interest as a modern reader in selected old books, but make those choices a matter of the appeal to individual readers of particular texts. They do not connect her choices to some coherent view of that writing *as American*.[28]

Tompkins needs anti-formalist theory to make the more general canonical critique that gives her work its prominence in the current critical debate about the future of American literary studies. But, strictly speaking, her historicism is inimical to her own program. Her assertion of modern feminist interests makes a hash of her effort to justify works by their appeal to nineteenth-century readers. Like Kolodny and a long line of earlier architects of an American literary tradition, Tompkins hurries back and forth between two incompatible positions—coherence and fragmentation, general claims and particular arguments, cultural values and literary readings—hoping that if she moves fast enough, she will find herself in both places at once.[29]

In general, I distrust the tendency of New Historicist practice, especially as it has been pursued in American Literary Scholarship, to define the nature of the relation between texts and culture in narrow terms that overdramatize the project of revision and make change sound easier than it is likely to be. By looking at these politically inspired revisionist approaches to American literature, I want to suggest that our attitudes toward particular texts are far more complex and profound than revisionists allow. While the interpretive attitudes behind any canon *are* necessarily historical, they are not so readily specifiable as Kolodny and Tompkins suggest by focusing their critique so narrowly on so-called modernist critical prejudices. And while such attitudes *do* inevitably change, that change does not come easily or quickly. There is, of course, no inherent, no absolute, reason for us to teach or write about any particular work. It is far less clear, however, that scholars can read differently than they do simply by deciding to.

The consequential questions this work raises about the interpretation of American texts are not, as they suggest, whether texts possess intrinsic value or whether changes in values and assumptions would lead to changes in the canon. These issues seem uncontroversial—at least to me. The consequential questions are whether the particular changes these revisionists recommend are practically possible, and whether *these* are the changes criticism needs. In saying this, I am not defending any established canon or criticizing possible alternatives. I am merely trying to suggest that, by and large, canonical works have assumed their importance for reasons much deeper than the literary critical assumptions about inherent or intrinsic value that Tompkins and Kolodny oppose. Their claim that "modernist prejudices" are responsible for the current canon misleadingly suggests that modernist prejudices are *all* that support that canon and that readers are attached to a canon by abstract critical principles extrinsic to the critics themselves.

In practice, the beliefs and assumptions that valorize canonical works are not so readily disposable as Tompkins and Kolodny imply, because they are not so artificial. Our tastes do not, as they would have it, merely restrict our seeing. Rather, as Stanley Fish has said, they are what we see *with*.[30] Our critical choices do not depend simply on an isolated collection of accidental attitudes about art that we can discard without otherwise altering our intellectual landscape. They are an inextricable part of all the convictions and interests we possess by virtue of our residence in our own time and place and our possession of the language we speak, that vast matrix of values from which our particular tastes can be abstracted. "A new theory," as Rorty says, "is simply a rather minor change in a vast network of beliefs."[31] There is no point in blaming our limited historical perspective only for choices we dislike. It is the context for everything we do or think, all that we like *and* dislike about our world. So, while I heartily agree with Tompkins's historicist point that inclusion in a canon has been and must be a matter of critical interests, I do not agree with her anti-historicist conclusion that "we can and should" therefore simply abandon those tastes along with the texts that accompany them. "An antifoundationalist," Fish asserts, "cannot (without at that moment becoming a foundationalist) reject something simply because its source has been shown to be human history as opposed to something independent of it" (p. 441).

In effect, I'm arguing that the attack on the canon that Kolodny and Tompkins mount does not carry its historicism far enough. Historicism is not a naive skepticism that, having discovered the fictitiousness of the world as it is, denies that world in a pique. This, as Fish rightly observes, is only a disguised version of the old faith. Historicism assumes that views produced by our time and place are all we have or can have.[32] To say that our readings depend on our particular position in space and time is not to expose a conspiracy. It is just to say that our opinions are a function of who we are. Our literary interpretations, like all of our understandings, are part of a vast web of related terms that extends as far as our understandings of the world and our practices in it. Changing a single element of that web is a myth. In practice, each change entails a vast restructuring of the web and all it touches. As Wittgenstein says, "It is true that we can compare a picture that is firmly rooted in us to a superstition; but it is equally true that we *always* eventually have to reach some firm ground, either a picture or something else, so that a picture which is at the root of all our thinking is to be respected and not treated as a superstition."[33] The failure to take account of the intransigence of our convictions is what I am complaining of in the particular changes recommended by the critics I have discussed here. Some New Historicists seem to want to take a shortcut that ignores the integration of our *literary* judgments into the larger field of our practices and beliefs. They use historicist arguments to deny the constraints of history.[34]

III

The need to make unjustifiable claims is the plague of American Literary Scholarship.[35] It is not so much a failing of individual scholars as a condition of argument in the field. The Americanist's uncomfortable obligation to account for the connection of American literary texts and American culture yields awkward apologetics in the most theoretically sophisticated work. The word *America* underwrites a characteristic critical narrative and provides an easy answer to the difficult but essential task of explaining the significance of scholarly literary history. It is in this sense that "America" has justified the relevance as well as the coherence of scholarly accounts.

The contemporary historicist critique of formalism in American Literary Scholarship is the heir of nineteenth-century scholarship's unacknowledged conflict between "scientific" history and spiritual coherence, and like those pioneering Americanists, contemporary historicists have adopted, for the most part, only the rhetoric of material fact, while still relying for narrative coherence on an idealist abstraction reshaped for modern consumption as culture or ideology. Critics like Tompkins, or like Philip Fisher in *Hard Facts*, argue that texts do "cultural work," that they change the world of which they are part. The trouble with these causal claims is that scholars seldom do (or really intend to do) the sort of study required to demonstrate them.[36] To carry his point that "popular" texts do the "cultural work" of making the "unimaginable" into the "obvious," Fisher would have to unpack a very complex cultural history. He would, at the very least, have to display the state of thinking about his subjects—slavery, Indians, cities—that prevailed before the texts he treats were written, examine the differences between that conceptual state of affairs and the concepts in the texts, describe the process by which the texts worked on cultural assumptions, and outline the new state of thought that prevailed in the culture after the texts had become popular.

This is the sort of empirical study mandated by Fisher's appeal to the importance of his texts as *agents* of cultural change; otherwise, how could we be persuaded that any change had taken place, much less that the particular texts he features had caused them? This is not, however, the sort of account offered by either Tompkins or Fisher. Like Tompkins's, Fisher's ideological readings dramatize the issues he has raised. Although Fisher's individual readings are fascinating and sophisticated interpretations of the texts at hand, they can be connected to the American cultural totality only by reducing them to ethico-political allegories, and such allegories are an inadequate substitute for demonstrating the influence on culture that, for the purposes of his argument, gives the texts he selects their importance.

The hard fact pressed home by this sort of work in American Literary Scholarship is that we do not, at the moment, have any very good explanations for the things Fisher and Tompkins are trying to explain (how books are chosen as classics, the relationship between texts and cultural change). By turning culture into an agent of that change, acting on its own behalf, Fisher preserves the *forms* of a causal narrative in hopes of harnessing its explanatory force.[37] Americanists are forced into such indefensible claims by the compulsion to attach texts to American culture. They want to read particular texts because those suit their political motives or fit their aesthetic tastes and thus justify their professional identity. They want to attach texts to culture because culture is something larger, more important, and not so "merely" textual. Yet, as it stands, literary scholarship does not know very much about how to attach texts to context, or even how to choose which context to attach them to—the context of modern debate over methods of interpretation, or politics, or economics or philosophy, or of equivalent past debates, and which ones, those that authors knew, contemporary ones they may not have known, those previous to the "production of the text," and so on. Nor have critics been clear about what kinds of claims they are making for the connections they do specify—causal, analogous, metaphorical, serendipitous—or about how those claims help justify the work they do, or how their claims correspond to their historicist assumptions. Enthusiasm for the historical project of placing works in the context of their time has diverted scholarship from those questions. The idea of cultural context replies to our vestigial need for mimesis, our desire to believe that our understandings are understandings *of* something. But in their polemical intensity, revisionists too often overlook the daunting task of accounting for their ability to constitute and read a particular cultural con-"text" and rely instead on a hypostatization of culture that begs all the questions that trouble historical understanding.[38] The current uncertainty about literary history is, in part at least, a measure of our dissatisfaction with the narratives we have so far invented to make these connections. And this continuing frustration marks the need for a criticism that makes claims of a different kind.

In *The Gold Standard and the Logic of Naturalism,* Walter Benn Michaels reacts against the programmatic readings that have been produced by political versions of historicism.[39] In a rhetorically complex narrative that is scrupulous to a fault in avoiding claims, Michaels attacks the moralism of much previous American Literary Scholarship rather than its aestheticism. For Michaels, texts are not agents of change. They do not "do the work of the present" as Fisher would have it. In fact, Michaels sees the whole effort to make this connection as wrongheaded. Using the critical discourse about "Naturalism" as a foil for voices in the contemporary critical debate in general, Michaels argues that criticism has been "caught up in endless theorizing about the nature and very possibility of realistic representation: do texts refer to social reality? if they do, do they merely reflect it or do they criticize it? and if they do not, do they try to escape it, or do they imagine utopian alternatives to it?" (p. 27).

Michaels makes an ambitious attempt to produce a literary history that avoids the difficulties of causal connections between texts and culture by treating the relationships between them as intertextual. Rather than being "caught up in endless theorizing" about the relation of literature and culture, he suggests, we should describe texts as examples of the waters of discourse in which they are submerged. His own intention, he says, in terms that clearly distinguish his aims from Fisher's "is not to identify a specific relation between literature and the real, or even a specific ideological function of literature in relation to the real" but to "map out the reality in which a certain literature finds its place." According to Michaels, texts are "exemplary" rather than formative of culture. "The only relation literature as such has to culture as such," he says, "is that it is part of it" (p. 27). Texts cannot criticize their culture, Michaels argues, because they cannot step outside it for an objective view. Reading Dreiser as a critic of capitalism, he says, would depend on "imagining a Dreiser outside of capitalism who could then be said to have attitudes toward it" (p. 19).

Despite Michaels's attempt to avoid the problems causal claims pose for work like Fisher's or Tompkins's, I would argue that he too is lured into unjustifiable claims—claims in excess of those his argument would strictly require or support—by the need to make statements about "America." While Michaels wants to avoid the difficulties of causal demonstration that trouble political accounts, he too wants to find significance in texts by referring them to something larger than themselves, to "structures whose coherence, interest, and effect may be greater than either author or text" (pp. 174–75). It is a peculiar feature of Michaels's criticism that it leans so heavily on the epistemological assumptions he says he has left behind. In Michaels's criticism everything is "inside" culture where connections are always already made, as it were. Nothing is "outside," where it would have to find a way in. In Michaels's work, cultural phenomena, texts, subjects as well as objects, dwell "inside" culture, "inside" a "logic," "inside" a cultural "moment." This strategy combats epistemological insecurity by seeming to unite fragmentary facts within a single identity. And it certainly smooths out the rough spots in the critical interpretation of varied discourses. It puts different phenomena "inside" a single "system of representation" (p. 20) where they speak the same language, as it were, making it easier to treat them as comparable and connected textual phenomena, interchangeable terms with a "common denominator." "The logic of capitalism," for example, "*produces* objects . . . as it *produces* subjects" (p. 20). No longer divided, with meaning wandering uncertainly between them, subject and object, in Michaels's view, mean within the coherent system that "produces" them (p. 27).

Reviewing Michaels's work, Brook Thomas describes it as avoiding the difficulties of both causal narrative and allegorical reading by describing phenomena as "connected by a structural homology."[40] This formulation is true to Michaels's attempt to remove "the focus of literary history from the individual text or author." But homological connections such as Michaels makes do not really explain much. Tracing the roots of the term homology to Structuralist criticism, Fredric Jameson has pointed out that "nothing is accomplished by the abstract assurance that [these] structures . . . are 'the same.' . . . There remains the danger that the identity holds good, not for the concrete realities themselves, but merely for the conceptual abstractions that have been derived from them."[41] In practice, Michaels uses this idea as a convenient way of justifying in advance the connections his narrative makes between excerpts from various roughly contemporaneous texts.

What Thomas describes as homologies, a description that ratifies Michaels's own focus on coherent "structures," might be better described, in Emerson's terms, simply as a "series of apposite metaphors." Having given up causality and allegory as tools for making coherence, Michaels begins to operate at a level of metaphoric abstraction that blends all particulars within the lively movement of his prose. Everything, in Michaels's account, depends on his dexterity in making connections, and on the particular connections he makes, connections between literature and other acts in culture, and connections within texts. Despite his implication that the "moments" he describes are "out there," his connections are both made and made significant *in* his own narrative. Whether or not we credit Michaels's claim that texts are wholly "within" the culture that produced them, it is clear that Michaels himself, like all contemporary readers, is not contained within that culture, and his metaphors are his own rather than intrinsic to the nineteenth century. They are the ones Michaels sees from a distance of 100 years, and he is able to see them and inclined to see them because of that distance.[42]

I mention these unglamorous commonplaces because blinking them prevents even Michaels's brilliant criticism from achieving the articulate literary history that is, I think, potentially implicit in the move to textuality. The final essay in the volume, "Writing and Photography," might stand as a fair example of the strengths and weaknesses of Michaels's method. It revolves, as do the others, around associations between a dazzling variety of terms: *accident, risk, the market, bodies, lines* (physical and textual), and *writing,* as they are taken up in texts on photography, economics, and gambling, and in Stephen Crane's "The Five White Mice" and Edith Wharton's *The House of Mirth*. With so many terms at work in so many texts, the principal point of this essay is buried, I think, in Michaels's remark that "in a market society, a great many actions look like gambling" (p. 225). Whether or not this particular observation is accurate, it is certainly true that, in Michaels's criticism, a great many things begin to look alike.

As Jameson warned, and like so many other accounts that relate American texts to American culture, Michaels's reading of *The House of Mirth* twists both text and culture into the shapes his theory requires. To achieve his characteristic reversal of the traditional critical view of the book, Michaels rejects the more traditional view that "the story told by *The House of Mirth* is the story of [Lily Bart's] inability" to "escape the market" (pp. 226–27) because, as he has argued earlier, such critique is impossible. At the center of his reading is Lily Bart's fatal "love of risk," a risk he identifies with the spirit of an inescapable market society. What I want to question about Michaels's reading is not whether Lily Bart *takes* risks; it is obvious that she does. What is questionable is Michaels's claim, generated by his insistence that *The House of Mirth* must necessarily exemplify "marketplace" culture, that, for Lily, risks themselves are "finally more attractive than the guarantee of freedom from them" (p. 229). This example is central to Michaels's larger argument. If Lily's choices do not depend on the motives Michaels attributes them to, then he cannot claim his reversal of the more conventional reading of the novel, that is, his claim that the "moments that seem to express her distaste for the commerce of Wall Street in fact express her complete commitment to the practices of speculation" (p. 228). And this claim is central to his larger point, that texts cannot really critique the culture of which they are a part.

However daring, even foolhardy, Michaels may wish Lily Bart to be, the Lily Bart of *The House of Mirth* is no adventurer. Like Edna Pontellier in *The Awakening,* she does not have "strong wings." It is her weakness that attracts her to the possibility of marriage with Selden, and it is her weakness that leads, in the decisive instance, to her death.[43] Lily does not exceed the prescribed dose of her sleeping potion because, as Michaels says, she has a "passion for giving up control" that is equivalent to her "passion for the market" (p. 230). She does so because she "must." "She knew she took a slight risk in doing so. . . . But after all that was but one chance in a hundred . . . and the addition of a few drops to the regular dose would probably do no more than procure for her the rest she so desperately needed . . . darkness, darkness was what she must have at any cost'' (p. 322). As this key passage shows, Lily calculates the risk as small, insofar as she thinks of it at all. And as we see elsewhere, Lily is not particularly good at calculation. She cannot even add up her bank balance accurately, erring, as she does in this fatal instance, to her own disadvantage by overestimating her fortunes. There is risk here, of course, but Lily does not act, here or anywhere else in the book, out of the love for the moment of risk that Michaels uses, rather narrowly, to characterize the market.

At the end of his "Introduction," Michaels asserts that his account is "meant to be a historical one," by which I take him to mean that his criticism makes no ahistorical theoretical claims, confining itself instead to particular descriptions of moments of discourse. As is well known, Michaels wants to distance himself from "theory." Referring to his reading of "The Yellow Wallpaper," he says that if his account is wrong, "it is wrong not because I have the wrong account of language but because I have the wrong account of Gilman" (28 n. 43). I agree that if Michaels's account of Wharton is wrong (and, clearly, I think it is), his errors reflect problems with his particular readings rather than some metatheoretical mistake. Yet even if we accept Michaels's point that he makes no large foundational claims that might be "theoretically" wrong, it is still the case that his small "t" theory, that is, his sense of what he is doing, his critical assumptions, lead to what is "wrong" with his particular readings. And, in turn, those readings are designed to illustrate and support his theoretical model of the relation of literary texts to culture.[44]

The strategies of Michaels's account are generated by his "theoretical" insistence that a book cannot be critical of its culture because it is inside that culture, that apparently critiquing the market, it must also express the market, and even embrace it. For Michaels, *The House of Mirth* cannot reject the marketplace because it is embroiled in the marketplace, and so it must be read as exemplifying market values. Hence, Lily loves risk. This critical reversal supports his "theory," and this theory generates the sort of critical reversals that make possible fresh readings of familiar texts. Yet, as we have seen, the weakness of Michaels's reading undermines his larger claim that texts cannot critique their culture from within. Michaels is able to make that reading work as well as it does only because, as Jameson points out, he has "read" both culture and text reductively. Like more obviously traditional American literary critics, Michaels has decided what American culture is and then, with impressive rhetorical adroitness, read particular texts as "exemplary" of that abstraction.

As we shall see in the next section, in American Literary Scholarship, that procedure is the norm rather than the exception. The way Michaels associates various cultural acts is not an example of a new American Literary Scholarship. It is one of the practices that any really new scholarship would replace. Though Michaels adopts his "inside" view as an alternative to the endless oscillation between subjective and objective models of interpretation that have preoccupied criticism, it seems to me to continue to subscribe to that model by assuming that an "objective" or "outside" view is necessary to critique. Although he has, rightly I believe, questioned the moral sentimentalism of various political attacks on the canon, his knowing (even cynical) acknowledgment of our inescapably fallen condition, our implication in the very system we abhor, has also been rightly criticized for its political quietism. Michaels's causation is static not because it is politically neutral but because it is everywhere, inescapable. If Tompkins makes change sound too easy, Michaels makes it sound impossible.[45]

I want to make it clear that I am not denying the theoretical possibility of establishing connections between texts and the world.[46] My complaint is a more narrow one about the particular way even revisionist critics have relied on a totalizing notion of American culture to connect textual and cultural facts in an oversimplified and hence reductive narrative coherence. The job of connecting literature with other discourses and, indeed, of describing the workings of individual texts, is bigger than the one recent historicist critics of American literature have undertaken. At bottom, the new historicists of American literature, by trying once more to connect literature and culture, have been after the wrong game. Michaels's claim to describe "the position of texts" within a "system of representation" or to "characterize a certain moment" in the appeal of indeterminacy moves too quickly past what seem to me the most important challenges for any new literary history: the need to specify the nature of relationships between signification in literature and in other cultural practices, and the coherence of relationships between particulars in history, most crucially, between past and present.[47]

If Americanists want to reclaim the cultural authority that the work of their professional predecessors derived from its nationalist focus, then they need to account not so much for the place of individual texts in the circumstances of their production as for their continuing interest (or lack of interest) over time for both professional and lay readers. The need for some such explanation applies as much to noncanonical as to canonical works. In both cases, critics have to explain better, to themselves as well as to nonspecialists, why they are reading books, especially *old* books. The explanations they develop will always and necessarily depend on local interests, but those interests are far more complex and less neatly causal than the formalist "prejudices" so many historicist critics have made their target.

The skeleton in the closet of Americanists' repudiation of formalism has been that their cultural alternative is also part of the old opposition and depends on it. The current political factionalism ignores the degree to which the cultural and formal postures are symbiotic. Both rely on an insupportable distinction between content and form and on measuring texts by finding textual meaning in their correspondence to something outside them. That unacknowledged incest leaks out here and there, however, as in Bercovitch's assertion that from his "ideological" perspective, "race, class and gender are *formal* principles of art."[48] Despite demands for cultural relevance, formalist rhetoric still sells, indeed, may still be essential to selling in the profession. The lingering power of this language, if it is not (and I think it is not) merely an institutional relic, discloses the inadequacy of the unproblematized turn to culture, just as the pseudoscientific rhetoric of early New Criticism hinted at limitations implicit in its aestheticism that are, by now, taken for granted.

This buried kinship may explain why, in some of its recent incarnations, the word *culture* seems to appear in surprisingly conservative contexts. "Our classic writers," Bercovitch asserts, "were accomplices of the culture in its complex totality."[49] With its bow toward a canon of classic writers, this formulation reveals the conservative potential that is unleashed when words like *ideology* are used to totalize American culture. It is not enough that ideology connects literature to culture. The best literature, the classic works must capture that culture with a unique richness and completeness. Thus, even as their users deride the American "myth," they express and reinforce that traditionally American democratic union of the individual and the nation. Like Ben Franklin or Walt Whitman, classic works are exceptional precisely because they are so typical. It is a powerful feature of the traditional story about American culture that it absorbs the atypical into itself. Though these arguments evoke deeply ingrained loyalties, they ride roughshod over all the doubts about established canons, nationalist bias, and aesthetic standards that are fundamental to the current revisionist debate in literary studies. Such claims appeal to venerable allegiances, but remaining as they do within the confines of the old debate, they resurrect the old problems, even as they reproduce the reassuring and familiar old stabilities.

My critique of the direction revisionism has taken in American literary studies is not founded on nostalgia for the professional *status quo ante*, a longing for the critical past. On the contrary, it is obvious that the conversation about American literature is more lively than it has been for many years, and that is undeniably to the good. My purpose here is to try to point out some of the traditional constraints that remain and prevent Americanists from pursuing still more vital lines of inquiry. In terms of professional training, pedagogy, and departmental structures, the implication of the revisionary gestures produced so far has been that we are revising American literature when we alter its content, that what we are revising is a canon rather than a wide range of institutionalized practices that spread their influences far beyond the well-defended borders of our own field. So far, this confusion has led Americanists who are interested in rehistoricizing American writing to concentrate more on demonstrating the conditionality of that canon than on developing a satisfactory redescription of literary study that articulates text and context by reconceiving both terms and confronting the broader implications of Romantic thinking for our own work. This may mean more than merely a new round of canonical expansion.[50]

In the context of historicist critiques, it begs too many important questions to say simply that Americanists should recognize and accommodate the diversity of the field. The effort in the name of diversity to enlist historicist theoretical approaches in the traditional project of outlining a history of American literature is both wrongheaded and deeply conservative. It is wrongheaded because it suggests that the variety of practices that the term *diversity* would ostensibly unite are merely alternate perspectives on the *same* subject or different routes to the *same* end. They might better be described as offering competing stories, alternate descriptions embracing different and, in the case of historicism at least, incompatible assumptions and aims. It is conservative because it pretends to a descriptive rather than an evaluative approach, while it actually legitimates the power of consensus and, thus, of the *status quo*.[51] By identifying the central business of the field as the competition between competing agendas, established institutions absorb dissent and exercise hegemonic power of the most disturbing sort, the power that prevents potentially disruptive issues—like the bankruptcy of the traditional concept of American literature—from becoming current in the conversation in the first place.

If we are to take the inconsistencies of foundationalist thinking as part of our acknowledged subject rather than simply rattling around within them, we must recognize our susceptibility not just to the "theoretical urge" for an explanatory umbrella but also to the positivist urge that makes us want to make unjustified claims about the connections between texts and something purportedly more real, to culture. Like the rest of the profession, American literary studies has only just begun to question the assumptions and methods that have supplied its intellectual and institutional foundations. Uncertain as we are where that questioning might lead, it ought to be clear that orthodoxies, with their firm formulations and reassuring rhetoric, can only stifle inquiry. We should not rush to establish new stabilities before we have exorcised the pervasive and still potent ghosts of the old. Among other things, banishing those ghosts means giving up the comfortable assumptions that, embodied in the word *America,* have both shaped the questions Americanists ask and supplied the answers. The long-term project of reconceiving literary history is changing the work of scholars in many fields. To take part in that change, Americanists will have to repeal the articles of scholarly faith that built the institution of American Literary Scholarship.

From the point of view I would like to see established, the institution of American Literary Scholarship looks less like the vanguard of change—a "new world" of criticism—than an isolated fortification protecting a (slowly) dying view of America and a dying form of historical narrative. Van Wyck Brooks's complaint about American culture seems to me true in spades for American Literary Scholarship. It "is filled with groups that do not stand for living issues, do not engage our personal energies. . . . They no longer touch men's vital instincts." In this light, American literary studies should not be too quick to congratulate itself on its ability to assimilate "hostile" theoretical forces and refit them to its own ends. Its flirtation with theory may have unexpected consequences. The flood of prescriptions for the perceived ills of literary studies share a desire to make the vitality of our work more apparent. Clearly, American literary studies shares with literary studies in general the need to rethink mimesis, to develop new terms for the relationship of literature and life.

If, as now seems to be the case, we want to abandon foundationalist and ahistorical debates, we will also have to abandon the terms we have used for more than a century to describe American literature. Looking back at their own professional past, contemporary scholars have generally viewed its monuments as more or less adequate approximations to modern scholarly standards of truth and accuracy and so have obscured the fact that the work of the inventors of the American literary tradition was a series of strategic efforts to deal with the problems of writing a coherent American literary history. This condescension to its own critical past has had the added (dis)advantage of helping contemporary scholarship forget that it too is a strategic project.[52]

« 2 »

Reading the Tradition: The Rhetoric of Transcendentalist Scholarship

When we speak of the Transcendental Movement . . . we
indulge in criticism in the very name.

H. C. GODDARD

Though it may be my particular vestige of the national chauvinism I
attack in this work, I believe that the history of American Literary
Scholarship displays with particular force the continuing problems of a
literary historiography that is still working its way out of idealism. As a
constraint on possible interpretations, the notion of "America" has
always both enabled and confined the beliefs even of its adherents. That
was, in fact, its purpose. The marks of that confinement appear in the
peculiar shapes American literary criticism has had to twist itself into to
describe its subject. The patient willingness of criticism to do so
measures the power of the idea. "America" was important enough to
make those rhetorical contortions worthwhile.

Since the eighteenth century, the demand to justify the idea of America
to the world has called out for confirming facts in a variety of voices,
some of which, like Noah Webster's in 1785, actually antedated the
nation's Constitution. By the beginning of the nineteenth century, British
doubters were arguing that time was flying and the promises of the
American experiment had begun to look like empty boasts. What had
America done that could justify shattering old cultural orders?[1] Commen-

39

taries and reviews like Sydney Smith's famous attack in the *Edinburgh Review* were characteristic of the breed, and seem driven by the anger of an outraged parent railing that a prodigal offspring, having deserted the rich family estate, will never amount to anything.[2] American writing, they say with all possible condescension, is just what one would expect from a wilderness: crude, unformed, low. Yet, at the same time, unwilling to let the prodigal off so easily, they argue that primitive conditions cannot excuse failure, and point to America's large population and bustling cities. So active a nation must be at fault if it has failed after so much time and such large promises to produce a literature of its own. Some of the more cheerfully pessimistic writers even doubted that literature would ever find a foothold in the New World.

These British doubts about the American cultural future may sound merely quaint to our ears, like predictions of the impossibility of manned flight or the impracticality of television. Nonetheless, this rhetoric had substantial consequences at the time, and its influence continues into ours. Even as they insisted on the originality of American writing and on its independence from British influences, American readers helplessly submitted to that influence in the most crucial way by taking up the defense of American writing in the terms that had been established by the British tradition, the only terms available to Americans even as they worked to assert their independence. In fact, there is not much point, on these issues, in calling them separate cultures, since to give them separate status is to beg the very question writers on both sides of the Atlantic were addressing.

Shaping the American response, British critiques determined the strategies that Americans would use to describe American writing for generations. Despite their insistent efforts to free themselves from British intellectual hegemony, American critics, too, were still constrained within the limits of this inherited language. The only terms they had for assessing literature were those they had inherited from their continuing residence within British culture, terms that had been designed around British texts. British writing was refined and polished, its diction and rhythms were the perfect models of writing in English. It showed artistic maturity and offered the intellectual and historical background without which literature could have no solid grounding and no very interesting subjects. Writing in America faced an impossible task. To be really American, it had to be new. But if it were really new, it could not be good.

For the first 100 years of the nation's history, the products of American letters looked, even to American observers, so relatively few in number, so scattered and miscellaneous, that they could hardly be said to constitute any sort of tradition at all. Instead of a great literary edifice proudly erected alongside the older European structures, American writing looked disturbingly like a few timid shacks huddled along the margin of a howling intellectual wilderness. Yet, it was inconceivable to American writers that a great nation would not produce a great literature. To say that another way, the lack of a great literature could not be imagined because it would cast unacceptable doubts on the greatness of the nation. These were the motives behind the idealist rhetoric that constituted American Literary Scholarship. With a nationalist zeal, nineteenth-century Americans called for a truly *native* literature to distinguish their new state from Britain culturally as well as politically, and ever since, American literary studies has conceived its subject on an idealist model. The rhetoric of American literature produced a tradition by fiat. Calling literature American became a way of justifying its value apart from established standards of value.

Insofar as scholarship has continued that preoccupation into the present, then, it still acts out conflicts grounded in far different circumstances. From the start, American Literary Scholarship has been part, and a rather reactionary part, of a debate over the sources of interpretive authority that has preoccupied Western thought since the breakdown of the ancient view of two worlds: conditional and ideal. That debate raged with particular ferocity in the third quarter of the nineteenth century, just as the institution of academic literary studies was being developed. American Literary Scholarship negotiated this debate in crucial and problematic terms by trying to identify worldly political orders with the ideal aesthetic order of literature, and each subsequent generation of Americans has described the subject in terms appropriate to its own time.

Increasingly, as American Literary Scholarship moved into the twentieth century, the peculiar project of American literary exegesis—to flesh out its enabling ideal with particulars—has been conditioned as much by changes in the emerging practice of professional scholarship as by new information about the subject. Over the past century, that inquiry has explored and exhausted spiritual, psychological, economic, and political models of explanation, as each scholarly generation has reshaped the arguments of the last to fit current critical fashion. Yet, through 100 years of trying, the imagined American Ideal has frustrated all efforts at specification. Like the perfect circle of the horizon, it has receded before the eager advance of criticism because, like the horizon, it has marked the limit of the beholder's view rather than the edge of the world.

The notion of Transcendentalism has been central to this project, central, that is, not so much to American writing as to American criticism of American writing. Like the American Renaissance it has grounded, Transcendentalism has been less an event in the world than an event in the minds of American scholars. It has been elevated in the service of much more powerful ideas, the notion of an American national ideal, the foundation of national identity and of the professional study of American literature. In American scholarship, Transcendentalism has housed critics' dreams for America and its literature, and critical descriptions of Transcendentalism have mirrored those dreams. Scholarly evaluations of American literature have always expressed a vision of the nation and its appropriate cultural expression, rather than any indwelling truth about the writing Americans have produced. While Emerson and his contemporaries called for a literature to match the promise of a new nation, by World War I, scholars were increasingly willing to assume that this call had been answered and were ready to demonstrate that American literature was the adequate voice of the national character.

Not described or describable itself, Transcendentalism enables the description of the rest by providing a center about which it can be ordered. If Puritan New England (rather than, say, commercial Jamestown) has been chosen as the historical origin of America, Transcendentalism has been designated its literary and intellectual origin.[3] Scholars engaged in the nineteenth-century search for origins used Transcendentalism as the funnel through which America's imagined Puritan origins passed to be transformed into the outburst of literary culture we have come to call the American Renaissance.[4] It represents the connection (absolutely essential for American Literary Scholarship) of America as literature to America as culture. The terms introduced into American discourse by Romantic writers like Emerson and Thoreau were co-opted and used to preserve an American corporate identity after the conditions that had justified America for earlier writers—a divine mission, external enemies, social and economic homogeneity—had become more rhetorical than real.[5] Nearly 100 years after the separation from Britain, anticipating the need to "bind up the nation's wounds," Abraham Lincoln and other rhetoricians of American identity described the national coherence in the popular rhetoric of moral idealism. Through all the differences that nearly destroyed the nation, they projected a pervasive American character or spirit that held the fragments together.

The word *Transcendentalism* has been used to help constitute an American literary tradition around the ideal notion of "America." The problems of reading Transcendentalist texts arise out of allegiance to that ideal and to the foundational thinking of which it is a dramatic example. In 1876, as the nation completed its 100th year, the profession of academic literary scholarship was just being born. And not surprisingly, the studies that sprang up to celebrate the American Centennial appropriated the idealist rhetoric of national unity to order the writing that Americans had produced in the decades since the Revolution. Conflating sentimental moralism and Christian idealism, the nineteenth-century inventors of Transcendentalism mined this rhetoric to describe a unified American cultural tradition independent of Europe. That assumption of *cultural* coherence supplied the key to *narrative* coherence in critical assessments of American literature, as the first American literary scholars worked to distinguish American writing from British in order to dignify it, the culture it represented, and not incidentally, their own scholarly interests.

The discourse about America may bristle with a rhetoric of adventure and the exploration of new territories, but explaining America has always been a conservative act, as interpreting the new to the old must be. The rhetoricians of American originality hastened to endow America with origins so as to give it a character where none had been. By doing so, they were not only distinguishing it, like a developing adolescent, from the British parent but controlling and determining its values and self-image so as to control potentially dangerous growth (and to rationalize existing directions). Their terms suggest a combined fascination with and fear of the created thing. Without such a defining explanation, America might look all too much like Frankenstein's monster, bolted together out of spare parts, full of vitality but out of control and alien to the rest of human culture. The Romantic ambivalence about forms that founded these attitudes has been crucial to criticism of Transcendentalism and lingers on in the antiformalism of current debates about the relations of literature and culture.

In this sense, the criticism of Transcendentalism has been criticism indeed. Not that O. B. Frothingham and subsequent, like-minded commentators were hostile to Transcendentalism.[6] They were not. But, as high priests of the Genteel Tradition, the scholars who gave shape to

Transcendentalism as an academic field were products of values and
assumptions akin to those against which Transcendentalism reacted in the
first place, however much those values may have assumed an aspect
derived from Transcendentalism to preserve them in a new age. As a
result, generations of scholars have both scorned and domesticated
Transcendentalist writing, turning it to their own purposes. Transcendentalism has been not so much a subject of study as a placeholder for the
ideologies and professional motives of its commentators. In effect, the
criticism of Transcendentalism, and of American literature, has been
entrusted to the Unitarians. The result is as predictable as if the history of
the American Indians had been written exclusively by the cowboys, as
until recently, it had.

Rooted in these nineteenth-century cultural debates, the critical discourse about Transcendentalism, like that about American literature, has
been preoccupied with early nineteenth-century concerns: with cultural
paranoia, with validating absolutes, with logical and aesthetic standards.
Those concerns have, in a remarkably consistent form, continued to
dominate scholarly discourse since the middle of the nineteenth century,
shaping discussion about Transcendentalism, and about American literature and culture for more than 100 years. By now, they have become so
familiar to us that we take them for features of the natural landscape. In
the great outburst of scholarship since World War II, they have not even
had to be explicitly stated. What started out as overt assumptions have
become unspoken intuitions.

As Richard Rorty says, "An intuition is never anything more than
familiarity with a language game, so to discover the source of our
intuitions is to relive the history of the philosophical language game we
find ourselves playing."[7] Like any descriptive term, the word *Transcendentalism* obscures as it illuminates. By examining the ways scholars
have used Transcendentalism to give coherence to their notions about
American literature, we may discover not only what that way of looking
at America has enabled us to see but what it has prevented us from seeing.
In reviewing the high points of Transcendentalist criticism, I am not
trying to write a professional history. I want to rehearse the development
and institutionalization of a particular critical discourse, a set of rhetorical strategies that have characterized and defined the practice of Transcendentalist studies, and of American Literary Scholarship. As Part 1
shows, these strategies, though in altered forms, remain central even to
contemporary theoretically informed discourse in the field.

A history of the scholarly portrait of Transcendentalism reveals the assumptions that have shaped prevailing accounts of American literature as a whole. That study traces the problems of Transcendentalist scholarship not so much to peculiarities of Transcendentalist writing as to the need to tell a particular kind of story about American writing, particularly to professional and political motives, and the critical strategies that installed Transcendentalism as the linchpin of the American literary tradition. In this reading, I am not trying to make space for new critical inquiry into the field by upsetting settled conclusions, nor am I trying to create new difficulties where critical contentment had reigned. On the contrary, my aim is to address issues that have been the preoccupation (if sometimes unspoken) of Transcendentalist scholarship starting with the first scholarly commentaries by writers who could claim firsthand experience of it.

The problems I shall point to are not products of imperfect knowledge or errors in reading. I am not going to offer new information that reshapes the old or bring to light passages from hitherto ''neglected'' texts that will correct the limited views of the critics who neglected them. My aims in reexamining these critical problems is not so much to resolve them by answering the questions they raise as to dissolve them altogether, to suggest that they no longer require answers. They are, from our point of view, or one I would like to be ours, the wrong questions, generated by outdated scholarly assumptions. However right (useful) those practices may have been in and for their time, they are wrong for ours. Discarding or reformulating them will not free us from all our critical problems. On the contrary, it will free us *for* them. It will confront us with the problems of our own time rather than of the nineteenth century, and with the job of producing another sort of understanding of what we have called Transcendentalism, of American writing, and of writing generally. That understanding will be ''better'' than the conventional one not because it is ''truer'' in any absolute sense, but because it works better, better fits the features of the texts we read, and better fits our uses for them. It would not claim superior knowledge or purer truth even if it could, because those are two of the key terms it makes problematical. I want to examine the convolutions that Transcendentalist criticism has thrown itself into for nearly 130 years as a way of clarifying why we ask the questions we ask and whether those questions are still the ones to which we most need answers.

O. B. FROTHINGHAM
Transcendentalism in New England
1876

The first major landmark of Transcendentalist criticism is O. B. Frothingham's *Transcendentalism in New England*.[8] Frothingham has a privileged place in the discourse about Transcendentalism. The son of N. L. Frothingham, whose prominence as minister to Boston's First Church put him at the center of Unitarian society, Frothingham knew the religious and social controversies of the 1840s firsthand. So, in addition to being the first "scholarly" study, *Transcendentalism in New England* might also be described as the last account by a "contemporary." Sydney Ahlstrom, editor of the 1959 reprinting of the book, like an anthropologist who had discovered a particularly cooperative informant, describes Frothingham's work as "the only serious historical effort written by a man deeply involved in the movement who yet lived long enough . . . to view matters with . . . a degree of objectivity. . . . It presents the movement's own estimate of its significance and place."

Though scholars like Ahlstrom have treated Frothingham as a sort of Transcendentalist, he seems less a radical thinker than a positively exemplary representative of Unitarian conservatism after 1850. In fact, it is a measure of the change in Unitarianism after midcentury that Frothingham's mentor, Theodore Parker, who had been one of the most influential advocates of change in the 1830s, moved into Andrews Norton's old position as *de facto* "pope" of the Boston church. As Parker's protégé, O. B. Frothingham was a perfect embodiment of the Unitarian establishment, and his work displays the strategies by which that establishment appropriated Transcendentalism for its own purposes.[9]

Ahlstrom's view of Frothingham epitomizes the conflict between subjective and objective models of interpretation that has been at the center of scholarly efforts to tie American texts to American culture, and that, as we saw in Michaels's work, continues to shape contemporary debates about new approaches to poststructuralist literary history. Another way of accounting for Frothingham's importance for modern scholars would be to say that he has helped them avoid the consequences of their distance from their subject. *Transcendentalism in New England* allows modern scholars to claim a direct connection through

Frothingham with their subject, much as Christ's elevation of Peter allows the church to claim a direct historical connection with God.

Frothingham himself expresses more modest scholarly aims. "This book," he says, "has but one purpose—to define the fundamental ideas of the philosophy, to trace them to their historical and speculative sources, and to show wither they tended." In its self-conscious directness and simplicity, this claim obscures the difficulties of nineteenth-century American literary historiography. It represses contradictory motives and ignores the narrative difficulties that shape, complicate, and ultimately frustrate Frothingham's attempt to present the straightforward history of Transcendentalism that he proposes. Despite his claims to objectivity, Frothingham does not actually try to describe Transcendentalism so much as to justify it to American readers who have been put off by its reputation for abstruse metaphysics and otherworldly mysticism. The necessity of placing Transcendentalism as the centerpiece of American letters conflicts with its alienation from the values of the American public and from the "official" pragmatic and everyday portrait of the American character. From the start, Frothingham strains to accommodate opposed claims on the national pride that inspired Centennial scholarship.

In the context of the scholarly discourse that was barely beginning to establish itself in America, Frothingham had to demonstrate that Transcendentalism was a participant in the intellectual conversation of its time and central to American culture, rather than a mere web of daydream and whimsy. This meant first connecting Transcendentalism to the major movements in European culture, and then, not altogether consistently, describing Transcendentalism as an American rather than a European product. American facts (and the fact of America) had, somehow, to be at once traditional and original, both a respectable part of the established European tradition and a fresh and unique event. Thus, in Frothingham's work, Transcendentalism becomes an epitome for the problematic relationship of past and present, or rather, from our point of view, an example of the persistent difficulties of making that relationship, as well as a figure for an American identity in scholarship.

Frothingham was "inventing" Transcendentalism in its modern sense to support a more general and largely implicit argument about America. As a distinctly American phenomenon and a coherent movement, an intellectually respectable *system* of thought, Transcendentalism becomes a key term in the domestication of America itself. The audience has changed over the years, but the project of justification that Frothingham established has characterized scholarship on Transcendentalism ever since. The issues that Frothingham faced in 1876 as a pioneering scholar in a still embryonic field and the terms he adopted in his effort to resolve them have been his most enduring legacy. More than 100 years later, they still preoccupy the study of Transcendentalism and of American literature.

Frothingham's narrative can be divided into two parts, reflecting the conflict between his needs to give Transcendentalism intellectual respectability in the larger context of European culture and to associate it with a distinctly American national identity. In the first half of his narrative, Frothingham turns his idealist rhetoric into a way of explaining cultural influence without incurring cultural debt. In the second, he unites the variety of American events into a unified "America" and demonstrates the centrality of Transcendentalism to that national identity. Idealism gave Frothingham a way of dissolving incongruent American facts into harmonious American essences. As the "miracles controversy" and Emerson's reservations about the Holy Supper show, the ineffectuality of Unitarian strategies for treating such relationships had been a principle inspiration for Transcendentalism in the first place. Frothingham's treatment displays the appropriation of potentially radical ideas like Emerson's by the conservative Unitarian social structure. Stripped of radical implications, they were put to the task of guaranteeing the moral order and assuring the spiritual foundations of everyday life, much as the Scottish Common Sense philosophy had done for an earlier generation trying to circumvent Lockean skepticism.

In the first section of his book, Frothingham provides Transcendentalism with a past, tracing its intellectual origins in European thought. How can Transcendentalism come from Europe and yet be uniquely American? Finding answers to this question has been a bustling subindustry in Transcendentalist scholarship, its mission captured in Perry Miller's famous rhetorical question, "Transcendentalism: Native or Imported?" Frothingham's strategy throughout this section is to treat his European subjects as precursors, steps on the path to "pure Transcendentalism," rather than examples of Transcendentalism itself, since that option would make Transcendentalism a European rather than an American invention. As Frothingham describes it, the influence of Kant, Schelling, Fichte, and Jacobi does not depend on their particular ideas, much less on any specifiable writings. The particulars of their work are abstracted and translated into character traits that mesh with the preconceived features of the American character. The acceptable terms are common to attempts to distinguish Europe from America. Europe is metaphysical and abstract; America is practical and concrete (p. 40).

By turning Transcendentalism into an abstraction, Frothingham can describe it as somehow preexisting the work of the writers he describes as its precursors. "They assumed its cardinal principles" (p. 57). Reflecting the still uncertain priorities of theological and historiographical rhetorics, he makes the process of historical influence an analog of spiritual inspiration. Like the inspirational sermon, the forms of the words were less important than the spiritual affections they generated in the audience. Regarding Kant, Jacobi, and Schelling, Frothingham asserts, despite his promise to describe the "beginnings of Transcendentalism," that "none of these writers taught formally the doctrines of the Transcendentalist philosophy, but they reflected one or another aspect of it" (p. 57). European thinkers did not infect Americans with a particular Transcendentalist philosophy. They "communicated its aroma, and so imparted the quickening breath of its soul to people who would have started back in alarm from its doctrines" (p. 57). These spiritual metaphors relieve Frothingham of the responsibility for describing the process of influence or the particular forms of the philosophy and permit him to portray Transcendentalism in more general (and generally acceptable) terms, the terms he applies to American culture: *spiritual, practical, undogmatic*. It is less than clear, however, how this character made it to the New World when none of those Frothingham cites as "communicators" actually communicated it.

Ultimately, Frothingham carries Transcendentalism from Europe to New England by sleight of hand. At the beginning of his chapter on the American avatars of Transcendentalism, "Transcendentalism in New England," he acknowledges the corner his conflicting assumptions have painted him into even as he tries to dance his way out of it. "The title of this Chapter," he admits, "is in a sense misleading. For with some truth it may be said that there never was such a thing as Transcendentalism out of New England" (p. 105). And in another question-begging metaphor, "Only in New England," he says, Transcendentalism "took root in the native soil and blossomed out in every form of social life." "When we speak of Transcendentalism," he now asserts, "we mean New England Transcendentalism."

This strategy is really very neat. Frothingham has been describing Transcendentalism as having been communicated from Europe in order to provide it with a respectable pedigree and also to avoid explaining just how, where, and when it was invented in America. But when he gets to America, he identifies the American version as the only "true" version, saying that America was the only place Transcendentalism "had a chance" to develop (p. 105). In this new context, the "old world" elements are not even the precursors of Transendentalism, but simply "such literature as there was" (p. 106), raw material indifferently supplied by surrounding culture. Americans "seized upon" this raw material and "dealt with it" in what Frothingham describes, without explanation, as "typical democratic fashion, paying no undue regard to its foreign reputation" (p. 106). The result, we are clearly intended to understand, was a decidedly American Transcendentalism, the inevitable and exclusive product of European materials adapted by characteristically American methods to uniquely American conditions.

Having established Transcendentalism (and his narrative) in America, Frothingham also takes on a new set of problems. In particular, he trades the conflicts between tradition (which he wants to assert) and foreign influence (which he wants to deny) for the questions of American (rather than European) origins and the essential compatibility of Transcendentalism with the dominant social values valorized as the "American national character." The problem of origins is complicated by the fact that Frothingham could not get around his own assumption that the roots of New England culture must somehow reach into Puritanism (a bias familiar to twentieth-century scholarship). But as a product himself of Unitarian dissent from what it imagined as Puritan dogmatism, Frothingham could not quiet his equally strong conviction that the authoritarian rigidity of Puritanism disqualified it as a fit model for American culture.

Faced with these incompatible motives, Frothingham rewrites history, revisioning the march of American Orthodoxy as an idealist parade.[10] Though, in his discussion of European sources, his first gesture had been to dismiss classical origins for Transcendentalism (p. 1), here he argues that Plato rather than Calvin was the mastermind of "Trinitarian" (as opposed to Puritan) faith. "The Platonic philosophy being transcendental in its essence and tendency, communicated this character to Christian speculation. The skeletons of ancient polemics were buried deep beneath the soil of orthodoxy. . . . The living faith of new England, in its spiritual aspects, betrayed its ancestry" (pp. 107–8). With this characterization, he softens the harsh *forms* of Puritanism that he found distasteful with a palatable idealist spirit.

Rewriting the history of American theology also entailed retouching his earlier portrait of the American intellectual landscape. In this revision, the Platonic undercurrent washed through the New England intellectual scene as well. Earlier he suggested that the doctrines of Transcendentalism were not naturally attractive to Americans and had to be smuggled into the country, but here Frothingham paints early nineteenth-century America as fertile ground for would-be Transcendentalists. Every feature of American life suited the development of the Transcendentalist temper. In addition to the beneficial influences of flexible laws, practical and independent habits, and a plastic social structure, the self-dependent habits of the new country made rigid Old World philosophies (by which he means Lockeanism) inherently unattractive. "The philosophy of sensation, making great account, as it did, of circumstances, arrangements, customs usages, rules of education and discipline, was alien and disagreeable to people who, having just emancipated themselves from political dependence on the mother country, were full of confidence in their ability to set up society for themselves" (pp. 106–7). Even before the Transcendentalist era, all America was natively and inherently idealist. This close association between idealism (which has become a synonym for Transcendentalism) and the American character has become so important to the coherence of Frothingham's account that it can brook no exceptions. With elaborate qualifications that disclose his impatience toward historical particulars that refuse to verify the truth as he knows it must be, Frothingham asserts that "every native New Englander was at heart, whether he suspected it or not, radically and instinctively a disciple of Fichte or Schelling, of Cousin or Jouffroy" (p. 107). Frothingham makes New England seem so ready for the Transcendentalist advent that one wonders how there could have been any opposition at all.

In Frothingham's new idealist history, the Lockean philosophy entered into New England like a sensuous serpent into an idealist paradise, tied not to Enlightenment confidence in reason but to an Orthodox dogmatism that, according to Frothingham, had twisted the true idealist spirit of Puritan faith. "Adherents of the sensuous philosophy" corrupted the sweet spirit of idealism that was essential to Puritanism and turned it into "the hard, external, dogmatical character which in new England provoked the Unitarian reaction'' (pp. 108–9). Yet, Unitarian thought cannot stand fast with idealism if it is to be superseded by Transcendentalism. Just as materialist philosophy turned Puritan Platonism into rigid doctrine, it twisted Unitarian respect for individual inquiry into a skepticism that threatened all faith and order. ''Skepticism throve by what it fed on; and, before they had become fully aware of the possible results of their diligent study, their powers had acquired a confidence that encouraged ventures beyond the walls of Zion . . . opened the door to the new speculation which carried unlooked-for heresies in its bosom; and before the gates could be closed the insidious enemy had penetrated to the citadel'' (pp. 114–15).

When Transcendentalism enters this scene, it comes not as a radical heresy from Unitarian common sense, as was popularly assumed, but as a conservative champion, the savior of traditional Christian idealism and a bastion against the ravages of skeptical insecurity. The possibility of unguided inquiry and ''the absolute freedom of the human mind'' (p. 114) without a ''system of philosophy on which a creed could be, by *common consent,* built'' reflects the fear of disorder that inspires Frothingham's insistent portrayal of Transcendentalism as systematic—fear of the very intellectual freedom he superficially embraces. Frothingham adopts idealist rhetoric to affirm the values of conservative Boston. It allows him to divide American culture into its ''real'' idealist component and its superficial sensualist one—Puritanism into doctrine and spirit, Unitarianism into thought and feeling. What was essential about America prepared the way for Transcendentalist thought (and for Frothingham's social world), while what might have opposed Transcendentalist thought was only an artificial overlay (of suspect European and metaphysical character) on the true American structure.

But this useful strategy contains its own problems. The myth of American idealism that Frothingham constructs to give coherence to his story of Transcendentalism as American ends by effacing all the features that might make the idealism he describes particularly American. Coherence, as we saw in Kolodny, frustrates diversity. ''Idealism,'' he asserts, ''is of no clime or age'' (p. 115). His idealist Puritanism, insofar as it is American, is only a Christianized version of Plato, and the idealist population of America that stood ready to welcome the birth of Transcendentalism apparently found their masters in Germany and France rather than in New England. Frothingham's demonstration of the affinity between Transcendentalism and American culture ends by implicitly reaffirming the debts American culture owed to Europe. Moreover, the idealizing of Transcendentalism that made its origins American conflicts with Frothingham's desire to characterize Transcendentalism as pragmatic and align it with the everyday values that fit his vision of America after the Civil War.

In effect, the image of Transcendentalism Frothingham finally presents is a nonimage, a refusal to specify Transcendentalism. For Frothingham and for subsequent scholars, this is a key strategy for domesticating it. By describing Transcendentalism as an ideal essence, a "spiritual tendency" that is only imperfectly manifested, when manifested at all, in any of the acts that have been associated with what he now calls the "Transcendentalist movement," Frothingham is free to attribute all the blame for Transcendentalist "excesses," to imperfect forms, which were not themselves Transcendentalism. These collected strategies—ambivalence about history, mixed allegiance to and avoidance of the past, and a complete unwillingness or inability to describe the present—characterize the American mythographer who seeks to wed an idealized past to a utopian American present. Unable to really leave the past behind, he ends up looking ever forward with fear and expectation toward a perfect future that never comes.

H. C. GODDARD

Studies in New England Transcendentalism
1908

The second major work devoted to Transcendentalism was intimately associated with the institutionalization of American Literary Scholarship. Both H. C. Goddard's *Studies in New England Transcendentalism* and his later chapter on Transcendentalism in *The Cambridge History of American Literature* were written under the supervision of W. P. Trent, who, as director of the *CHAL* project, did as much as any single scholar to shape the course of academic inquiry into American writing before World War I.[11] For Goddard no less than Frothingham, Transcendentalism was a means to an end. *Studies* was Goddard's dissertation at Columbia and had been directed by Trent, who schooled Goddard in his own moral conservatism and in the need to accommodate his subject to the "needs of a healthy-minded, sound-hearted people."[12]

Like Goddard's work, the earliest academic studies that began to appear in the first decade of this century were self-conscious exercises by apprentices in an embryonic field. These works are sensitive to their own status as fledgling professional efforts (dissertations), as well as pioneering ones in a subject area still foreign to American departments of English.[13] As a result, they confronted for the first time the conflict between the discipline-justifying need to distinguish America from its transatlantic roots and the scholarly imperative to acknowledge the countless debts American writers owed to Europe.

Goddard's task in the first years of the twentieth century was not precisely the same as Frothingham's a generation earlier. Frothingham wrote to distinguish a unified American culture from European culture, and though, by Goddard's time, the particular insecurities that motivated Frothingham had faded, his terms remain largely the same because they operate within a smaller sphere, the professional. He writes not to distinguish American from European culture but to distinguish, among professionals, between American and European literature. Frothingham focused on the Americanness of Transcendentalism and on influence, softened Transcendentalist radicalism with his own genteel culture, and severed the historical connection between Europe and America in order to minimize European influence. Goddard, on the other hand, concentrates on historical change. He wants to refute the charge of absurdity that disqualifies Transcendentalism for serious scholarly study and to show how Transcendentalism fits into the existing framework of historical understanding. Unlike Frothingham, Goddard wants to preserve the historical connections that give Transcendentalism and American literature a place in the historical field.

Schooled in positivist historiography, Goddard assumes that a "coherent story about America" can be discovered amongst the fragments of observable fact. Improved understanding simply requires additional scholarly scrutiny. Earlier studies, he explains, have been too brief, the key questions have been "treated only incidentally . . . the pertinent facts being scattered through many pages; and even though these matters had been handled exhaustively in every case, it is quite conceivable that the individual results might take on an entirely new meaning when considered collectively" (p. 11). The scholar's role here is the humble and disinterested one of gathering and arranging all the pertinent information so that it can, more or less on its own, assume the shape of truth. The authority of Goddard's account does not depend, as Frothingham's did at least in part, on his own unique perspective. It depends on his ability to provide what he calls a "massing of evidence." The truth lies concealed somewhere and will reveal itself in a natural pattern if only enough facts are laid end to end.[14]

Goddard's participation in the rhetoric of scientific history is complicated, however, by competing motives. In effect, Goddard wants to tell two stories at once. The first is a scholarly story of sources and influence that identifies him with prevailing practice in his new profession, and the second an ideological story that will give his subject intellectual importance and respectability. The latter proclaims the unity of American literature and asserts its unique historical role as the reconciler of the divided practical and the spiritual strains of European culture. Each of these stories is crucial to his problematical role as "American" "Scholar," but, like his professional heirs, Goddard cannot tell one coherent story embodying both aims. So, he has to tell them serially. And although he initially asserts that a resolution of the problems Transcendentalism presents can be found in careful scholarship, his historical narrative ultimately turns to ideology to resolve what he calls the "paradox" of Transcendentalism (p. 148).

From the start, the word Frothingham treated as a hook to hang his American values on seems to Goddard more like the multipointed horns of a scholarly dilemma on which he is all too likely to hang himself if he is not careful. The nature of Transcendentalism, he asserts in the manner of Frothingham and with no more justification, is not in dispute. "The fact is that [Transcendental philosophy] is about the least mooted point in the whole discussion" (p. 2). The word had "a quite definite and unmistakable meaning, nor can that meaning be said to have undergone any development or change." The defining features he offers—divine immanence, the part in the whole, a soul pervading man and the world, life as growth, natural beauty as a route to God—and his abundant list of "minor" corollaries (self-reliance, individualism, universalism, evil as a negative force, anti-authoritarianism) take in a lot of ground, but even so, they only partly coincide with those Frothingham had proclaimed as central thirty years earlier: the worth of man, divinity in instinct, and the divinity of nature. Such agreement as there is seems too general to be very useful. Yet, Goddard insists that Transcendentalism not only does but must have one clear meaning "if names are to correspond with realities" (p. 21).

In examining the slippery term *Transcendentalism* Goddard is caught between conflicting desires for order and accuracy, between his desire to have the word mean only "one thing" as the center of American letters, and his recognition that the facts are complex and obscure categorical boundaries. In a passage that might summarize the problems of subsequent Transcendentalist studies, Goddard admits that

> all the radical tendencies of that day may be considered, perhaps, as parts of a single movement, and even the extremes . . . may seem to blend quite imperceptibly together. But the point is that if we glibly call the whole Transcendentalism, we shall certainly be meaning something very different from what we mean when we speak of the Transcendentalism of Emerson or Parker. No one can dictate how the term shall finally be used, but we shall inevitably fall into great confusion if we employ it in several senses, or if he who criticizes means one thing while he who reads may understand another. (p. 7)

Sensitive to this truth, subsequent scholars have been careful to use the word *Transcendentalism* to mean only one thing, but they have managed this trick only by not inquiring too deeply into what that thing is.

In practice, scholarship carries Goddard not from the thicket into the clearing but from one thicket into another. Learning does not take him toward the unity and order he requires; it only multiplies distinctions. His opening question, "What was the nature of the Transcendental movement in New England?" seems to have no one answer. Instead, there is always another opposition, another set of extremes. In its stubbornly multiple meanings, the word *Transcendentalism* ensures confusion and clouds objective scholarship by luring scholars into dangerous interpretation. "When we speak of the Elizabethan Age, of the Restoration Drama, of the Victorian Poets, we use terms purely or mainly temporal in their significance. But when we speak of the Transcendental Movement, we go further, we indulge in criticism in the very name." And with an insight that resonates throughout the practice of American Literary Scholarship, he goes on: "This is likely to prove dangerous, for we are tempted, if not compelled, to assume at the beginning what really should be the outcome of our discussion—a definition of transcendentalism" (p. 8). This prophetic remark reveals that even this early in Transcendentalist studies, Goddard sensed the pitfalls of the field, though he was as helpless as his successors to avoid them.

Despite Goddard's allegiance to scholarly objectivity, his narrative is shaped largely by the need to justify American literature to a professional academic audience. Several recent studies of the institutionalization of literary scholarship in American universities have stressed the influence of the German scientific model in establishing philology and historical scholarship as the dominant methodological models in the early years of the profession. But Goddard's example complicates this view by suggesting that the relationship of scientific and ideological terms was more complex, their rhetorical implications more interwoven, than such a schematic model of influence would suggest.[15] In American Literary Scholarship, at least, it appears that scholars like Goddard assumed the trappings of scientific history to rationalize their ideologically driven professional practice. Without numbers, power, or professional organizations of their own, they adopted the dominant style to make a place for themselves in the professional discourse around them.

Ideology and method were in symbiosis. Idealist ideology justified scholarly practice by giving it a mission—the coherence of American literature—apart from the abstract pursuit of knowledge for its own sake, which would not have appealed to an American scholarship predicated, as we have seen, on the practical. In turn, empirical scholarship reinforced the validity of ideological claims with the growing prestige of professional academic knowledge. The result mirrored the opposition between form and spirit, realism and idealism that echoes throughout Romantic writing.

Yet, for all their mutual support, the two strains led in opposite directions. In Goddard's case, the split between methodological and ideological motives is so sharp that it generates two distinct tables of contents, two separate rationalizing orders for his material that suggest sharply divergent uses for his book and opposed approaches to historiography. Each of these two stories is equally essential to Goddard's work, but they conflict in style and method, as well as in their implicit conclusions. The first makes modest claims to amassing dispersed facts and assessing (not necessarily refuting) charges of Transcendentalist absurdity. The second interprets facts to make ideological claims about American Transcendentalism as midwife to the modern world, delivering culture from the eighteenth century to the nineteenth.

The first table of contents, the official one, portrays the work as a traditional piece of scientific scholarship and represents Goddard's desires to bring the study of Transcendentalism (and thus himself) into the world of respectable scholarly discourse. The first chapter, "Unitarianism and Transcendentalism," establishes the intellectual and social context. The second, "Intellectual and Literary Influences Affecting the Transcendentalists," traces the sources of their thought. The third and fourth, on "The Transcendentalists and Practical Life" address the Transcendentalist violations of "common sense" that discourage serious scholarly consideration of the subject. These, Goddard claims, are the areas that have been neglected in previous studies, making them the appropriate theme of scholarship conceived as the bringer of new light into dark places.

The second table of contents, however, suggests the co-presence of a different set of motives. It redescribes the study as an analysis of the ways Transcendentalism blends European and native traditions, the intellectual tendencies of the eighteenth century with those of the nineteenth. Goddard describes the passage between the two as an age of transition from a period in which reason and passion run in parallel but divided streams to one in which they are rejoined. In the process, it identifies Transcendentalism with the inevitable march of progress, and makes Transcendentalism, and the American literary tradition he finds rooted there, into the foundation of the modern world as he would like to conceive it. What he calls the "revolutionary age" united the divided streams of eighteenth-century reason and Romantic feeling, and Transcendentalism is his messenger of that age to America. Viewed in this way, Transcendentalism becomes more than just another subject for scholarship, as respectable as the more-established study of British subjects. It becomes the key to understanding the modern world, just as respectable as British literature but better.

The ideological reading of Goddard's work provides coherence for his narrative. It domesticates to American values not merely Transcendentalism (that had been Frothingham's task) but historical change itself, producing certain and reassuringly acceptable meanings out of the historical flux. As an instrument of this professional project, the word *Transcendentalism* becomes a label that Goddard applies to the appearance, as inevitable as passing time, of the American nineteenth century. The unifying "Spirit of the Age" (p. 31) is not simply an abstraction from historical events; it is a veritable spirit indeed, hard at work making history. Even if, as he remarks, it arrives a little late in America, the nineteenth century was bound to come (p. 26).

The scholarly clarity Goddard prized and aspired to is more helpful, not to say attainable, in principle than in practice. It cannot protect Transcendentalist writing from charges of absurdity. The chapter that

Goddard advertises as an unprejudiced investigation of the popular charges against Transcendentalism ends by recapitulating and confirming them. Goddard is forced to concede that "the popular criticism of the Transcendentalists has beyond doubt a basis in real fact" (p. 148). Having made this admission, Goddard abandons the questions that have led him into this thicket for others that he hopes will be more productive. "The vital question has not yet been asked. That question is not, How far would it seem that these men *must* have been out of touch with practical life? but rather, How far *were* they out of touch with it?" (p. 148). Having rejected Transcendentalist expression in favor of its "thought," he now rejects Transcendentalist "thought" in favor of the practical lives of the thinkers. The distinction between thought and expression preserves the value of Transcendentalism as "thought," and also allows Goddard to validate cultural values as scholarly imperatives—seriousness, balance, conformity to rule—and thus to wed scholarship with ideology. As in Frothingham, the lives of the Transcendentalists correspond to their particularly "American" contribution, while their speculative thought (which had until now been the particular subject of Goddard's scholarship) is implicitly derivative from Europe and hence can be discounted.

Yet, even this formulation does not give Goddard the coherent portrait of Transcendentalism he is seeking. As it is represented by the lives of its members, Transcendentalism still suffers from a stubborn internal split between the concrete and the ideal: Alcott, the man of speculation, a latter-day Don Quixote, struggling manfully if pathetically, to make his way in a world for which he was not made. Parker balancing Alcott, a man of "prodigious . . . labor of the most exhausting, varied unselfish, and productive kind," fitted to action by temperament and training, a lover of the "simple and the concrete" (p. 165), the symbol of conscience and pragmatism, and so (quoting Frothingham) "the best working plan of an American yet produced" (p. 166). Emerson is full of "respect and love for the simple, plain, concrete things of life" (p. 175), but Goddard admits that "tried by any such standard of activity as that which Theodore Parker set, Emerson's life was inactive and out of relation to the practical." Fuller, too, "united apparently contradictory elements." (p. 180).

Goddard's portraits of individual Transcendentalists do not reconcile the conflict between facts and accepted social values that caused dissatisfaction with their writing. They only reveal individuals torn apart by irreconcilable motives. Although he wants to say that Transcendentalism is the "union of two contrasting elements, the product of two opposing forces" (p. 183), he shows only the "contrasts and oppositions," leaving the principle of their union obscure. And Goddard finally has to admit that there are "two Margaret Fullers," "two Channings," "two Emersons," "two Parkers and two Alcotts" (p. 182).

Goddard's scholarship cannot discover a coherent American tradition. On the contrary, facts proliferate beyond all shaping, and Goddard is drowning in them. The deeper into the facts he goes, the more diffuse his subject gets until he asks, almost as if he were talking to himself, "Into the wilderness of names with which this survey . . . of these Transcendentalists has surrounded us, how will it be possible to bring any meaning?" (p. 106). "Once more, what is the meaning of all this?" he repeats, and again, "How will it be possible to bring any meaning?" (p. 107). Going down for the third time in the sea of particulars, Goddard reaches out for the Americanist's well-worn lifeline of abstraction. But in the increasingly empirical scholarly context, he cannot cling to it even for his life without suggesting its inadequacy. "It may seem equivalent to abandoning the inquiry as hopeless to say that the real origin of the movement was 'influences in the air,'" he admits, yet goes on to the ironically minimal claim that "to put it so would doubtless leave an impression much nearer the truth than to assign any one writer or group of writers as its source" (p. 107).

Faced with the refusal of the historical particulars to assume the coherent "American" form of Transcendentalism he had imagined for them, Goddard retreats from facts entirely, even from the facts of his own earlier account, and takes up the traditional story of American national identity that served so well in the nineteenth century. To salvage a sense of coherence out of contradiction, Goddard invokes the Puritan spirit. This ritual incantation is an abrupt about-face from his earlier treatment of the Puritans, whose only role so far was as the dogmatic villain in Channing's struggle for free thought. But now, in a paragraph so artificially appended that it rings of *non sequitur,* Goddard reaches once again for the assured tone. It is a fact, he says, "repeatedly brought out in the course of the discussion" and one "for the purposes of our study . . . of unsurpassed importance" that "the most conspicuous similarity of these Transcendentalists was simply their *Puritan character*" (p. 183).

This astonishing conclusion to his inquiry, bearing as it does despite his claims to the contrary, so obscure a relation to any facts he has so far presented, cannot be explained in the scholarly terms he has espoused so far. In this case, he gives up all pretence of attending to empirical fact and falls back entirely on a moralistic interpretation that sounds like a quotation from Frothingham. "They . . . had the same moral courage, the same adherence to principle, the same purity, nobility, elevation of spirit that belonged to the best of the old New England" (p. 183). In a pinch, Goddard appeals unblushingly to the American tradition. The "best of the old New England" excludes Puritan dogmatism as it had for Frothingham, and, once again, removes the identifying principle of Transcendentalism out of the world of action, indeed out of the nineteenth century, and identifies it with the suddenly unproblematical imagined origins of the American experience.

As soon as Goddard assumes this position, it becomes the centerpiece of his, now overtly nationalistic, conclusion. There, he minimizes European influences in Frothingham's terms. Europe provides an "indispensable emotional atmosphere" (p. 186). And he repudiates the stale conservatism of Unitarianism as an adequate preparation for this new spirit. Its "indigenous elements" were not "merely those indirect and preparatory ones already traced in the story of Unitarianism" (p. 188). "The fact of paramount importance is that these influences came to a group of men who were embodiments in its noblest form of the old New England character. *They were Puritans to the core. This . . . was the signally American contribution to transcendentalism"* (p. 188), and again, "the Puritan blood was still within their veins" (p. 191). The moral inheritance from "old New England" does not merely explain away Transcendentalist defects; Christ-like, it "redeems Transcendentalism" and "preserved [Transcendentalism] from those romantic and anarchical excesses to which [in Europe] rapture and evolution, morally unrestrained, had led" (p. 199). Goddard's scholarship submits to his ideology in this conclusion, and it proves so weak a vessel because Goddard's real interest here is not scholarly fact but correspondence with the cultural myth preserved in the popular view of Transcendentalism of which Goddard's scholarly aspirations made him so critical at the start.

I have examined the work of Frothingham and Goddard at such length because the narrative strategies they developed have, with an astonishing and distressing consistency, echoed through Transcendentalist criticism ever since. Modern scholarship has not inherited their particular portraits of Transcendentalism, for, as we have seen, the cumulative effect of their strategies is to muddle the meaning of Transcendentalism so thoroughly that Goddard had to abandon his original empirical aims for a nationalist formula that (in its evocation of Puritan roots among other things) contradicts his earlier story. What modern scholarship inherited from these pioneering scholars is the program of scholarship their strategies initiated.

Goddard's work is both the last and the first of its kind. Coming near the turn of the century, it asserts for the last time the nineteenth-century way of talking about Transcendentalism and reveals the weakness of that myth: its uncomfortable fit with the emerging standards of modern scholarship. The idealist assumptions on which Frothingham relies throughout and to which Goddard finally must retreat in desperation were, by Goddard's time, already awkward and outdated. They seemed plausible enough amidst the euphoria of new nationhood 100 years earlier, and they had been therapeutic as a restorative to national consciousness after the Civil War. But the obvious artificiality of the arguments Goddard rushes into service to preserve the myth of America suggest how unpersuasive these notions seemed in 1908 when offered in terms of a shopworn idealism that demanded the identity of the ideal spirit with the nation. Though Goddard produced these strategies to serve the professional aspirations of his field, in subsequent scholarship they have taken on a life of their own and appear not as alternative models of historical coherence that the scholarship of Goddard's time made available to him but as features in the landscape of the subject itself, as officially sanctioned issues in the study of Transcendentalism.

But Goddard's inability to demonstrate the coincidence of fact and spirit hints, even at the beginning of American Literary Scholarship, at the implications of scholarly methods for the idealist assumptions that have governed America's self-image since Unitarianism turned Transcendentalist rhetoric to its own needs. To assert an American identity, Goddard finally had to abandon his reliance on fact and on the scholarly methods that were rapidly becoming essential to literary study. Because it forced scholars to measure their conclusions by the standard of correspondence to an ever-widening field of facts, scholarly methodology was (and is) a threat to the idealist coherence at the root of Transcendentalist and American literary studies. For this reason, the rise of the model of empirical scholarship may be seen as the first step in the fall of the American Ideal.

VAN WYCK BROOKS
"America's Coming of Age"
1916

In the years surrounding World War I, critics were less inclined than Goddard to blink recalcitrant facts. Despite Goddard's own retreat into a traditional reliance on an idealist foundation for historical coherence, his inability to reconcile American lives with an overarching American Ideal forecast the relocation of those foundations and of the ''true'' reality they represented in order to acknowledge the unpleasant facts of history. The most perceptive observers of this change were also its principal instigators. Among the foremost of these, Van Wyck Brooks records the change in terms that cannot obscure the continuing power of the passing idealist vision. In his famous essay ''America's Coming of Age,'' Brooks writes, ''It is amazing how that fabric of ideas and assumptions, of sentiments and memories and attitudes which made up the civilization of our fathers has melted away like snow uncovering the sordid facts of a society that seems to us now so little advanced on the path of spiritual evolution.''[16]

As Brooks's remarks show, the new generation of writers about Transcendentalism did not abandon the American Ideal as a unifying concept. They made it historical. The unchanging essence of America became an ideal as yet unfulfilled but awaiting future fulfillment. The debate about America had become political rather than moral. These critics see Transcendentalism as dissenting from American cultural values and approve or disapprove it as they approve or disapprove such dissent—as they support or dissent from the values of their own culture. Writers like More, Sherman, and Babbitt picked up the conservative implications of Goddard's work. Arguing for standards (as did its earlier detractors), they saw Transcendentalism as a threat. Mencken, Parrington and Mumford, on the other hand, saw the same things in Transcendentalism but approved them as necessary criticisms of an overly material and superficial age.[17] For all these writers, the nation had become a place rather than an ideal. As a place America could be multiple, and imperfect, while as an ideal its multiplicity had to be explained as a mere appearance, its imperfection as a result of incomplete fulfillment. While both of the earlier writers had to tidy up Transcendentalism to suit American genteel society, Brooks produced a multifaceted portrait that mirrored all he saw as wrong with America as well as what he saw as right.

Brooks's work is remarkable because for the first time in Transcendentalist scholarship, defensiveness does not dominate criticism. Disappointment with the facts of American life reshaped writing about Transcendentalism during the teens and twenties. Yet, Brooks is not so much the cynic as the disillusioned idealist, still wedded to his ideals but frustrated that reality has not yet caught up with them. He does not identify himself with American culture, as Goddard did. As critic rather than spokesman, he is not interested in defending Transcendentalism against its attackers. On the contrary, Brooks uses Transcendentalism as a weapon against the failures of his own time. What had for Goddard and Frothingham been a desirable and defining external split between Europe and America becomes an undesirable internal discrepancy between America as it is and America as it was or will be or ought to be. America as an ideal has been replaced with ideals for America. A spiritual vision has been replaced with a political one. Goddard's opposition between European theory and American practicality has hardened in Brooks's hands into two equally unacceptable aspects of American life. While he notes that "no European can exist without a thousand subterranean relationships," that is virtually his only transatlantic glance.

Brooks's problem is not his relation to the past but his relation to the present. Brooks's famous distinction between "highbrow" ideals made hopelessly ineffectual by their abstraction from everyday life, and "lowbrow" mercantilism blind to everything but selfish gain is too familiar to need detailed treatment here. To his mind, the "typical" American lives a rigidly divided life. "The theoretical atmosphere in which he has lived [at college] is one that bears no relation to society, the practical atmosphere in which he has lived bears no relation to ideals." It is that failure, the failure of America to unite its opposed impulses into a coherent and admirable culture, that preoccupies Brooks. Goddard had stumbled over his inability to find the values and coherence he sought in the material facts of the lives of the Transcendentalists and had retreated instead into an inherited idealist myth of American national identity.

Brooks, however, revised those terms and so indicated the *possibility* of a radically new direction for Goddard's dead-end debate and for twentieth-century narratives about American culture. In a move that neither Frothingham or Goddard could have contemplated, Brooks made literature the middle term between opposed ideal and material values.

"Everything, no doubt, depends on evidence," he says, "and . . . an appeal to American literature, if literature really does record the spirit of a people, is an appeal that leads, I think, to evidence of a material sort" (p. 20). To support his argument about the division of American culture into "highbrow" and "lowbrow," and to mediate between abstract idealism and crass materialsm, Brooks substitutes the "material" evidence of literary *art* for Goddard's material *lives*. Literature, Brooks asserts, "record[s] [and thus makes material] the spirit of a people" (p. 20) that gives coherence to American culture.

The consequences of marshaling the "material" evidence of literature to support his arguments about America runs in two directions: one self-conscious; the other, perhaps, not. Both have their analogs in contemporary revisionist debate. The self-conscious consequence of using literature as the emblem of the national spirit is Brooks's well-known doctrine of "use." As he applies it here, this notion has a specific political agenda that links his judgment of America with his judgment of its literature.[18] "Not one of them," he says, referring to the nineteenth-century classics, "not all of them, have had the power to move the soul of America from the accumulation of dollars; and when one has said this one has arrived at some sort of basis for literary criticism" (p. 23). This formulation prefigures contemporary critical appeals to direct social influence or "cultural work."

But, like Tompkins or Michaels, Brooks also wants to use literature to make a larger case about America. By making literature empirical rather than ideal, an object *in* culture, representative *of* culture, rather than a repository of otherworldly truths, Brooks changes the focus of American Literary Scholarship. He seeks a coherence in literature that will prove his case about American society. If the facts of life in America prove unruly, refusing the coherence that permits generalization, literary orders may prove more satisfactory. He is trying to show, he says, in "what way a survey of American literature would inevitably lead us to certain facts about American life" (p. 25).

In his eagerness for an "inevitable" relationship between American literature and American life, Brooks assumes (as Goddard warned one must assume) all that such a study would try to prove. The failure of Transcendentalist writers becomes the failure to describe (and thus to help create) the ideal unity of America. For Brooks, Emerson only contributed to the split in American culture, fathering American saints and American millionaires alike. He was made up of equal parts otherworldly elevation and nose-to-the-ground shrewdness. But in him, these qualities lay side by side, isolated and therefore sterile. Under these circumstances, it is hard to say whether Brooks condemns Emerson more for his influence or for his lack of influence—his inability to enact an effective social ideal.[19]

Not only does Transcendentalism, in Brooks's view, forecast *both* of the opposed and equally inadequate lines of development in American society, it also contains, in embryo, the resolution of their sterile conflict. As a result, many of the features of Transcendentalism that Goddard had worked to obscure, Brooks brought out and brushed off for display. Brooks located the fertile germ of his own ideal for American culture in Emerson's "disciple," Walt Whitman. And Brooks's brief discussion of Whitman ushers forth the idealism that was implicit as "the path of spiritual evolution" in his judgment of American culture. Talking about Whitman, Brooks turns from the concrete to the spiritual, from American "life" to American "character." He sounds more and more like the American mythographers of the Gilded Age and less and less like a disillusioned critic of the new century.

Whitman's advent transforms "America" from a sadly split personality to a desirable but not yet manifest ideal embracing the opposed values of high and low, theory and action. Brooks's critique of American culture and literature had been predicated on that split between "equally undesirable . . . and incompatible" forces that "divide American life between them" (p. 4). Whitman, however, represents "the rudiments of a middle tradition . . . that effectively combines theory and action," and conveys "the sense of something organic in American life." In doing so, he "precipitated the American character." Despite his realistic critique of American culture, Brooks, too, finally needed an American myth, an ideal American identity, in order to preserve his hopes for the nation. He found it in Whitman. "In him the hitherto incompatible extremes of the American temperament were fused" (p. 59).

Instead of escaping the moral ideal of the Genteel Tradition and the real/ideal split of which it was one side, Brooks finally can only translate it into literary terms, continuing the line of American literature scholars who give up facts for ideals. At the outset of his argument, literature was to supply "evidence of a material sort" for the fatal fragmentation of American culture. By the end, however, literature supplies terms for the coherence of American culture, terms that are so *far* from material that they defy specification. "A *focal centre*—that is the first requisite of a great people," Brooks now insists, but it becomes clear that he is not referring to any socio-political compact.

> I mean that national "point of rest," . . . upon which the harmony of a work of art is founded and to which everything in the composition is more or less unconsciously referred; that secure and unobtrusive element of national character, taken for granted, and providing a certain underlying coherence and background of mutual understanding. [In] this element . . . everything admirably characteristic of a people sums itself up, . . . radiates outward and articulates the entire living fabric of a race. (p. 63)

Like the efforts to provide coherence for American culture that had preceded it, like the notion of Transcendentalism itself, this literary vision remains imprisoned within the ideal.

Literature, here, is not evidence for generalizations about American culture, as Brooks argued earlier. It is a *substitute* for American culture. This is America *as* literary ideal. Brooks is not making a statement about the facts of American life, or about American literature. He identifies American cultural coherence with a principle of aesthetic coherence, reconceiving American culture as a work of art. In this turn to literature as a mediatory term between the historical and the ideal America, we see both the isolation from life that troubles contemporary critics in the formalism that soon followed and the precedent for contemporary theoretical strategies that elide textuality and culture.[20]

Despite this ideal vision and all his own efforts, Brooks as critic of his own culture, could not finally avoid reiterating the cultural debate he wanted to criticize. Even his literary ideal finally falls apart. For opposed and incompatible "highbrow" and "lowbrow" he substituted opposed and incompatible "literature" and "action," and the frustration of his efforts to locate a middle ground appears clearly in his criticisms of the inadequacies he sees on all sides. Brooks had made Transcendentalism the figure for all America, for all he disliked, highbrow and lowbrow, and for all he hoped for. And he divided literature along similar lines; it was alternately attached to the "actual," a justification of the commercial, and an ideal aesthetic standard that could fulfill its true potential by moving the hearts of society to a higher moral plane.

Even Whitman finally could not unify these imperatives for Brooks. The very idealist rhetoric that identifies in Whitman the cultural coherence Brooks seeks also reminds him of the practical failings of that ideal. Reality, and thus "judgment" comes into play, and "at this point," he says, "one has to discriminate" (p. 64). The need to "discriminate" calls on standards of coherence that have been consistently hostile to writing like Whitman's or Emerson's. Judgment predictably affirms the value of the world of judgment, of the actual, of reason over "instinct," "art," "emotion." From this "colder" perspective, Whitman is "a collection of raw materials . . . which take shape only in an emotional form." And although he was "perfectly right so long as he kept to the plane of instinct, he was lost on the plane of ideas" (p. 64). Thought and feeling, the two cultural strains that Transcendentalism had unified for Goddard, remain unresolved for and in Brooks. Whitman's idealist acceptance of life in all its variety promised to unify the fragments of life into a coherent culture. But Brooks finds, as Goddard did, and as Whitman himself did still earlier, that facts lead only to more facts. Reason balks that the connections Whitman makes are not logical and hence not practical. "On the plane of ideas," Brooks says, "the practical effect is that, in accepting everything he accepts the confusion of things" (p. 66). Brooks won't see "things" in the saddle. His program for an America reborn, like all such programs past and present, requires a principle of coherence.

What America and Brooks need for coherence, he asserts, *pace* the problems of Emerson's intellectual book-ridden abstraction reborn in Whitman's excessive passivity, are the *ideas* Whitman lacked. "By adding intellect to emotion—the social ideal the raw materials of which had been provided by Whitman must be formulated and driven home." And the agent of this change, from Brooks's critical perspective, is not far to seek. If the poet alone flew too high above the world on his cloud of emotion to move an earthbound society, Brooks imagines a better blended class merging intellect and art. "How much talent goes to waste," he asserts, "because there is no criticism, no standard, no authority to trip it up and shake it and make it think!" (p. 68).

These are not the abstract and merely academic scholars he derides as the ultimate triumph of theory over practice. They are a new breed of trained and judicious observers of their own world, the "trained gardeners" who can work its emotional raw materials into a productive plot as rigorously coherent as the one Brooks tries to construct to usher in "America's Coming of Age." Brooks defines "the first work" of these "thinkers" as raising the "issues that make the life of a society," and balancing between the worlds of art and fact that he is still unable to join, says that these issues must be "discovered like principles of science," or

"almost . . . created like works of art" (p. 85). This dramatic ambivalence between science and art to the end of reversing the spiritual
direction of the nation begins to sound more and more like an act of
national salvation, and in harmony with this familiar rhetoric, the
nation's "thinkers" coalesce into a single figure, yet another new
American Christ, "the man out of a hundred million" who can "throw
American life into relief." "How shall we know him when he comes?"
Brooks asks, sounding like the prophet of his coming.[21]

But even this vision proves inadequate, sounding, as it does, all too
much like the individual isolation from society at large that Brooks
condemned in Emerson's unrepresentative *Representative Men*. In its
place, and as his final formulation of the progress in American culture he
hoped for, Brooks offers the image of the "old Yankee stalk" that "will
begin to stir and send forth shoots and burst into a storm of blossoms"
after the "women of America have collected all the culture in the world,
and the men have gathered together all the money."[22] In this metaphor of
an idealized future, Brooks joins all the terms—social, empirical, and
aesthetic—that he could not unite discursively.

At its outset, Brooks's work promised a truly radical revision of
American literary studies by offering a new model for scholarly thinking
about America, one that cast aside, or at least deferred, the notion of
America as the real-world embodiment of humanity's highest aspirations
for itself. His hostility toward what he saw as the blind complacency of
the Genteel Tradition reflected the bankruptcy of the idealist model that
had shaped the work of both Frothingham and Goddard. By describing
American culture as an ongoing conflict between equally unacceptable
idealist and materialist factions, highbrow and lowbrow, Brooks told a
story that he and his contemporaries could find more believable because it
seemed to them less a fairy tale. But the cost of credibility proved too
high, since it meant abandoning the concept of a unified American culture
that had been the founding principle behind American literary studies in
the first place.

Worse still, it was a depressing story, despite its ill-fitting idealist
ending. It meant giving up notions—American cultural unity, the progress of America toward an ideal destiny, the image of Americans as a
uniquely blessed chosen people and of America as the stage on which the
divine destiny would be worked out—that had been central to the national
self-image and to all previous studies of the subject. In place of these self-
affirmations, it proposed a far less heroic portrayal of America as simply

one more product of squabbles among fallible individuals collectively muddling through—by American standards, a national disappointment. Facing this prospect, Brooks dropped his alternate model of an America in conflict and returned to a more traditional idealistic view.

But even when he abandoned his new "realistic" view of American culture, Brooks could not simply reassume the old vision of ideal unity. He had developed his new model of America as a nation in conflict with itself precisely because even before the war, contemporary perceptions of the facts exploded the old story of an ideal America. The realities that had inspired his innovation in the first place, the conflicts between American idealism and materialism, still prevented him from offering a single unified vision, and as we have seen, he offered a metaphor that embraced his distinction between highbrow and lowbrow without practically uniting them. Unable to resolve the conflicts he inherited from his predecessors, he passed them on, fuel to feed the growing critical fires of American Literary Scholarship.

LEWIS MUMFORD
The Golden Day
1926

The options between which Brooks suspends himself at the end of "America's Coming of Age" reflect the division between idealist and realist approaches that characterized debate about Transcendentalism from the beginning and that becomes still sharper after World War I. Unable to reconcile these two positions, Brooks tried finally to occupy both camps at once, his awkward split an imitation of the divided America he criticized. Most inquirers who followed him have simplified the problem by assuming only half of the controversy he insisted on looking at whole. The idealist approach found an influential champion in Lewis Mumford, whose The Golden Day, as has often been noted, finally gave the critical stamp of approval to Transcendentalist literature.[23] But we should not too quickly credit Mumford's good taste merely because he brings critical judgment in line with our own. Mumford finds literary value in Transcendentalist writing only because he embraces the literary idealism that Brooks found inadequate and rejected. By doing so, he resurrects the idealism of Frothingham or Goddard and therefore necessarily meets their fate, the same fate that Brooks criticized in genteel culture. Like Brooks, Mumford turns to literature for coherence. But where Brooks looked to literature either for *evidence* of a coherent argument about American culture or for the unfulfilled hint of what American culture *might* be, Mumford seeks and finds there a *real* cultural coherence. By approving Transcendentalist literature as the repository of the American Ideal, Mumford effectively divides the past from the present. Like those New Historicists who pursue relevance by locating the meaning of texts in their surrounding social contexts, he ends up isolating that ideal and the literature that embodies it from American life in his own time.

While he retains many of Brooks's criticisms of America, Mumford makes a fundamental change in Brooks's argument. Instead of placing his cultural ideal, the synthesis of conflicting factions, in some imagined and idealized future, Mumford locates it in history and makes it a specifiable object against which all subsequent experience must be measured. Like Frothingham or Goddard, Mumford insists on the reality of the American Ideal and locates it in Transcendentalism. For Mumford, the Transcendentalist period was the epitome and fulfillment of American possibilities. "An imaginative New World came to birth during this period," he says, "a new hemisphere in the geography of the mind. That world was the climax of American experience. What preceded led up to it: what followed, dwindled away from it" (p. 91). By turning in this way from dialectic to drama, from Brooks's vision of ongoing literary and cultural conflict to a story about the fulfillment and subsequent decline of a social ideal—the "Golden Day" in American life—Mumford elaborates the traditional view of American writing from which Brooks had been an apostate.

But the distaste for the present state of American culture Mumford shares with Brooks creates problems for him that Frothingham and Goddard did not have to face. It turns his focus away from the rise of the American Ideal out of nature or European origins and toward the loss of that ideal amidst Gilded Age commercialism. Thus it calls for a new plot that can portray this cultural tragedy as a sort of American divine comedy. It demands the reemergence of a new Golden Day. For Mumford, America, by which he means the "best" of America, is an organic break with the European past that unites the best of both worlds, East and West. America is "life," the present moving toward the future; Europe is the "having lived," the dead past. "Life only avails, not the having lived. There is the kernel of the Emersonian doctrine of self-reliance: it is the answer which the American, in the day of his confidence and achievement, flung back into the face of Europe, where the 'having lived' has always been so conspicuous and formidable'' (p. 93). In this passage we can see that, for Mumford, the past, though dead, is still dangerous enough to force a defensive posture. He cannot, as Brooks proposed, invent a "usable past" to improve the present. On the contrary, his adherence to the American Ideal breeds hostility to the past, at least to the immediate past, proportionate to his dissatisfaction with America in his own time. By insisting on a real ideal in a real history, he cuts himself and his time off from the values he prizes.

This defensiveness reflects not only Mumford's continuing participation in the long-standing American paranoia about its own identity but the unresolvable conflicts imposed by his commitment to an American Ideal that can never be adequately embodied in particular forms. The Civil War is Mumford's dividing line between a period of ideal purity and the imperfect present. The transition is apocalyptic rather than evolutionary. Unlike Brooks, he cannot afford to find any germ of the commercial disease in the pure ante-bellum atmosphere. After the war, Mumford argues, industrialism and commercialism appeared "overnight." "All that was left of Transcendentalism in the Gilded Age was . . . 'an inner elegance,'" he says. "The guts of idealism were gone" (pp. 165, 166). Such irreconcilable oppositions, unbridgeable chasms, are characteristic of inquiries that treat American writing in terms of the opposition between the real and the ideal. Frothingham and Goddard had split American literary history along similar lines to distinguish the good sense, social values, and scientific sophistication of their own time from the dangerous imbalance between uncontrolled subjectivity and the sterile materialism of the earlier period. Then, in terms much like Mumford's, they, somewhat paradoxically, divided the pragmatic innovation of that earlier time from the sterile dogmatism of Europe. By returning to the idealist posture of these earlier writers, Mumford returns to their views of historical schism as well, though he reverses their evaluation to reflect his preference for the ideal world of the imagination over the limitations of mundane reality.

This reversal was facilitated by changes in the American literary pantheon. When Brooks pictured American writing, he saw Emerson and Whitman standing out against the domestic figures of Whittier and Holmes and Longfellow. Nineteenth-century American writing still meant the Genteel Tradition that Brooks blamed for the fecklessness of highbrow culture. But only a few years later, when Mumford looked at that picture, its features had changed. Emerson, Thoreau, and Whitman no longer stood uneasily around the domestic fireside talking at cross-purposes with their genteel fellows, they were "on the tramp" in the world, interrogating it for its hidden meaning along with Hawthorne and Melville. In this new context, Transcendentalism no longer seemed an elevating but ultimately bland and unrealistic optimism. As the harbinger of nineteenth-century American fiction, it provided a foundation for profound metaphysical inquiry, and contributed to the "rebellious" terms that have typified twentieth-century characterizations of the "American identity."

In the new literary fraternity that persists through Matthiessen into our own time, Emerson and Melville, however sharp the contrasts between them, were essentially complementary figures. They divided the human soul, exploring between them the full range of human experience. "The sunlight had in Emerson and Whitman penetrated to every spot, and in its presence, the dark corners became more intense. If one explored the white summits of the glacier with Emerson, one might also fall into the abyss with Melville. One climbed high; and when one fell, the fall was deep" (p. 142). Frothingham and Goddard, along with most of their contemporaries, had to deny the existence of "dark corners" because they seemed to pose a real danger to society and to society's acceptance of Transcendentalism. But Mumford revels in them. But we should not forget that he can do so with little apparent discomfort partly because they are, in literature, safely isolated from life.

At this point in his argument, that isolation is central. It marks the new prestige of the American *literary* tradition as the field established itself as a subject for serious discourse, a prestige that reflected the growing influence of modernist literary assumptions among American intellectuals. Mumford made the American Ideal literary rather than moral, made it depend on technique rather than middle-class moral values and proper behavior. "At heart," Mumford asserts, "the American novelists were all transcendental. The scene was a symbol: they scarcely had the patience to describe it" (p. 140). For Mumford, this is no mere "side-effect"; it is a crucial strategy. While Brooks idealized literature in general and prized American literature for the insights it provided into American culture, he repeatedly described American writing as narrow, flawed, and, for all its evocation of spirit, implicitly inferior to British writing. Mumford, however, relies on literature not to reinforce his attack on American culture but to salvage his hopes for it. American cultural coherence, the "wholeness" Mumford values, appears in poetry not in society. Whitman's poetry produces a synthesis of the "quaker, the

puritan, the cosmopolitan, the pioneer, the republican'' into a union of
science and philosophy full of the ''doubts, searching, quests, achieve-
ments, and consummations which are the stuff of life itself'' (p. 127).
Thus Whitman embodies Mumford's notion of the ''mission of creative
thought,'' ''to gather into it all the living sources of its day . . . in the
practical life . . . in science . . . in the social heritage and, recasting
these things into new forms and symbols, to react upon the blind drift of
convention and habit and routine'' (p. 166).

Literature preserves values that had died out of America with the Civil
War—values that were identical with ''America'' itself. ''The promise
of America had not disappeared.'' Mumford says, ''If it was absent from
the immediate scene, it had nevertheless taken form in [Whitman's]
poems; and his poems were still waiting to shape a new America'' (p.
125). The passing of the Golden Day has not diminished the value of its
products. ''What Thoreau left behind is still precious; men may still go
out and make over America in the image of Thoreau'' (p. 120). Literature
was an agent in the future of American society. Emerson and Whitman
had ''continued the old voyages of exploration on the plane of the mind''
(p. 277). And although ''we cannot return to the America of the Golden
Day,'' the literature they produced preserved ''the essential characteristics that *still lie under the surface*'' (p. 279). This essence of the
American experience provides Mumford with a different sort of instrument than Brooks imagined for reshaping America through an act of the
imagination. Mumford imagines the literature of the Golden Day as a sort
of time capsule preserving the ideal from the ravages of historical change
and carrying it into the future to exercise its transforming influence.
Literature links an idealized past to an idealized future, distracting our
attention from an unsatisfactory present.

Mumford avoids disappointment at the failure of the Golden Day to
realize fully its ideals by relocating the ideal wholeness he prizes not in
particular literary forms but in an ideal ''vision,'' a literary analog for
spirit. Summing up the significance of the literature of America's Golden
Day, Mumford reveals his own willingness to accept the potential of
unexpressed spirit over the constraints of reality.

> The attempt to prefigure in the imagination a culture which should grow out
> of and refine the experiences the transplanted European encountered on the
> new soil, mingling the social heritage of the past with the experience of the
> present, was the great activity of the Golden Day: the essays of Emerson,

the poems of Whitman, the solitary musings of Melville all clustered around
this central need. None of these men was caught by the dominant abstractions: each saw life whole, and sought a whole life. (p. 278)

Mumford so willingly opts for the wholeness these men "saw," for
vision, rather than insisting on the fulfillment they "sought" because that
one "concession" gives unity to so many troublingly divided concepts:
Old World and New, past and present, imagination and culture, individual and society. Behind his elevation of the Golden Day over the Gilded
Age is his preference for "the spiritual fact" over "things." This
preference, which I have been describing as a central strategy of
American Literary Scholarship, finally cuts literature off from life and (in
its earlier manifestations) isolates it in aesthetic superiority, independent
of actions, including the action of a completed text.

Brooks urged critical thinkers to reformulate the terms of American
experience in ways that unite its divided streams and produce a unity that
embodies its ideals in action. Mumford would have us bring to light the
existing "essence" that is currently hidden. He enacted Brooks's highbrow idealism by describing the Golden Day as the real, if momentary,
incarnation of an American Ideal that subsequently went underground in
literature, awaiting its own second coming. But this exclusively literary
incarnation of the old ideal falls so far short of all that had been invested in
the promise of America that, despite its unmistakable echoes of
Whitman, it finally rings hollow. Its highbrow roots show in its isolation
from real life within the airy world of art. And it was just such isolation
from practical life that Brooks had objected to in the genteel portrayal of
American culture. American culture has, in effect, been embedded in the
collection of texts that constitute the tradition. Critical approaches to
American writing from New Criticism to New Historicism will, in their
different ways, depend on that step.

VERNON LEWIS PARRINGTON
Main Currents in American Thought
1927–1930

Vernon Parrington put America between hard covers. The force of that
fact, so important to his contemporaries, has faded for more recent

critics, who have featured methodological issues of a more narrowly professional interest. Some, testing his status as a founder of "intellectual history," have criticized his work as insufficiently scientific. Others, more literary in their inclinations, have portrayed him as blinded by his emphasis on ideas to the appeal and authority of art. For most of his contemporaries, however, Parrington's achievement in *Main Currents in American Thought* lay in the scope of his account.[24] Parrington aspired to one coherent story about American culture (and with it, American writing) from the seventeenth to the twentieth century. He was the first to try to tell the "whole story" of American culture, and so enlisted himself and his work in the conflict he saw as central to the American life he wanted to describe. "The problem of America," he wrote, "is the problem of how to achieve in the midst of the jungle an intellectual and spiritual reintegration—to learn to live once more in the whole."[25]

This problem places Parrington's work squarely in the traditions of Romantic historiography and associates it with the modernist distaste for American commercialism. It aligns him with writers like Mumford and Brooks in the project of explicating the American Ideal. Parrington was less interested than some of his commentators have claimed in producing a "scientific" history of America or an "economic" interpretation of America, or even a history of ideas in America. He wanted to tell a coherent story about America, a story that held together and made sense because American culture itself held together and made sense. In this respect, his aims were essentially the same as Frothingham's or Goddard's, though his ambitions were larger. His work is not notable for recasting the critical view of Transcendentalism. On the contrary, although it is often treated as iconoclastic, his portrait of Transcendentalism preserves intact the vision of the subject that he inherited from Brooks and from Frothingham and Goddard. Frothingham set the agenda for Transcendentalist scholarship, and Mumford adapted Frothingham's vision to the revised canon that Americanists developed in the 1920s. Parrington, in turn, despite his hostility toward the scholarly establishment from which he felt so excluded, translated the study of American culture into a new idiom that spoke to the changing standards of academic discourse after World War I.

Parrington's work seemed so powerful partly because it managed to incorporate many of the material or "lowbrow" facts of American life into a story that renews the idealist vision Brooks had temporarily abandoned. Retaining Brooks's social agenda, Parrington finds a way of reincorporating social criticism into a new version of the old idealist model.[26] The result was a story about America that echoes Brooks's antipathy for the increasingly commercial cast of American life but manages to avoid shattering the American Ideal into warring camps.

Transcendentalism is central to this argument and at the center of his book. It is also in the middle of all the difficulties Parrington encountered as he tried to make his story of American culture coherent. Although he felt that the importance of New England thought had been exaggerated in previous scholarship, and he intended to minimize its role in his work, like other idealist historians, he sees Transcendentalism as a privileged moment in American history. It stood at the center of those "revolutions in thought" that were an interlude between eighteenth-century skepticism and nineteenth-century commercial greed. "For a brief time, at least," he said, "liberal ideas found a welcome in homes where they had hitherto been strangers; for a brief time the intellectual and not the merchant dominated New England" (2: 279). The similarities of this view to Mumford's nostalgia for a lost ideal are clear enough. Only a sentimental idealist would argue that "the intellectual" actually dominated New England, however briefly. Thoreau would never have said so.[27]

Parrington uses "idealism" to oppose the commercial trends in American culture that he despises. He sees Transcendentalism as a point of view, the embodiment not of an ideal but of an idealistic perspective, a set of values, from which American life might be judged. He hopes not for an ideal world but for an idealistic attitude toward the world. New England thought, he says, is central to the "development of American idealism" (2: 271). Idealism is the truly American posture, the stance appropriate to the possibility America represents. It is the functional equivalent of "character" in Frothingham and Goddard, both a national characteristic and an individual trait. By treating Transcendentalism as a way of seeing, a point of view rather than an embodied ideal, Parrington avoids all the problems attendant on locating Transcendentalism in history and associating it with the national identity. He avoids the need to explain away its imperfections, or to account for its passing, or to predict its return.

To his chagrin, however, Parrington finds, in his quest for the continuity of American ideas, that the ideas he opposes are no less continuous and no less a part of American experience than those he favors. He discovers the seeds of commercialism and the downfall of the democratic ideal in the very origins of the nation itself with the movement toward central government that gave birth to America as a political reality. "Americanism superseded colonialism. . . . This marked the turning point in American development. . . . The history of the rise of the coercive state in America, with the ultimate arrest of all centrifugal tendencies, was implicit in that momentous movement" (1: 196–97). The very unity that made the nation, and that gives it a political version of the coherence that Parrington would like to describe, leads inevitably to the commercialism that destroys his ideal. Logically, therefore, the America he idealizes never was. It was always, as long as there has been an America, a national *ideal* rather than a reality. To Parrington, Transcendentalism represents (rather than embodies or expresses) that admirable ideal in the century after the founding just as commercialism was coming to dominance.

When Parrington makes Transcendentalism represent the American Ideal, he also makes it embody the problems of coherence that trouble his view of America as a whole. But the continuity that Parrington tries to establish in these idealist terms cannot disguise the echo of his own ongoing debate between the disparate facts of American life and his assumptions about what is essentially American. The portrait of Transcendentalism that Parrington produces ends up reflecting both the idealism that links him to Mumford, Goddard, and Frothingham, and the movement toward empirical scholarship that Brooks prepared for with his transformation of the American story from a moral and spiritual tale to a conflict of human attitudes. Parrington accommodates both only in the sense that he includes them within the larger structure of his book, but he cannot truly unite them. The New England Renaissance confronted Parrington with the problem implicit in his whole project: how to explain a unified culture in terms of individuals, how to make the parts cohere into a whole.

Transcendentalism seemed, even more than other "movements" he described, merely a collection of independent individuals. "How shall we explain a movement," he wonders echoing Goddard, "that embraced such different men as Everett and Channing and Parker and Garrison and Whittier and Emerson and Longfellow and Holmes; men often mutually repellent, sometimes sharply critical of each other?" (2: 319). Parrington unites these disparate men by subordinating the facts that divide them to shared ideas, or in this case, their shared protest against the "aspirations of the middle class" (2: 320). The various "isms" (individualism, liberalism, optimism, idealism) that Parrington offers interchangeably as the central issue of American thought represent aspects of a single gesture toward a coherence of ideas. Emerson's individualism was only

> the final transcendental form of . . . the same revolutionary conception that Channing had come upon, that Jefferson had come upon, that Rousseau had come upon—the idea which in the guise of political romanticism had disintegrated the *ancien régime,* and in the form of philosophical romanticism had disintegrated eighteenth-century rationalism—the idea that was providing Utopian dreams for an ebullient democratic faith. (2: 390)

As always, coherence tends to erase national boundaries, and the internal coherence of Transcendentalism proved even more difficult to establish.

This conflict between organizing ideas and facts persists throughout Parrington's account of Transcendentalism, appearing most prominently in the contrast between his introductory generalizations and the biographical sketches that purport to illustrate them. Parrington's introductory section on Transcendentalism dwells at a level of generality that blurs any boundaries between stubbornly independent parts. Parrington's generalizations all tend to associate Transcendentalism with New England culture at large as agents of the "romantic revolution in thought." The result could be an abstract from Frothingham or Goddard. It emphasizes mysticism, individualism, love of the new, and optimism. It bristles with the metaphors that carry so much argumentative freight throughout Parrington's writing, associating concepts figuratively that could never be joined discursively. The generalizations Parrington makes are so broad, so detached from specifics against which they might be tested, and so thoroughly infused with revered assumptions about America that they are unchallengeable. They are a triumph of characterization, of a familiar and reassuring myth, over any actual reading of Transcendentalist texts. In fact, they substitute for such reading, presenting the expected and acceptable caricature in its place. This introductory section seems designed to conjure the ideal of which the individual portraits that follow are, necessarily, only partial fulfillments.

If the coherent story of the introductory remarks operates at a level of generalization too high to question, the individual portraits to which his cultural critique is confined raise issues entirely unrelated to those that made for coherence in the introduction. Thus, Parrington's interest in telling a coherent story about America conflicts with his criticisms of commercial culture. Without discarding the traditional view of Transcendentalism as the linchpin of his argument for cultural coherence, he isolates it in a section of introductory generalization, then ignores it in the individual portraits that put individual Transcendentalists at odds with their world to make them allies in his attack on cultural trends he opposed. The traditional Emerson, for example, the one who fits the introductory portrait of Transcendentalism Parrington has just offered, is, in this new context, not the most essential or interesting one. There is, he says, another Emerson "too much obscured to common view." This Emerson is not the dispenser of aphoristic wisdom but the social critic who speaks Parrington's own rejection of commercial interests.

Finally, however, even Transcendentalist "individualism" looks, as it had to Brooks, like the high road to Social Darwinism. The new age demanded a social conscience and group identity that made Transcendental self-reliance look suddenly culpable. "The hermit Thoreau in his cabin at Walden Pond was no symbol of a generous democratic future" (3: 76). And Parrington abandons his original terms for the American Ideal and retreats, as Mumford had, though with more apparent discomfort, into the isolated world of literature.[28] With Transcendentalism displaced from the center of Parrington's American portrait, Whitman moved in. Whitman's work somehow combined unity and diversity, the voice of "this great shapeless America," in which "all limitations and skepticisms were swept away by the feeling of comradeship" (3: 76–77). The coherence Whitman represents to Parrington is a "diminished thing." Whitman's work captures America and tells its story simply by reflecting its diversity, its lack of coherence, producing the "feeling" rather than the substantial reality of comradeship.

Parrington's vision—of America and of a complete story about American writing—is unfulfilled. The American Revolution, inspired by the ideals Parrington reveres, was echoed by Transcendentalism, a "revolution in thought" inspired by the same ideals. But those ideals were too lofty, too thoroughly individualistic, to effect practical social change. They could only inspire admiration. "That [Jefferson's effort to preserve American democracy] was foredoomed to failure . . . cannot detract from the nobility of his ideal, or the inspiration of his life" (1: 362). In the fallen world from which Parrington looked back on American possibilities, ideal sentiments are noble and worthy of admiration in themselves despite the impossibility of living them.

But, however depressing as a portrait of American culture, Parrington's account was a powerful model for subsequent professional literary scholarship. The consequences of Parrington's revision of Transcendentalism were a broadening of interest in the details of Transcendentalism as a historical movement (rather than a way of thinking) within the new context of an intellectual history that was more accommodating to the aesthetic limitations (in conventional terms) of many American texts. In Parrington's hands, Transcendentalism became a "fact" displayed in documents. His work turned it from an ephemeral spiritual experience that evaded capture by any action or text into a concrete historical object, a cultural movement, that scholarship could study without apology.

F. O. MATTHIESSEN
American Renaissance
1941

The approach of another war brought with it the beginnings of what might be called the modern age of Transcendentalism scholarship. F. O. Matthiessen's *American Renaissance,* arguably the most influential work in modern American literary studies, illustrates the persistence of the nineteenth-century idealist model in even the very best scholarship in the field.[29] Matthiessen anticipated (and thereby played a large part in creating) a new wave in American literary and cultural criticism that combined New Critical close reading and aesthetic values with a restatement of the ideological vision that had moved critics from Frothingham on.

In Parrington's work and that of earlier scholars, art and life had remained stubbornly divided. Art represented the spiritual ideal, and life, individual or national, represented the worldly ideal. In the 1870s, Moses Coit Tyler and O. B. Frothingham were unable to praise much American writing as art. They turned for the order they sought to the lives and characters of individual writers and to the national character. Fifty years later, Lewis Mumford had become sure enough of the merit of writers like Melville that he could afford to take the aesthetic high road, praising them as "transcendental." But even as Parrington wrote, the precepts of the New Criticism were infiltrating the profession, and subsequent critics of Parrington's work, judging him by standards he could not have recognized, have repeatedly complained about his "insensitivity" to literary issues.

The mission for American Literary Scholarship after Parrington— Matthiessen's mission—was to attach the American Ideal, a vision of American culture, to a tradition of literary excellence. *American Renaissance* earned its influence in the profession by responding so fully to this challenge. Matthiessen's approach to American writing was powerful because he made *art* an equal term with *life* in a balanced equation. He insisted that the creative individual use "such gifts as [he] possesses for . . . the people" (p. xvi). Pioneering the problem that still challenges contemporary literary history, Matthiessen sought a notion of art that made it not only compatible with but essential to social justice.

Matthiessen himself was the greatest of the Romantics in American Literary Scholarship. Like idealist commentators from 1840 on, he assumed that a fundamental unity must underlie the worldly flux, and he expected art to provide insight into that unity by representing it to this world. Brooks had insisted on the necessary conflict between highbrow and lowbrow and praised Emerson as a poet of the spirit. Parrington had made him a political radical. Matthiessen, on the other hand, demands, as he claims his subjects demanded, the unity of "untrammeled speculation and Yankee practicality" (p. 15), and he demands this ideal unity be established on solid ground, the ground of life, rather than on the ideal ground favored by earlier idealist critics. In language, Matthiessen wants the perfect union of words and things; in literary forms, the ideal coincidence of content and form; in the creative act, a perfect balance of spontaneity and craft; and as a result of the work of art, the establishment of a perfect relationship between art and life and thus between the individual (represented by the artist) and society. His primary concern, he says, is with what these books were "as works of art, with evaluating their fusions of form and content" (p. vii). But the American art he prizes is one with life. "All five writers" desired "that there should be no split between art and the other functions of the community, that there should be an organic union between labor and culture" (pp. xiv–xv). Art had to carry the artist beyond himself and unite him with his society. Individual expression had to produce an adequate portrait of the cultural whole.

This insistence on the "common life" of America as the foundation for art is the ultimate embodiment of the American Ideal in criticism. It promises that a truly American art will be an expression of a truly American people. This is the famous unifying principle he claimed for his own work from the start. "The one common denominator of my five writers, uniting even Hawthorne and Whitman, was their devotion to the possibilities of democracy" (p. ix). Matthiessen enlarged Parrington's "New England Renaissance" into a truly American Renaissance (p. 271).[30]

As always, however, American facts frustrate American coherence. Complicating Matthiessen's quest for a unified vision of American art and society was the fact that each of his authors is devoted to democracy in a different way. Because each is an individual and not a people, limited in perspective rather than all-encompassing, each is only an angle, imperfect, incomplete. Each represents an alternative blend of social and aesthetic values, or an alternative version of their incompatibility, and each thereby plays a different role in Matthiessen's composition of a literary tradition that reflects his version of the American Ideal. His discussion of these writers can be read as an exploration of the possibilities for the cultural unity and aesthetic coherence he idealizes and of the consequences of failing to achieve it.

Matthiessen's discussion of American literature is framed by discussions of Emerson and Thoreau at one end and Whitman at the other. Emerson "made one of the most challenging quests for a form that would express his deepest convictions, and that would bring him at the same time into vital communication with his society" (p. 5). As art, his writing does not meet Matthiessen's standards for literature any better than it met the standards of Emerson's contemporaries, and Matthiessen can explain away Emerson's contradictions only by appealing, like his predecessors, to "the wholeness of character lying behind" the "multiplicity of his conflicting statements" (p. 3). Moreover, as the pure idealist, Emerson represents all the deficiencies of elitist abstraction. All Emerson's weakness comes from his adherence to the inner voice. All his (limited) success comes from the relationship of his writing to life. "His word corresponds so naturally to his life that it constitutes the purest example of what individualism could produce," Matthiessen says. But in light of his condemnation of Emerson's writing, this seems faint praise indeed. As the archetypal representative of "the individual," Emerson is detached from the nation as a whole, and offers only one side of the equation that Matthiessen must balance to see greatness in American art.

Thoreau represents the other. He was the "hands" of Transcendentalism while Emerson was all "eyes." Thoreau used all of his senses and lived the common life that was missing in Emerson's writing. But his virtues also created problems for Matthiessen, who had to explain how this rustic existence could produce art that was more coherent and unified than Emerson's more elevated one. Matthiessen's solution is a typically romantic blurring of the distinction between nature and art. Thoreau's "craftsmanship" first takes on connotations that have "been thought of more often in connection with Indian baskets or Yankee tankards and hearth-tools than with the so-called fine arts" (p. 172). Then, despite his repeated emphasis in his discussion of Emerson on deliberate construction, it becomes compatible with unselfconscious expression. "Thoreau's very lack of invention," Matthiessen argues, portraying Thoreau as an early avatar of William Carlos Williams, "brings him closer to the essential attributes of craftsmanship, if by that term we mean the strict, even spare, almost impersonal 'revelation of the object'" (p. 173).

In this discussion, Matthiessen's aesthetic is at war with his ethics. His aesthetic observation that Thoreau's unselfconsciousness removes the observing individual from between object and audience directly contradicts his ethical criticism of Thoreau for espousing "left-wing individualism" rather than socialism as the proper direction for American social thought. In a social context, closeness to nature is excessive individualism. In an artistic context, it is an approach to the universality that produces great art. "By following to its uncompromising conclusion his belief that great art can grow from the center of the simplest life, [Thoreau] was able to be universal" (p. 175). The preference for the common over the elite, the concrete over the abstract, to which Matthiessen was committed repeats the oppositions between theory and practice, content and form, literature and life that had, even then, characterized Transcendentalist criticism for nearly 100 years.[31] Yet, like Brooks, Matthiessen is unwilling to sacrifice one to the other. And this persistent contradiction reflects Matthiessen's determination to respond to Thoreau's writing as art and to explain it in terms that are consistent with his social ideals.

The center of Matthiessen's argument makes his priorities clear. After his more elaborate discussion of Emerson in Book I, Matthiessen's treatment of him at the beginning of Book II seems designed to erect an Emersonian straw man designed to get the stuffing knocked out of him by Hawthorne and Melville, who possessed "the substance the philosopher lacked" (p. 186). Both Emerson and Thoreau, it begins to seem, are important to Matthiessen's argument mainly for what they lack. They lack the tragic vision that the twentieth century made a prerequisite to any art with claims to truth. And they lack the inclusiveness, the common touch, the stamp of the people that Matthiessen gestures toward throughout the book whenever Whitman appears and reappears, the inevitable end toward which each of the other writers, and the book as a whole, leads. Just as Whitman's name echoes throughout the chapters on Emerson, an incantatory refrain representing the aesthetic fulfillment of Emerson's disembodied theory, so Emerson's is invoked in the chapters on Hawthorne and Melville as the spirit of optimism and moral innocence to contrast with their darker and therefore "fuller" and more "balanced" visions.

Like critics before and since, Matthiessen cannot find a fully adequate embodiment of the American Ideal either in the past or the present. Following Mumford, he locates it in literature. Matthiessen's literary ideal appears in no single revelatory act of expression. It is embodied in no one writer of the *American Renaissance* but in *all* of them, in the American literary tradition that, collectively, they both represent and create. "Literature for our democracy," Matthiessen says, "emerges from the total pattern of their achievement" (p. xv). That literary tradition unites the elements that remain "infinitely repellent particles" in the work of any one writer. To fulfill itself, Matthiessen implies, America must unite its opposed elements to become a sort of national poem. *American Renaissance* idealizes America itself as a work of perfect art. Like Melville and Hawthorne, it includes tragedy. Like Whitman, it embraces "the people." Like Emerson, it expresses the individual mind, and like Thoreau, it enacts the simple life. This perfection resides in their imagined corporate identity and in works yet to be produced on their model, not the least of which, as Matthiessen hopes in his "Preface," may be *American Renaissance* itself.

Matthiessen's work carries the legacy of the critical past into the critical present, and like other profoundly powerful formulations of the American literary tradition, Matthiessen's work was imperialistic. It synthesized all the terms that had preoccupied scholarly discourse about America: the moral seriousness of nineteenth-century scholarship; the ideological commitment of Brooks, Mumford, or Parrington; and New Critical aestheticism. By translating the American literary identity into the modern idiom, Matthiessen was refilling for his own time a critical prescription that had been written 150 years earlier, and has been renewed time and again since then in terms consistent with the discourse of the day by scholars from Moses Coit Tyler to Sacvan Bercovitch. It located nineteenth-century American writing at the center of a continuous American tradition between early and modern American writing and made American literature respectable *vis-à-vis* the British tradition. And it did all this while stressing individualism, democratic principles, and the practical life of the common man.

In a sense, *American Renaissance* succeeded so well because it told us what we already knew, but more fully and interestingly than it had ever been told before. It set the modern agenda for critical practice in American literary studies by recasting the spiritual idealism of earlier scholarship into a powerful amalgam of aesthetic and political idealisms. As a result, it not only established its own supremacy in American literary criticism for the next forty years but also virtually stifled alternative attempts to describe American writing. By capturing the scholarly past so completely and translating that tradition into contemporary critical terms, Matthiessen's work prolonged the reign of the nineteenth-century project of American Literary Scholarship long beyond its own time and into the last quarter of the twentieth century.

LAWRENCE BUELL
Literary Transcendentalism
1973

Amidst all the changes that have shaken the modern study of literature, scholarship in Transcendentalism continues to hoe the rows laid out by pioneers in the field. The notions of Transcendentalism formulated in the nineteenth century meshed with ideal values that were, in turn, associated with "America": independence, genteel virtues, liberalism and individualism, democracy. But, in our own time, the discounting of these ideal motives has left Transcendentalist criticism without any grounding purpose, and like the cartoon figure who rushes off a cliff, it has been running in the air for forty years, prevented from falling only because it refuses to look down and discover its situation.

One hundred years after Frothingham established the terms for Transcendentalist scholarship, Lawrence Buell approached the subject once again from the same direction and wielding the same critical tools. His *Literary Transcendentalism,* the most important book-length general reconsideration of Transcendentalism since Goddard, exemplifies the very best of modern Transcendentalist scholarship.[32] Yet, it seems peculiar that after a century of inquiry, its introduction must still contend with all the questions that have faced and defeated previous inquirers. To his task, Buell brings the full weight of the accumulated knowledge in the field. And it is only fair to say that no one is more aware of the historical difficulty in defining Transcendentalism than Buell.[33] Few scholars know so well the complexities Transcendentalism presents or the difficulties of previous criticism. As a result, Buell's book is both the most authoritative contemporary exemplar of the tradition of Transcendentalist scholarship and, as an exercise within the constraints of that genre by an unusually able and well-prepared scholar, a demonstration of its limits.

Like most of his predecessors, Buell is troubled by the need to define Transcendentalism so that he can study it and justify that study. Against all the evidence of widespread disputes among them, Transcendentalist scholars from Frothingham and Goddard on have claimed agreement about the central points precisely because any serious inquiry into the subject tended to show that, like Pascal's God, the center of Transcendentalism was everywhere, its circumference nowhere. In short, there was too little agreement about absolutely essential points to allow them to become subjects of critical debate. Like Goddard, Buell recounts the well-known obscurities of previous definitions. Transcendentalism means "vagueness." It inherited its name from its enemies. It had no program or causes and was constantly in flux. Its membership had little cohesion. But Buell repeats this litany only to reassure us, again like his predecessors, that through all these difficulties, modern scholarship can discern a distinct center, an absolute nugget, "an accepted core of meaning" (p. 3). But Buell's reassuring figures cannot entirely obscure the troubling question of why, as Buell himself has just pointed out, in the face of such simple truth, the nature of Transcendentalism has seemed so elusive for so long.

When Buell turns from these general assertions to particular descriptions, he rediscovers familiar problems and rehearses familiar strategies for resolving them, strategies that had been tried and exhausted a century earlier. These alternative definitions enact centripetal and centrifugal impulses, competing gestures toward fidelity to particular facts and ideal coherence that have, as we have seen, for all practical purposes defined the project of American Literary Scholarship. Each of these strategies has its own limitations, and Buell presses those limits before he un-ceremoniously abandons the project of definition altogether.

Buell's first gesture toward definition is a familiar intellectual history that recapitualtes Frothingham or Goddard, or more recently Alexander Kern or Henry Pochmann, and has the disadvantages as well as the advantages of those earlier accounts. Rather than moving inward to essence, as his earlier reference to a "core" would suggest, it moves outward, as Frothingham had done, to historical context, presenting Transcendentalism as an intellectual system growing out of Kant and mediated by English and German Romanticism. While this intellectual history makes Transcendentalism available to scholarly scrutiny by locating it at the end of a coherent historical development, it also displaces its identity, the coherent "core" of Transcendentalism, into its surrounding cultural context and the work of figures who, by definition, do not represent it. As Goddard found, the subjects of such historical narratives have no unifying core, they expand ever outward, enlisting more and more facts, obscuring any possible identity in a blizzard of information. Seeking the meaning of a fact in its connection to previous facts produces an infinite regress that moves ever outward from the object whose center it is seeking.

Buell's account follows along in this centrifugal movement. Transcendentalism is dissatisfaction with Unitarianism, Unitarianism with Congregationalism, Congregationalism (we know) is dissatisfaction with Protestantism, Protestantism with Catholicism, and so on. "Where amidst all these facts," as Goddard said, "do we find Transcendentalism?" Even as it tries to be all-encompassing, this strategy cannot avoid being selective. Though, like Frothingham's similar one, this tale ties Transcendentalism to the American context as a local variant of European Romanticism, it frustrates the desire for definition by leaving out so many of the problems scholars have raised about Transcendentalism: the well-known differences among Transcendentalists, the respective influences of other philosophers like Cousin or Swedenborg, its relation to a literary tradition. My point here is not that Buell does not know about these complicating factors. On the contrary, as I have said, few scholars know them so well. But the necessity of defining Transcendentalism as a field-constituting category and the limitations of the kind of narratives available to him prevent Buell from doing justice to his own better knowledge.

To give *coherence* to Transcendentalism, to keep it from dispersing amidst the surrounding facts, Buell has to reverse his field. As his second strategy, he focuses on a single, central idea, the notion of "reason." Reason, he asserts, is the "heart" ("center" "core" "essence") of Transcendentalism. Yet, here again, he raises more problems than he can solve. As a daunting abundance of scholarship makes clear, *reason* is a still more vexed term than *Transcendentalism*. It has been a rhetorical battleground for 200 years, as Romantic writers have tried to use it as an antidote to skepticism, and its implications have remained problematic throughout the history of writing about Transcendentalism and Romantic writing in general.[34] Buell is far from blind to these disputes. But to use "reason" as the promised "heart" of Transcendentalism, the common ground onto which all its varied manifestations can crowd together, Buell would have to explain, if not resolve, the differences that have produced so many disagreements about it even among those Buell wants to call Transcendentalists. Such a resolution has evaded scholarship for 100 years, and it would be unreasonable to expect sudden clarity here. As it turns out, rather than explaining these differences, Buell explains them away by dismissing them as merely superficial. Although different Transcendentalists called reason by different names and attributed different qualities to it, Buell assures us, only the "names" and characteristics of reason differ—not its essence. The complications of the term, he argues in a note, result from calling "the intuitive faculty by the name of reason," an unfortunate "semantic paradox," a matter of mere words, rather than a conceptual conflict that might threaten the ideal identity of Transcendentalism. Not only does this explanation merely displace from "Transcendentalism" onto "reason" the distinction between identifying "characteristics" and ephemeral "essence," but Buell's note also seems to suggest that had they been more sophisticated or better informed, or clearer minded, had they chosen their words better, the Transcendentalists might have avoided this difficulty entirely, saving twentieth-century scholarship no end of trouble.

Probing for the "heart" of Transcendentalism, Buell's formidable learning insistently reminds him that Transcendentalism seems to be a beast with many hearts or (more threatening still) with no heart at all. He preserves its unity by cutting off loose ends rather than weaving them in. The coherence of the concept and of the field depends on denying stubborn differences. To close the discussion of reason and to provide closure on what might seem to "have been an unacceptably nebulous situation." Buell offers what amounts to a *non sequitur*. "In fact," he says, the differences among Transcendentalists were no greater than those between Kant and his "German successors" (p. 5). However true, the relevance of this analogy is uncertain because no one is building a national literary tradition on the claim that post-Kantian philosophy constituted a coherent movement.

After this effort, the claims of coherence give way, understandably enough, to those of particulars. Buell's third attempt to "define" Transcendentalism is a membership list, though he cannot offer it without preparatory qualifications that would seem to undermine the project even before it begins. The difficulties of definition, "the vagueness of the principle 'uniting' the Transcendentalists" (p. 5), he begins, becomes still more difficult if we focus on Transcendentalist membership (and in light of what has gone before, it is hard to imagine why Buell would want to make things any harder). The disclaimer implicit in his quotation marks is only the first in a volley of scholarly qualifications that prepares for Buell's assault on a defining list of Transcendentalists: Unitarians often sound like Transcendentalists, the idea of intuition "crops up" elsewhere as well, non-Transcendentalists "might be called Transcendentalists of a sort" (p. 6). Where, amidst all these hedged bets, we might ask, are the Transcendentalists?

Migrating once again toward coherence, Buell reassures us, in the midst of his discussion of membership, that the problems he has just emphasized, like those surrounding a "core" meaning, need not be troublesome. They simply "disappear" if we view Transcendentalism as a "state of mind" to which he extends solidity by placing its origins within a "specific matrix" in the "reaction against rationalism in Unitarian thought" (p. 6). Like a Neoplatonic principle of divine creation, this "state of mind" unites particular facts by "emanating outward" from its origins, embracing the fringes and "arising coincidentally in a number of other places . . . under similar intellectual conditions." It resolves the question of membership by absorbing it, but as a "history-of-ideas" version of the nineteenth-century notion of a "national spirit," it also dissolves cultural origins, historical influence, and distinct identity. Moreover, whether or not we think the "reaction against rationalism in Unitarian thought" ought to be characterized as a "matrix," it becomes harder to credit that intellectual break as the historical origin of Transcendentalism when Buell explicitly denies that notion later in his introduction and when, throughout the book, he argues the continuity of Unitarianism and Transcendentalism over their antagonism. Buell's metaphor raises more questions than it answers—questions about transmission and influence, identity amidst difference, and scholarly practices that had first been raised and in similar terms by Frothingham. How does a "state of mind" emanate? Are the unspecified alternate manifestations of the Transcendentalist "state of mind" to which Buell refers also Transcendentalism? If so, why have they not been treated as such in Transcendentalist scholarship? If not, why not? Buell's disclaimers, like Goddard's "Geist" or Frothingham's "character," assert coherence in advance for a collection of famously incompatible individuals. They evaporate all the facts that have always both fragmented and constituted the field.

The membership list that Buell goes on to superimpose on this unifying "state of mind" incorporates alternate strategies of its own. It starts out as a (qualified) hierarchical schema, moving from the "more or less central" to the "more or less peripheral" in expanding circles of declining importance (ordered alphabetically). The first—Alcott to Very—includes seventeen names. The next "circle of importance"— Brooks to Wheeler—covers eighteen. But then Buell shifts to a genetic model, listing "harbingers" and "third generation keepers of the faith," before returning to hierarchy with "eminent peripheral figures" from Bancroft to Whitman. Long as this list may seem, Buell admits that it could be vastly expanded if one wanted to include either individuals associated with utopian experiments like Brook Farm that are, in turn, often associated with Transcendentalism, or others like Emily Dickinson, who "had imbibed large doses of Emersonianism"—the emanation metaphor turned pharmaceutical and conflating without explanation two equally problematic terms: *Emersonianism* and *Transcendentalism*.

Extensive and qualified as it is, this list cannot conceal the false assumption on which it rests: that the Transcendentalist status of *any* individual has been immune from question. In fact, as Conrad Wright ruefully observes, no one (not even, not especially, Emerson) has been so immune in the give-and-take of Transcendentalist scholarly definition.[35] Ultimately, the only limit on the names that might be included is the space available, and by the end of his list, Buell finds himself, like Whitman, on "a verge of the usual mistake," the realization that lists do not deliver unity. They record miscellany and can lead only to dispersion and fragmentation.

So Buell backs away from his unboundable list, and for his final shot at a definition of *Transcendentalism* that both attends to and unifies its particulars, he seizes on a sort of statistical summary, a "general profile" of a Transcendentalist (one can only imagine what Emerson would have thought about being profiled in this way). In considering this profile, one might ask how many of the individuals on Buell's earlier list fit each (or all) of these new categories? Even better, how many others would fit who would not make anyone's list of Transcendentalists? Excluding the question-begging requirement that they reach Transcendentalism by way of Unitarianism by age 30, how many conservative Unitarians were raised in Boston, educated at Harvard, trained for the Unitarian clergy, came from genteel backgrounds, of old New England stock, supported ("with varying degrees of enthusiasm") the moral reforms of the day, and were ("in some degree") "literary" in their inclinations. A list of such people would surely dwarf even the quadrupled list of Transcendentalists that Buell earlier shrinks from producing, and might easily dwarf the entire membership of the First Church. If this "general profile" cannot even distinguish between Transcendentalists and their Boston neighbors, what hope for definition? Like Buell's list, his "profile" covers a lot of ground without getting any closer to it destination. After this, Buell unceremoniously drops his attempt to describe Transcendentalism as a movement.

Deprived of the ideological glue that, however tenuously, held together the narrative visions of his predecessors, Buell's effort at a coherent view of Transcendentalism leads only to evident frustration. In a sense, he knows too much. So many recalcitrant facts refuse to fit neatly into prevenient categories. Boundaries are blurred and ultimately the facts disperse the categories instead of being organized within them. Like Goddard, Buell is trapped between competing desires to separate Transcendentalism from the historical background he knows so well, and to demonstrate its continuity with its context (which he proposes as the "corrective" thrust of his study). This competition pits his desire to unify Transcendentalism and affirm the professional identity conferred by his field against his desire to respect the elements of his own knowledge and the scholarly methodology that mandated and produced it. That unresolvable conflict, as we have seen, has defined scholarship in the field for more than 100 years.

« 3 »

Time and Textuality

As the conflicts within the critical narrative tradition suggest, Transcendentalism does not provide the theory about which the classic American writing organized itself. It does not symbolize the birth of a truly American character, or represent a coherent literary and social movement with lines of influence reaching down to Gandhi and modern environmentalism. In this altered light, Transcendentalism is not only a critical invention but an *obsolete* critical invention, and discarding it leaves us with just that feature that has most troubled and dissatisfied criticism, a collection of texts that have no categorical home.

Just as Transcendentalism has been used to blend the early American aesthetic wasteland into the belletristic flowering of the American Renaissance, it has also been, throughout the history of the term, the no-man's-land in the nearly continuous skirmishing between literary and cultural studies. This ambivalence accounts for its centrality in American literary studies (which obsesses about that connection), but it also explains the discomfort of critics with writing that violates categories of literary excellence rather than fitting neatly inside them. By working from the same assumptions that Transcendentalists debated, critics of Transcendentalist writing have been practicing Romanticism rather than studying it. They worry about originality, formal coherence, influences, relations of particulars and universals, personal and social speech, logic and feeling. Like Buell, what they seem to want is some amalgam or compromise—Emerson laments the spirit of "cowardly compromise" abroad in the land—that would unite both terms of incompatible pairs. They want a unique literature that meets established formal standards, a logical art, spontaneous craftsmanship. And these oxymorons have remained the consistent subjects of works in the field for a century and a half, from Henry Dana, Sr., to Lawrence Buell.

The study of Transcendentalist writing, like that of American literature in general and for similar reasons, has always needed justification. With the advent of the New Criticism, as Melville took his place in the literary pantheon, Transcendentalism, like Puritanism, dropped behind, leaning on national pride and its small but enthusiastic professional constituency for support. During this period, the great unaskable question has been, why should we read Emerson, or Thoreau, or Margaret Fuller when we could be reading Dickens, or Shakespeare, or Melville, or James?

Hostility to Transcendentalist texts has been a peculiar and consistent feature of that critical tradition. Critics put Transcendentalism at the center of American literature not because they admired it but because it was central to their larger project. It gave criticism the intellectual lever it needed to pry a mature native literature out of the hard and uncultivated American soil. But in our own time, the importance that these nationalistic assumptions have given Transcendentalism has too often seemed, even to its most enthusiastic students, oddly out of proportion with any identifiable literary merit. This sense of disproportion, in turn, has prompted much of the scholarly debate in the field as criticism defends both Transcendentalism and the vision of a uniquely American literature it supports by conjuring up the obscure beauties of Transcendentalist writing. Transcendentalist texts were so far from anything Frothingham could accept as either American or as art that he virtually ignored them in his effort to identify Transcendentalism with the American "spirit." Transcendentalism, he said, is whatever it is apart from texts (p. 123). Even works like Emerson's *Nature* fit into Frothingham's scheme not as worthy of study in themselves but as events in the "zeitgeist," indicators of the changing social atmosphere. The texts that Frothingham would have preferred, the perfect Transcendentalist texts, avoided the formal limitations of Emerson's essays. They were the ones Theodore Parker (Frothingham's favorite Transcendentalist) never wrote. Indeed, the best parts of Transcendentalism, the parts that satisfied scholarly ideals, have always been unwritten, a matter of spirit. At bottom, Frothingham's objection is not merely to Transcendentalist texts, though he certainly does object to them, it is a refusal to accept the limits of particular forms, one ratified though not, perhaps, created by his appropriation of Transcendentalism to justify and domesticate an America without a formal track record.

Goddard's similar discussion of Transcendentalist "absurdities," picks up Frothingham's idealist distinction between Transcendentalist "thought" and "expression" to excuse Transcendentalist excesses.

Awkward phrases in Alcott's writing "inevitably provoke a smile" not so much because of the "character of the thought" as because "Alcott was very far from being a master of expression" (p. 118). The famous "transparent eyeball" passage in *Nature* (everybody's favorite whipping boy in this sort of discussion) "is ridiculous quite apart from its truth or falsity. We may agree entirely or we may disagree with the philosophic thought, but we must surely admit that the sentence is grossly unpoetic and wholly deserving of the cartoons it called forth" (p. 119). The binary oppositions of these approaches to Transcendentalist writing reflect the idealist model of art that generates them and that survives into our own day in the one-sided argument between New Critical formalism and New Historicist polemic. Frothingham divides Transcendentalism from forms of any kind, including texts, Goddard divides thought from expression, Matthiessen divides theory from literature. And these are Transcendentalism's *fans*.[1] The fact is these critics cannot see a writer like Emerson as great by any standard they can specify, but he is central to the tradition that is central to their professional field, and moreover, they really feel, despite their inability to justify it, that he *is* a great writer. In part, their confusion represents their frustration at this contradiction.

The problem critics have in reading Transcendentalist writing is analogous to those critics have had in trying to make coherent sense of American facts for 200 years. To his credit, Lawrence Buell acknowledged these difficulties before many of his contemporaries did and called for a solution, another way of talking about texts that overlap the usual categories. But the particular solutions Buell proposes, the application of new generic categories, for example, does not meet the need that inspired the attempt. Comparing Transcendentalist writing to "conversation" seems less a way to get new insight on its excellence than a way to disguise its deficiencies.

The particulars of Transcendentalist writing repeatedly frustrate critical gestures toward resolution. Even when a scholar like Buell sets out to demonstrate the artistry and coherence of Emerson's essays, his meager claims sound more like condemnation.[2] Like Brooks, when critical judgment is called to the bar, Buell cannot escape his own verdict that Transcendentalist ideas are "half-baked" and their style "inchoate." Having started with the assumption that Emerson must be a self-conscious artist, Buell has to go on to assume that, to be valued, Emerson's self-consciousness must produce forms of coherence consistent with established aesthetic or logical models. But the infamous fragmentation of Emerson's prose makes Buell cautious about his claims. Emerson's prose, he ventures, can be seen as a series of "propositions," but even here, he has to admit that this approach "hardly captures the greatness of Emerson." What does capture that greatness he never makes clear. The most he can risk, after a long list of Emerson's deficiencies, is that "the essay has method," "a form distinct enough for the careful reader to perceive." And, allegedly in Emerson's defense, he affirms that "the essay does fall apart about three-quarters of the way through, but until then Emerson has his material well in hand" (p. 407).

It is simply astonishing that the work of a writer considered so central to the national tradition can be portrayed in such terms by a scholar who has taken his work as a special area of study and is, I am certain, sincerely interested in demonstrating his greatness. Buell's disapproval of Emerson's prose measures how confined he is within the tradition of Transcendentalist criticism that he represents so well and hence how helpless to imagine the antiformal literature toward which he tentatively gestures. Indeed, assumptions like Buell's lead inevitably to a devaluation of Transcendentalist writing, a condescension and even scorn that seem out of place coming from its foremost contemporary commentators but are actually all too typical of Transcendentalist scholarship.

Convinced, like Buell, of the centrality of Transcendentalist texts, but unable to justify it, American scholarship has tried to believe that Transcendentalist writing is the ugly duckling of American literature and would prove a lovely swan at last. But time and all the efforts of criticism have not turned the duckling into a swan. After 100 years of scholarly nurture, Transcendentalist writing is still a duck, and it has become increasingly clear that criticism will have to deal with it as it is. Scholars will have to learn how to explain it as historical without making it the cart horse for a nationalist criticism, how to produce accounts of the problems Transcendentalist writing raises without merely continuing them.

In the past few years, this process has been begun, though not, as a rule, by scholars who could be called students of Transcendentalism in the traditional sense. Following the lead of Harold Bloom and Stanley Cavell, some of the newer generation of critics who have grown up with theoretical vocabulary have made Emerson central to their project. Of course, there is nothing unusual about that. Emerson has been central to every critical project in American literature since the nineteenth century, even for those critics, like Matthiessen, who could not justify his centrality on aesthetic grounds. That very conflict can, in fact, be identified as instrumental in forcing criticism to trade in one interpretive paradigm for another.

One of the great advantages of poststructuralist criticism is that it has provided terms for discussing texts apart from the standards of aesthetic coherence that have caused such complications for critical accounts of Transcendentalist writing. In some cases, however, the adoption of theoretical assumptions that make hay out of the very gaps in texts that criticism has always found so troubling in Emerson produces surprisingly conservative results. In *Emerson's Romantic Style,* for example, Julie Ellison superimposes a Bloomian model of reading and writing on an aesthetic appropriated from English Romanticism. For Ellison, Emerson's writing is "organized by antagonism," and he uses it "for aggressive purposes."[3] Like many revisionist critics of American literature, Ellison seems to bring a critical perspective ready-made to Emerson's texts. Emerson is only an instance of the more general fact that "writing is always resistance" (p. 3).

The advantage of Ellison's approach is that it gives her space to describe Emerson's discontinuities rather than trying to explain them away. Unlike Buell, she is not tied to a model of self-conscious artistry. "A man's style," she quotes Emerson, "is his intellectual voice only in part under his controul [*sic*]."[4] Freed in this way, she can describe the movement of Emerson's prose without seeing that very movement as evidence of aesthetic failure. Like any critical methodology, however, Ellison's also carries its attendant disadvantages. Starting with discontinuity, Ellison is unable to acknowledge even the minimal coherence Buell discovered. "There is," she says, "no flow of argument or exposition, but rather a series of discrete acts of substitution" (p. 10).

More troubling, however, Ellison wanders simultaneously into pitfalls of the tradition and of contemporary criticism. She sees Emerson, ahistorically, as an exemplar of contemporary critical assumptions, and yet fails to find any substantial significance in his writing that could explain its importance to generations of critics and especially to modern readers. She also reveals the tendency, often noted among poststructuralist critics, to thematize her own activity in the texts she reads. Emerson's prose, she says, is "a drama of interpretation, of theorizing."[5] On the other hand, she gains credence of Emerson and for her own argument by fitting Emerson into traditional literary critical categories, showing how he is part of traditional discourse about Romantic writing. Just as the New Criticism raised the status of American writing by promoting a transnational universal aesthetic, Ellison promotes a subjective aesthetic of personal feeling. Emerson's writing, she says, seeks "the gratifications of the sublime." He is "motivated by his desire to repeat the movement from deprived ambition to aggressive criticism. . . . His greatest pleasure is in the willing reenactment" of that movement (p. 140). While this move is, in one sense, worth applauding because it breaks down the nationalist isolation that, as I argue, generally characterizes American literary scholarship, it does so only by trivializing Emerson's writing in the process. From Ellison's point of view, Emerson has no more substantial aims than the repeated enjoyment of this peculiar pleasure. Though Ellison's approach recognizes, without disapproving, discontinuity, it does so only by depriving Emerson's prose of all sense of argument, the sense that there is anything at stake.

Moreover, her ability to accommodate Emerson's illogic does not prevent Ellison from falling into the traditional critical inability to take Emerson's writing as it is. Like earlier critics who wish Emerson would be just a bit more clear, or less bizarre, Ellison can't help wishing Emerson conformed more closely to her own "aggressive" ideal. Emerson triumphs for Ellison when he "rises into the mastering phase of the sublime" (p. 46). But as numerous critics have observed, Emerson's prose never stays on the heights for long. "I confess," she says, "that I am always disappointed to find Emerson backing away from his courageous acceptance of the necessary aggressiveness of thought and lapsing—I cannot help seeing it as that—into the desire for 'consanguinity' with nature" (p. 95). This is a confession indeed. Like a long line of earlier critics, Ellison simply prefers one side of Emerson's internal debate, and so ignores the problems that Emerson sees better than she and that consequently make him swing back to the other. In this sense, Ellison's really *is* a discourse of power, one that illustrates the way the criticism of power asserts the power of criticism.[6]

Other critics like Donald Pease, Richard Poirier, and Stanley Cavell have begun, in different ways, to develop an account of Emerson's and Thoreau's prose that explains its discontinuities without denying the meaningful coherence that would justify its centrality for 150 years of criticism. Pease dislodges Emerson from the "revolutionary" rhetoric of American literary scholarship that would portray all American writers as iconoclastic individualists, thus freeing himself to acknowledge the conservative motives that have been obscured by traditional critical assumptions. Poirier has offered a sophisticated general description of the working of Emerson's prose, and Cavell has accounted most fully for the complexity of Emerson's (and of Thoreau's) accounts, and they address issues about which we still ought to be concerned. This is the line I hope to extend here by describing the way Emerson's and Thoreau's writing encompasses temporality and thus acknowledges in its very form its own place in history.[7]

In this chapter and the next, I want to suggest that Emerson's and Thoreau's prose enacts a thinking through of alternatives to the conventional understandings that were proving inadequate to social and moral action in the nineteenth century. However radical its linguistic and social implications, their project was a deeply conservative one. Emerging from idealist beliefs, they were consumed with discovering a ground of coherence *in* fragmented human experience that could replace the traditional foundations that had been eroded by developments in science, philosophy, and scriptural scholarship. But precisely because their writing so thoroughly explored, and ultimately discarded, the alternatives available for such foundations in their time, they ended up developing a language and a narrative form that speaks to their (and our) world without foundations.

In the process, Emerson and Thoreau produce altered terms and conditions for understanding. Rather than formulating a Romantic epistemology, as scholars have often asserted, Transcendentalist texts dramatize the abandonment of epistemology. Their effort to renew, in modern terms, the assurances that Enlightenment empiricism had banished issued in another sort of truth altogether, one conditioned by and bound up with historical circumstances and shaped in and by their contingent writing. Freighted with vestigial idealist aspirations, they pursued their timeless goals through the transformations of a relentlessly temporal medium and thus assured the frustration that appears in the peculiar and fascinating forms of their prose.

That writing raises the issues and explores the strategies that continue to preoccupy us. My readings of Emerson and Thoreau are attempts at talking about their literary practice in ways that avoid the insecurities about aesthetic and intellectual coherence that we have inherited from the nineteenth century and at establishing a more productive relationship between our present and our past as it appears in these texts. That relationship must not merely rehash the oppositions that generated nineteenth-century debate. If, as professors of literature we are to speak to contemporary needs rather than to issues that Transcendentalist writing dissolved a century and a half ago and give our work a shot at exercising the influence I think it deserves, we need to develop ways of talking about literature that do not depend on contemporary redactions of idealism.

Between Metaphor and Metaphysics: Reading Emerson as "Onward Thinking"

> I fear that the progress of metaphysical philosophy may be found to consist in nothing else than the progressive introduction of apposite metaphors.
>
> EMERSON

I

Emerson's writing, of which his essay "The Transcendentalist" will serve as an example, provides a counterpoint to scholarly descriptions of the same subject. But more than that, it provides an example of a strategy for revising the explanatory narratives that have lingered in historical scholarship. In "The Transcendentalist," Emerson first takes part in and then transcends the debate between realism and idealism that has dominated American literary scholarship. Like so many of the critics who took him as their subject, Emerson seeks a language that will mediate the division between spiritual and material models of coherence. At stake is the possibility of finding order among the fragments of material fact, the hope of reconciling individual with public truth, and the possibility of producing coherent narrative accounts within the constraints of a historical and conditional world. This chapter aims at a description of Emerson's prose that suggests ways of developing modern tools for examining Transcendentalism, tools that are designed to meet our own needs rather than those that prevailed when American literary studies were in their infancy. With these new tools in hand, we need not either deny Emerson's self-contradiction or condemn him for it, and we need not pursue inevitably strained attempts to save his art by discovering its hidden unity. Without having either to reconstruct or deconstruct an Emersonian philosophy, or to uncover a previously obscure aesthetic beauty, we can see his prose as participating in the composition of an alternative philosophy, or better perhaps, an alternative *to* metaphysical philosophy with important implications for literary history.[8] That view would examine the language in which Emerson tried to recapture unity when conventional language could not, and describe the role of that language in the radicalization of prose that gained momentum in the nineteenth century.

This is not to say that Emerson had discovered the truth that remains obscure to us. Emerson's own treatment of Transcendentalism in "The Transcendentalist" is no less troubled than the descriptions of his contemporaries or of ours. It claims our attention not because it succeeds where others have failed in pinning Transcendentalism down for scrutiny but because it defuses all attempts to do so, and in the process, casts a peculiar light both on the scholarly image of Transcendentalism and on the historical criticism that has produced it.

In "The Transcendentalist," Emerson is characteristically coy about explicitly defining his subject. Nevertheless, critics desperate for something solid to hold onto have made his only apparently explicit definition one of the more often quoted lines of an author who, like the *Bible*, has prospered primarily in quotation. "Transcendentalism," Emerson is commonly quoted as saying, "is Idealism . . . as it appears in 1842."[9] This remark has been the *locus classicus* for scholarly arguments about Emerson's historical and philosophical naivete. It fits neatly with the assumption (endemic to Transcendentalist scholarship from Lawrence Buell back to O. B. Frothingham) that Transcendentalist writing is neither philosophical fish nor literary fowl, that it lacks intellectual coherence and formal beauty, dwelling uneasily in Buell's terms, "somewhere between metaphor and metaphysics."[10] Back in its place amidst the language from which quotation removes it, however, Emerson's "definition" of Transcendentalism looks less simple and the usual critical oppositions less applicable.[11] It expresses a struggle with meaning more complex than criticism has allowed and more like the critic's own, one that ought to evade the historian's condescension because it undermines the very documentary treatment of texts that has supported historical scholarship while dividing meaning and language, intellectual and aesthetic coherence.

The first thing we have to say respecting what are called *new views* here in New England, at the present time, is, that they are not new, but the very oldest of thoughts cast into the mold of these new times. The light is always

identical in its composition, but it falls on a great variety of objects, and by
so falling is first revealed to us, not in its own form, for it is formless, but in
theirs; in like manner, thought only appears in the objects it classifies. What
is popularly called Transcendentalism among us, is idealism; Idealism as it
appears in 1842.

This passage does not offer a decorative figure for Transcendentalism
that must be boiled down for clarity into some discursive proposition:
"Transcendentalism is Idealism reflected from nineteenth-century concerns." Emerson's opening paragraph is a sequence of formulations in
dialogue with one another. Each of the incompatible images that Emerson presents in this series takes a different angle on the relationship
between form and essence, and their uneasy cohabitation in this paragraph frustrates any attempt to reduce them to a neat formula that
criticism could portray as Emerson's doctrine on the subject. The first
metaphor ("cast into the mold of these new times") suggests that the
particular determines the shape of the universal. The second responds to
the material bias of the first by describing the universal as an immaterial
"formless" essence that only "appears" as it is reflected from particulars. The third ("thought . . . appears in the objects it classifies")
portrays the universal as an intellectual ordering principle that arranges
particular phenomena and appears only implicitly in that order.

"Inconsistent" passages like this are just the sort that criticism tried
for so long to explain away or argue around, but their ubiquity in
Emerson's writing suggests that they are characteristic of his prose and
central to the problems of Transcendentalist criticism. Emerson's writing
unceasingly adapts old terms to new conditions, aiming to produce true
accounts of a persistently new world rather than to develop a systematic
philosophy. On a small scale in this passage and on a larger and more
ambitious scale in the essay as a whole, Emerson does not just alter his
arguments, revising or finding new justifications for his views. He alters
the meaning, significance, and associations of words themselves as he
alters their uses. They change from sentence to sentence, paragraph to
paragraph, patching holes in previous formulations but inevitably opening new ones, trying the power of each expression in an inherited
language to convey fresh and individual truths.[12]

In the context of the conflicting images that precede it, Emerson's
famous definition does not present the identifying essence of Transcendentalism. It floats one more strategy, the fourth in this first paragraph,

for uniting resistant terms. It is an attempt to *do* something that previous statements had not done rather than a representation of Emerson's settled convictions. Each of Emerson's earlier formulations took an angle on the question of whether reality is actively or passively constituted. But this one incorporates conflict into itself, the first of a series of internal splits in "The Transcendentalist." The two sides of Emerson's definition embody contradictory views of the relation of words and world that entail differing notions of the influence of history on meaning. Transcendentalism may be idealism "as it appears" in 1842, but whether historical circumstances obscure, alter, influence, or determine the way Transcendentalism "appears" is precisely what is being negotiated in this paragraph and in the rest of the essay. How are we to discover coherence amidst the changes in history, or, which may be the same thing, in narrative? Read in this way, his pithy description does not answer our doubts about the identity of idealism as essence or form. It leaves us asking how we are to know idealism *as* idealism if its appearance is always changing? It embodies, even as it launches, the struggle between material and spiritual models of knowledge that shapes the rest of the essay.

Emerson's strategies are compressed in this first paragraph, and the problems he faces here characterize "The Transcendentalist" and Emerson's writing in general. Emerson's essay divides along the same ideal and material lines as his famous "definition." It starts off with an abstract and theoretical division between the idealist and the materialist in the first section only to divide itself again into a second section that amounts to a new beginning, a reconsideration of earlier abstract issues in practical, social, and historical terms that create new conditions for Emerson's narrative.

The first section of the essay features balance and abstraction. Both materialism and idealism are described, in an objective third person, as timeless concepts, untouched by particular circumstances: "mankind have *ever* been divided into two sects, Materialists and Idealists." The terms that dominate the essay at this point come readily enough to hand from the rhetoric of Christian Platonism. In that tradition, the division between material and ideal worlds implies the *superiority* of the latter. The materialist "insists on facts . . . history . . . circumstances . . . the animal wants of man; the idealist . . . thought . . . will . . . miracle . . . individual culture" (p. 201). The universal prevails over the particular or individual, the timeless over the temporal, both in preference and in power. Yet, the opening of the essay has already advertised the inadequacy of these traditional oppositions.

Every statement in the early paragraphs that depends on this opposition divides experience in halves, each necessarily "incomplete." Each division calls the description that offers it into question, leading to the need for another corrective (but also inevitably incomplete) substitute.[13] Emerson cannot simply adopt a Pauline repudiation of things in favor of spirit any more than he could opt to return to a pre-Lockean world. He has to account for a world in which apparently fragmentary natural facts necessarily found even higher knowledge. This is a version of the same project that preoccupied scholars of American literature from Frothingham to Buell, who tried to weave the facts of American experience into a coherent story about the nation. At stake is the very possibility of worldly order and the means of producing it.

Emerson begins to revise his own traditional Neoplatonic terms almost as soon as he offers them. Opposition between two worlds, ideal and real, becomes hierarchy in the natural one. Both are "natural," he says, but idealism is "in higher nature." The idealist, Emerson asserts, affirms "facts" that "appear" to him according to a "manner of looking at things" that "needs a retirement from the senses to discern" (pp. 201–2). This passage denies the authority of the senses even as it depends on the language of sensation, and its ambivalence toward ocular metaphors illustrates Locke's continuing grip, at this stage, on Emerson's descriptions of experience.[14] If the idealist "affirms *facts* not affected by the illusions of sense," what is the relation between such immaterial "facts" and the more familiar material ones, where do the former come from, and how does the idealist get them?

Emerson's first response to these implicit questions makes speech the generative link between natural and spiritual facts. Nature itself becomes an original language, the servant of spirit. Spiritual facts, Emerson ventures, "assume a native superiority to material facts, degrading these into a language by which the first are to be spoken" (pp. 201–2). This move completes the process by which a difference in kind (spirit/world) is converted into an expressive relation. But the passive verb "are to be spoken" leaves the process of this conversion in doubt. Emerson has made spirit dependent on the mediation of speech, but in order to keep subjectivity at bay, he has left the potentially formative speaker out of the equation.

But when Emerson applies this idea in the real world, by giving a particular speaker the power to produce spirit out of material truth, revision begins in earnest. His conventional Romantic metaphor of nature as a "language" takes a turn that profoundly extends its implications. "The Idealist, in *speaking* of events, *sees* them as spirits" (p. 202). By so conflating speaking and seeing, Emerson works a change on the traditional metaphysical association of sight with knowledge, where knowledge is conceived as the accurate representation of the world in the mind. The idealist speaker sees/knows the spiritual by *speaking* the material. By conflating words and things, Emerson straddles the crucial boundary between reality represented and reality created about which the traditional debate rages, and on which it depends. And neither side alone is acceptable in any terms Emerson can imagine. Such speaking sight stretches to the breaking point the traditional implications of the perceptual metaphor as the passive imaging of external reality in the mind. In the Idealist's hands, speech becomes a transforming activity, turning matter into spirit, revising the world rather than merely reflecting it.

Having introduced subjectivity in the speaking idealist, the following paragraphs proceed to explore its implications and make disturbing discoveries. As Emerson points out, this way of speaking and seeing "transfers every object in nature from an independent . . . position without there, into consciousness" (p. 202), repairing in the mind the breech that had troubled Emerson in nature. Just as contemporary theorists have debated subjective and objective models of textual meaning, Emerson struggled with an epistemological tradition in which the only alternative to an objective view of external objects was identity with them. As a result, Emerson's insistence that nature must be not merely fragmentary, "independent and anomalous," and unconnected to man, but that it "nearly concerns him" moves him to transfer "every object in nature . . . into the consciousness." To "nearly concern man," facts must be connected to him as part of "consciousness." Despite Emerson's earlier assurance that the Idealist does not deny natural facts, the logic of his move into consciousness seems to require just that. "Mind," Emerson says, "is the only reality" (p. 203). The events that had provided spirit with an expressive language are now themselves products of consciousness. "Nature, literature, history, are only subjective phenomena," and the Idealist even "degrade[s] persons into representatives of truths." "His thought,—that is the Universe" (p. 203). Emerson's use of "consciousness" produces unity, but only by solipsistically absorbing everything else that counts as human experience.[15]

Emerson aimed to secure knowledge of the world by bringing the world and its ideal foundations together in "consciousness." He accuses the materialist, by contrast, of embracing a view of the world "built up on . . . strange and quaking foundations." But on what foundations is the Idealist's "consciousness" built (p. 203)? Once it is placed in the human mind, the ideal foundation of experience becomes part of experience itself and loses its foundational ideality. Particular thoughts in individual minds (as opposed to abstract "thought") are knowable, worldly, and therefore contingent. Emerson is struggling here with competing imperatives for foundational purity on one hand and for access to foundational truth on the other. By definition, anything with which the conditional knower can make contact must also be conditional and is thus disqualified as a candidate for ordering foundation of all knowledge. Emerson has caught himself in an infinite regress. If his thought is the universe, then the absolute ground of that universe must be unthinkable. Yet, to be of use, to give experience unity and order, it must be accessible, which is why Emerson located it in the mind in the first place.

In the ensuing discussion, Emerson is a character in the continuing dialogue between the material and the ideal, taking each part in turn.[16] While he is immersed in consciousness, Emerson conflates the story of the inquirer with the story of the ideal coherence that he seeks to know. "I," he says and then qualifies and revises, "this thought which is called I—is the mold into which the world is poured like melted wax. This mold is invisible, but the world betrays the shape of the mold" (p. 204). This description reiterates the essay's first paragraph, with the "I" taking the place of the "ideal." Like the earlier term, the "I" is a "thought," is invisible in itself, is only "called" "I," and becomes apparent only in the forms of the world. But in this second version, the ideal *self* is the mold giving shape to the world as the world gave shape to the ideal at the start.

Locating reality in the mind leads to the apotheosis of the self, which becomes identified with ideal spirit. When Emerson refers to the Transcendentalist at these moments, he does so in the first person. "They" becomes "I" or "we" as Emerson makes the voice of the Transcendentalist his own (much as he does to speak as the "Orphic Poet" in *Nature*), offering truths unavailable to any objective view. But it also raises other and more troublesome implications. By withdrawing into the mind, Emerson also moves into an adversarial relation with his own worldly audience. His unavoidable advocacy makes it clear, finally, that this is not just a conflict within consciousness, but one between individual and culture. As the debate develops, his tone becomes almost hostile as he refers to the audience as "you," rejecting "all that you call the world," and implicitly condemning the common view of the world as artificial, a fraud (p. 204).

Working out the implications of the ideal has changed the balance of issues in Emerson's discussion. Increasingly, the essay replaces the "idealist/materialist" split with an opposition between the "Transcendentalist" individual and society, and the discussion swings between opposed authorities for judgment rather than alternative worlds of experience. Pressed to its extreme, "consciousness" as the seat of meaning produces unacceptable conclusions and yields a new emphasis on materiality to control the increasingly anarchic impulses of the divine self. The first hints of this change follow hard upon the assertion that "mind is the only reality." They are inspired by the disturbing subjectivity of all nature, literature, and history, and the dangerous admission that the Idealist "does not respect labor, or . . . property . . . he does not respect government . . . nor the church." Amidst these anarchic offspring of the mind's hegemony, Emerson first introduces what will become a crucial distinction *within* the Idealist between "thought" and "action." The "order of thought" produces threatening isolation, and in response, the Idealist shows a "warmly cooperating" relation with other men, though to do so he has to be *"overpowered* by the laws of action" (p. 203). Only the necessity of worldly action, imposed by social need, breaks down the isolation of thought.

In the rest of the essay, an epistemological quest for knowledge becomes a practical quest for relationship. The original effort to find a place for the ideal in the world turns into an effort to locate the idealized individual in society. It is in this context that Emerson first refers to the "Transcendentalist" rather than the "Idealist," a move that signals a turn in the essay from timeless abstractions to historical particulars. In this new historical and social context, Emerson has to reconcile individual with social authority rather than spiritual essences with worldly forms. At first, the "Transcendentalist" still reflects the authority of mind that prompted his appearance. His steadfast allegiance to an inner authority "resists" all worldly "rules and measures." He is so abstract, refusing "any thing *positive,* [or] *personal,"* that it is hard to imagine his *doing* anything at all. The necessary imperfection of worldly forms leads to the well-known conclusion (one it is in my interest to be particularly fond of) that "there is no such thing as a Transcendental *party;* that there is no pure Transcendentalist." The first part of the essay ends by denying the existence of its subject.

Unable to resolve the inherent incompatibilities between ideal essence and material particulars in the first part of the essay, Emerson starts all over again with a second and revised account of his subject, this time in terms of temporal action. This second time around, Emerson avoids his earlier conflict between world and idea by describing Transcendentalism not as a spiritual object in or out of the world but as a historical *movement* toward fulfillment, a "tendency" to trust the intuitions. "The history of genius in these times," he asserts, "will be the history of this tendency" (p. 207). In a historical world, one in which meaning cannot be found by appealing to a higher and timeless realm, Emerson's subject is material for *interpretation* rather than an object of immediate *perception*. Emerson's focus on worldly action has made both opposition and the resolution of opposition a matter of time. The imperfection of present action hints at a more satisfactory future of which present imperfect individuals are merely "prophets and heralds." But like Emerson's other strategies, this apparent promise only recasts and further complicates the problem by revising the terms and conditions under which it must be considered.

As always, the problem is how to specify the connection between the longed-for ideal and present facts. As Emerson tries, in the paragraphs that follow, to describe the "persons" who represent this "tendency," he evades specificity with all his might. They are not, of course, "Transcendentalists" and, in fact, he goes to extraordinary lengths to avoid naming them at all. For the rest of the essay Emerson moves between an elaborately evasive third person—"these companions and contemporaries," "these exacting children," "this class," "these seething brains, these admirable radicals, these unsocial worshippers, these talkers"—and a first person who subsumes "them" into himself, depending on whether he is speaking to Transcendentalist imperfection or to society's intolerance and superficiality. Although the essay aims, ostensibly, at reconciliation between these opposed camps, the implications of each position, as Emerson unfolds them, increasingly distance the Transcendentalist ideal from the world, first by alienating the Transcendentalist from society and then by separating him from the ideal in himself.

Passivity and withdrawal, rather than harmonious relationship, are the first features of these "persons." "They hold themselves aloof" disdaining the work of the mundane world, and what they do, they do only because they are "overpowered by the humanities that speak on all sides" (p. 207), just as earlier the "Idealist" has to be "overpowered by the laws of action" in order to submit to worldly orders. Abstract "thought" might passively and invisibly shape the world, but the worldly force, even if it is, as he says, only a "tendency," ought to produce some worldly result. The rest of the essay reflects this ambivalence, moving back and forth between demands that these "dreamers" *do* something useful and assertions that none but the perfect action is worth doing.

How can Emerson describe a relationship between "these persons" and the rest of society? Like most of Emerson's inquiries, his effort to do so takes its own direction, ending finally in an isolation that reiterates, in social terms, the solipsistic withdrawal into consciousness at the beginning of the essay. When the world, frustrated by Transcendentalist disdain for worldly activity, accuses them of insensitivity, Emerson replies, in their defense, that, despite their withdrawal from an imperfect world, "they are not stockish or brute,—but joyous, susceptible, affectionate; they have even more than others a great wish to be loved" (p. 208). Emerson uses *love* here to rebut accusations of Transcendentalist indifference, and it is the *fulfillment* of such love, the integration of Transcendentalist and the world, that Emerson is seeking. But Emerson cannot get halfway through a paragraph describing such relationships before their implications generate an alternate movement. Social relationship, human love, threatens the ideality and integrity of the individual consciousness, and as his plaintive quotation of Mozart suggests (Mozart is "ready to cry ten times a day, 'but, are you sure you love me?'") it undermines individual self-sufficiency (p. 208).

In the world of particulars, the real world, "love" puts unacceptable constraints on ideal purity, and even as Emerson offers it, he seems to step back from these and the word begins to take on more elevated and abstract connotations. In place of his original assertion Emerson offers their "whole thought" to replace the now merely accidental and personal ones that seemed so needy (p. 208). "Love" now has no connection with any personal relationship between individuals. It attaches itself to nature in general, as its last and highest gift, a revision that effectively depersonalizes love and associates it with universal spirit. The resulting tenuous relationships hardly involve people at all. "Their faces are perhaps unknown,'' Emerson explains, ''but in their hearts'' (rather than actively in the world) the Transcendentalists thank them daily for existing (p. 208). Transcendent love is diluted to a passive beholding of spiritual beauty in distant, admirable others, a tenuous and abstract relationship that penetrates Transcendentalist isolation in spirit only. The indifferent sort of love Emerson develops here proves indifferent as well to Emerson's original uses for it, for by inspiring impatience with the general run of humanity who are not worthy of this rarified sentiment, it leads to just the sort of isolation that Emerson set out to deny. ''I will not molest myself for you,'' Emerson concludes, speaking in the place of the Transcendentalist, ''I do not wish to be profaned.'' Since ''they'' cannot approve of men enough to associate with them, it is not surprising that ''loneliness, and not . . . love, would prevail in their circumstances'' (p. 209).

Emerson's strategy comes full circle, putting him in the very position he started out to repudiate. His rhetorical gymnastics in this passage, his characteristic movement between opposed positions, is particularly compressed. In this one paragraph, he begins in third-person objectivity, moves to first-person identification, adopts a middle ground, detached from both parties (*''They* cannot gossip with *you''*), and ends up in a narrative first person (''Love me, they say'') that elides identity and difference. His ambivalence about the relationship he is trying to describe is performed in the flexibility of his own position.

The next section begins where the last left off, with human imperfection as it appears to these ''most exacting and extortionate critics.'' But like the last, it tacks in midstream. Scholars have often interpreted this passage as Emerson's rueful comment on his Transcendentalist contemporaries and on himself. ''So many promising youths, and never a finished man!'' But the facts that it is ''their quarrel with *every* man'' and that it is their *criticism* that inspires a ''strange disappointment'' with *''every* youth'' make it clear that the well-known line that follows refers to all men, to human imperfection in general, including but not at all limited to Emerson's acquaintances (p. 209). As in the earlier discussion of the ''tendency'' toward *''transcendental''* thinking, the specter of present imperfection leads here to a desire for signs of progress, but the historical development that seemed a mark of progress at the relatively abstract beginning of this second half of the essay looks, in the context of individuals, like a decline. The ''divine idea'' seems confined to youth. It seeps away with the passing of time, which no longer preserves or perfects but kills "the high idea" in its contingent human (and hence mortal) manifestation. In this passage, time leads not to fulfillment of promise but to loneliness, separation, and limitation. What started as a revision of the static and irresolvable opposition between contingent forms and timeless essence has sprouted problems of its own.

The more Emerson says about the failings of humanity in general, the more sympathetic he becomes to the alienation of "this class" from the rest of the race. In light of the low condition of humanity, "their" very dissatisfaction becomes a form of public service. By alerting us to the folly of our own expectations for men, "they have not been without service to the race of man," though they "eat clouds, and drink wind." Emerson has found a way for "them" to be useful without being productive. This seems an ironic mission for the harbingers of a perfected humanity. But as Emerson's sympathies move back toward "these persons," he becomes less and less concerned with humanity at large. Indeed, society itself is redefined. "They" "shun what is called society" (p. 210), a superficial and false name that echoes "what are called new views" and "what is popularly called Transcendentalism" from the first paragraph of the essay, as well as the more emphatic "What you call the world." This dissatisfaction with the world moves Emerson back into the isolated individual mind. They "find [true] society for their hope and religion" by "taking themselves to friend." Their imaginations "can give them often forms so vivid that these for the time shall seem real, and society the illusion." But, in the earlier more abstract formulation, mind was the *only* reality, whereas this one cannot escape limits, particularly temporal ones ("often," "for the time") that qualify modern critical assumptions about the flights of Romantic imagination, and call to mind Frost's more modest claim for poetry as a "momentary stay against confusion."[17]

Now, when the issue of productive work comes up, Emerson stands with "these persons" and against society, but his position very quickly rehearses its own futility. He first produces a reply to society's criticisms that recalls the oddly ambivalent position at the end of the section on love, placing himself between society and "this class," by referring to both in the third person ("What you call your fundamental institutions . . . seem to them . . . paltry matters") (p. 211). Then he engages in a diatribe against the meanness of a common life shaped by "a spirit of cowardly compromise" that makes life "an activity without an aim." And finally he returns to the rebellious first person ("unless the action

is . . . adequate, I do not wish to perform it") and to an inaction
(" 'We will wait' ") that seems, under its sympathetic defensiveness, to
identify "their" posture as an aim without an activity (p. 211). All of
these issues sprang up with the need to be in the world, to produce
worldly "action," and Emerson dispenses with them here by repudiating
the term that produced them. He retreats into "patience and truth,"
which amounts to inaction and silence, and defines virtue negatively as
the avoidance of vice. "All that is clearly due today is not to lie" (p.
212). The remedy for the world's disharmony is still displaced into the
future, but the agent of change, the source of "the highest command," is
even less certain.

Emerson's argument now reiterates its movement in the first section
from a division between world and mind to a division within the mind
between "consciousness" and the "Unknown Center." In this second,
materially oriented part of the essay, the distinction is temporal, an
alternation between radically opposed states of awareness, rather than an
inevitable logical division between self-awareness and its absolute foundations. In place of the division between "Them" and society, it offers a
division *within* "these persons" between "superficial life" and "flash-
of-lightning faith" (p. 213).

Recapitulating its earlier gestures, the essay also begins to re-collect its
earlier terms and strategies. Emerson has carried available terms as far as
they will go without success, and has no other language available to him.
He first responds to this latest irreconcilable conflict with a metaphor
reminiscent of the first paragraphs of the essay, in which "my faith" and
"I" are identified and described as "a thought" and "an abode in the
deep blue sky." But this apparent alternative to the internal conflict that
preceded it immediately becomes only a phase in a temporal process, a
momentary perfect vision ("Presently the clouds shut down again"), and
when this vision of unity is lost, he is thrown back on mere possibility and
inaction—"we retain [only] the belief" in a future beauty, to be awaited
with "patience" (p. 214).

By this point, it is clear that "The Transcendentalist" is not "going
somewhere" in any conventional sense. It is not a series of progressive
propositions that follow a straight argumentative line. Though Emerson
seems to be trying to come "a little closer to the secret" of his subject,
that secret recedes at least a step for each step he takes, and as we have
seen, when he reaches the end of any particular path, he opens a new one
that recovers old ground. Failing to reach his original goals, he changes

the subject. The quest is not over, however, even if it begins to sound more and more like a strategic withdrawal. Still trying to locate the ideal that he cannot discover in "action" or in a list of traits, Emerson introduces still one more division, this time *between* rather than within "these persons." They are, he says, "of unequal strength, and do not *all* prosper." "The strong spirits overpower those around them," while the "strength and spirit" of the weak are "wasted in rejection." But simply by invoking these "strong spirits," Emerson invites more of the questions about "action," that caused him so much trouble earlier. What have these strong spirits done? By what acts can they be recognized? Under this pressure, the class of "strong spirits" turns out to be merely a theoretical and empty one. "*All* these of whom I speak are not proficients" (as opposed to "do not *all* prosper," which leaves open the hope that *some* do). Inevitable imperfection prevents harmonious relationship, leaving Emerson only a call for tolerance and forbearance by society toward these "novices," who point out, despite their failings, "the road in which man should travel" (p. 215).

The undeniable rhetorical power and appeal of Emerson's dramatic final paragraph (the kind of statement professors of literature often wish they could make their students *believe*) cannot conceal the fact that it does not resolve any of the issues Emerson has raised in the essay. On the contrary, it works so powerfully largely by returning for closure to the traditional oppositions the essay had abandoned. The metaphors he uses to describe "this class"—"a few finer instruments," "a few persons of purer fire kept specially as gauges," "persons of a fine, detecting instinct," "collectors of the heavenly spark," "superior chronometers"—are no more individually satisfactory or mutually compatible than the ones he used in the first paragraph. The opposition between transitory "mechanical inventions" and ideal "thoughts" is no nearer resolution. Not only is a "fuller union" displaced into an inaccessible future but "these few hermits" have receded into the past tense, only their insubstantial "thoughts" "abide" (p. 216). The present offers no hope. Emerson gives up his claims for their usefulness and rejects the transient superficial world in favor of "thoughts" that are as permanent as the "oldest thoughts" of the first paragraph. Yet, in their timelessness, these thoughts can only anticipate their worldly fulfillment in the further reaches of that history that is, for Emerson, both the great problem and the only imaginable remedy.

II

As Emerson reopens the debate between realism and idealism in "The Transcendentalist," he does not, despite his own best efforts, or, perhaps, because of them, come down on one side or the other. He does not, because he cannot, consistently argue a logical position. His investigation first explores and then exhausts the potentials of both traditional models. He does not, however, formulate an alternative, a revolutionary philosophy of meaning—just another theory into the fray. He pushes back and forth between the available, equally unacceptable, traditional alternatives, pressing their conflict to its limits. In the process, his writing performs (as opposed to "discovering") a different sort of meaning altogether.

This prose upsets the traditional model of knowledge grounded on ideal foundations by articulating temporal change *as* conceptual and narrative change. Emerson's search for a perfect relationship between his initially opposed terms, *idealism* and *materialism,* and for the perfect knowledge and universal coherence it would produce, issues in neither the achievement nor the failure of relationship, knowledge, or coherence. It produces the far more consequential substitution of one way of "knowing" for another. Mastery and possession give way to a conversation with one's self, a way of speaking suited to rigorously conditional experience. Such speech depends on constantly changing linguistic relationships rather than on a verifiable connection between words and objects in the world. By recasting his original subject, the relation of spirit to material forms, as a relation between self and world, Emerson quashes the possibility of independent inquiry and, more important, of a reality independent of descriptions.

Although Emerson's contemporaries and modern critics alike have viewed his project with distrust as fuzzy-headed and dangerously anarchical, he understood authority better than they have imagined. Emerson knew that, in traditional terms, authority in interpretation requires an unshakable foundation. Having given up such unconditioned grounds, he tried to imagine, in "The Transcendentalist" as in other essays, what authority could mean in modern, conditional terms. The resulting prose anticipates Saussure's dictum that "in language, there are only differences without positive terms" that we can extract to represent independent positions.[18] Emerson's words do not cling to intrinsic and thus consistent meanings. His use for them depends on associated terms, on the needs of the moment. Words do not stand for essential meanings independent of language and traceable to the ideal ground of all human experience. They lead only to problematical images and other words—interdependent human acts in a contingent world. Under these conditions, conceptual change is complex and difficult in just the ways many revisionist critics seem reluctant to acknowledge. To change one term is to change myriad related terms. And this process violates all the rules. Emerson crosses conceptual boundaries not with logic but with gradual modulations of meaning, alterations of emphasis, reapplications of old terms in new and transforming contexts, compelling but skewed metaphors. His sentences have their meanings not as independent syntactical units that express or represent settled convictions but exclusively in the field of the statements that surround them, as exploratory gestures toward understanding in a culture that had made meaning problematical.[19]

It its frustrated (and for us, often, frustrating) movements, Emerson's prose renders the constraints on meaning under which he worked and exemplifies both the new forms meaning takes and the old ones it refuses when it gives up its old ground (or for that matter, any ground) replacing the standard of fidelity to an external reality with—it knows not what—an ongoing experimental improvisation, a progressive thinking aloud that Emerson calls ''onward thinking,'' an internal (il)logic that evades all standards.

Emerson's unexplainable prose may frustrate our desires for critical consistency and system, but we need to recall that, in Emerson's essay, consistency and system stood with the materialist opposition in Emerson's debate over foundations for knowledge and feel the full force of his critique. My aim here is to suggest that the difficulty of reading Emerson has been infinitely increased, and the place of his writing in the writing of his time profoundly distorted, by the insistence, despite all these troubling transformations, that his words ought to mean the same things from sentence to sentence, as if they referred to some extrinsic standard for their meaning.

Scholarly discourse encourages critics to make Emerson speak for one view or another: antiformalism, or Marxism, or individualism, or self-help, or self-culture, or even ''Emersonianism.'' Stable meaning makes for neat scholarly arguments and papers of manageable length. But the example of ''The Transcendentalist'' questions the whole business of finding systematic thought in Emerson's texts because it denies the critical assumption that particular sentences represent, or ought to represent, a consistent ''view.'' Emerson's protean writing does not deliver the authoritative information that scholarship has made its stock-in-trade. The old grounded and substantial authorities have no place in it, hence the frustrations of his writing for knowledge-hungry scholars, who seek there a solid fare he does not serve.

As Emerson always claimed, his prose gives up "argument" altogether. Each term is, at each moment, in its place (hence the temptation to find an Emersonian system), but that place is inevitably different from previous ones and from those that follow (hence the impossibility of finding an Emersonian system). No one formulation can ever fairly represent Emerson's "view" because no one relation among terms in Emerson's prose ever fulfills all his hopes. The possibility or impossibility of such perfect fulfillment, of perfect form and thus of any consistent view at all is, as we have seen, an issue he is struggling with. Emerson's shiftiness is not inconsistency. It is acquiesence to the necessity of historical change. Emerson's effort to make his accounts reflect their own historicity forces him to refuse the comforts of systematic argument. He recognizes that no available vantage could give him an objective view. Man, he says, is to be explained only by "all his history." Yet "the whole of history is in one man."[20] Trapped on this hermeneutic merry-go-round, the carnival ride of historical understanding that can never lead outside itself to some real world of fixed knowledge, Emerson notes that there is no stopping for explanations. "Why," he says, "must the philosopher . . . fatigue us with explanation?"[21]

Emerson's distaste for "explanation" was no disguised confession of fuzzy-mindedness. It was his typically indirect and anti-programmatic insistence on the need to maintain descriptive freedom so he can describe changing circumstances. "I cannot define and I care not to define," he says. "It is man's business to observe."[22] As Paul Feyerabend points out, argument can inhibit thinking by imposing fixity on change, and the history of scientific change as it is described by historians like Feyerabend and Thomas Kuhn is largely an account of acts of rhetorical "trickery," much like Emerson's insistent blurring and eliding of established terms.[23] "Without a consistent misuse of language," Feyerabend asserts, "there cannot be any discovery, any progress."[24] For Emerson, to use language truly was to misuse it.[25] When we seek stable meanings in Emerson's text to justify critical claims about his "thought," we are doing something that Emerson strenuously refused to do himself. In a letter to Henry Ware, Jr., during the flap over the

"Divinity School Address," Emerson wrote, "I could not possibly give you one of the 'arguments' on which . . . any position of mine stands. For I do not know, I confess, what arguments mean in reference to any expression of a thought. I delight in telling what I think, but if you ask me how I dare say so or why it is so I am the most helpless of mortal men; I see not even that either of these questions admit of an answer."[26] Emerson is (apologetically or ironically) sketching out the distinction between having "views" that express fixed principles to which they can be retraced, and "saying things" that, having no principled foundation, must perforce carry all their own authority. Emerson realized that he could not "explain" what he had said except by "saying" something else, which would then require further explanation. It is in this sense, rather than as some information from another world, that Emerson's writing is like Scripture.

My point here is that Emerson's texts are historical not merely because they participate in a debate in ways characteristic "of his time," and not just because he acknowledges the historicity of his own views. His texts are historical in the most radical and formative sense because they *render in language* the historicity of understanding. Emerson's is a language of performatives rather than of truth statements. It displays strategic and necessarily partial attempts to articulate intuitions, and its changes and contradictions enact the limits of those strategies and the conflicts between incompatible intuitions. Heidegger says that with such speech "the point is not to listen to a series of propositions, but rather to follow the movement of showing." Emerson's writing should be viewed "not as land looks on a map, but as sea bord seen by men sailing."[27] While historians have implicitly treated Transcendentalist texts as finished forms that reflect changes that have occurred outside them in biography or culture, Emerson's essay locates the important changes in its own unfolding language. His linguistic transformations express the predicament of the author suspended between old meanings of his language and new circumstances. The point is not to reduce such writing into terms that convey "clear" understanding. The point is to trace the conflicts and movements that reflect Emerson's refusal to impose clarity amidst the inadequacy of all available terms. When scholars do not take Emerson's own reluctance seriously, they uncritically assume a metaphysical posture Emerson's writing reveals as inadequate and abandons. The limitation of that metaphysic represents a great lesson of his prose, one that we should consider for our own.

As Emerson discovered, *both* objective and subjective approaches to knowledge work only within unacceptable limits. He vacillates in this essay between subjective and objective notions of meaning, between unity with and alienation from Transcendentalism, because he worked (indeed, he *had* to work) within the assumptions of a metaphysical language that insisted on Cartesian distinctions between form and substance, manifestation and essence, and offered him only subjectivity and objectivity as options. Because he had no alternative, he continued to conceive of form as separable from the thing formed, to believe that a form is a form *of* something; matter the worldly form of spirit, words of thought, thoughts of divine reason, although the intellectual and cultural foundations for such beliefs were no longer viable. Within this inherited system, knowledge required either unity with the thing known or distance from it, and each had its price. Unity cost him either the thing (solipsism) or himself (pantheism, panentheism); distance consigned him to superficiality and skepticism. Emerson's interest for us is in his refusal, despite the lack of established options, to accept either sacrifice, to rest in either position, and in his rigorous investigation of their limits. When he exhausted those limits, he turned to history, though it offered him, as it did Parrington or Mumford, only the empty promise of a solution to his problems.

One of the lessons I want to take from Emerson is that our greater temporal distance from 1842, our scholarly expertise, gives us no special privileges, no more solid ground for establishing the authority of our views than he enjoyed. That lesson seems to me to apply not only to the ways we pursue our scholarship but to the ways we communicate it, the claims we make to justify it, and thus to the place of our work in our culture. It is not limited to the (by now familiar) notion that historians shape history. Such subjectivist views of historical meaning reflect only one side in the debate that Emerson both engages in and transcends in this essay. For students of Transcendentalism, "The Transcendentalist" reinforces the conclusions of the critical history I offered in Parts 1 and 2. It suggests that we need not treat Transcendentalism as a discrete historical entity, analogous to an individual, with relatives, ancestors, and heirs, or as an empirical object, with a definite shape, measurements, and observable composition. It is not an object in history on which historical distance will give us a better view. Attempts to describe Transcendentalism as a coherent system of thought, or as a set of philosophical propositions, or as a particular group of men and women are limited by their foundationalist assumptions, just as the need for absolute grounds constrained

Emerson's descriptions of Transcendentalism. If Transcendentalism "is" anything, it is an object of our belief, and its only validity has come from its coherence with the other things we have believed. That coherence, among other things, is what I want to call into question here.

For 100 years, scholarship has used the word *Transcendentalism* as the linchpin for beliefs about the meaning of America and its literature. Although Emerson shared in that nationalist vision, he had no particular stake in the word. As we have seen, he used it interchangeably with others as a strategy for unifying conditional facts on absolute ground, or failing that, for locating some new ground on which they might be reunited. He was looking for language that would fuse incompatible systems of belief he categorizes as idealism and materialism. He called Transcendentalism "idealism" not because that was its "true name" or even because that word best embodied his convictions but because his culture gave him only those terms to work with. He had to say something, but all the words he tried carried consequences he could not abide along with those that suited him.

I have tried to suggest that modern criticism suffers from a similar condition. It owes the well-known problems of Transcendentalist criticism neither to imperfect knowledge nor to scholarly misreading. It simply inherited them from its professional ancestors, who formulated them to meet their own needs. In the early years of American literary study, those nationalist assumptions and methods were justified by their demonstrable usefulness. But our concerns are not those of Paul Elmer More and Van Wyck Brooks. With the prestige of American texts firmly, if sometimes grudgingly, established in the profession, and considering our increasing disenchantment with the dream of national destiny, Americanists no longer need to justify reading and teaching texts outside the English canon by discovering the uniquely American character of a distinct literary tradition.

The lesson of Transcendentalist writing for scholars trying to define Transcendentalism (to figure out what unites all those people—Emerson and his friends—into a Transcendentalist "movement") is that there is no principle of unity, that there are only differences and the unities we see are made by us to serve our purposes. Transcendentalism is simply a term about which we organize, as we have always organized, our interest in American writing. It embodies and fulfills our desire for coherence in that writing, and the ways we have used it have reflected the particular kinds of coherence we have desired. If our interpretations take their value from their ability to fulfill our needs—to do what we want them to do—then we need to figure out just what those needs are.[28] This will undoubtedly be an uncomfortable process. But if we learn to think of *Transcendentalism* as a word that must find its place among the other words we use, rather than as a meaning-full historical object, we shall more comfortably treat it as a tool we can continue thinking with *as long as it serves us well*. On the other hand, continuing to think of Transcendentalism as a "natural fact" rather than as a "description" only encourages us to forget that it is *our* tool, and keeps us from asking how it's being used and for what purpose.

By now we ought to be looking for other ways to describe American writing and account for its place in the tradition of writing in English of which it is so important a part. My aim here is not so much to solve the problems that have generated debate about Transcendentalism as to exorcise them as phantoms of a discarded vision, no more (or less) real or in need of attention than storm gods, or bodily humors, or the Northwest Passage. We have to ask not what Transcendentalism is but what orders best suit our current interests. Can we continue to have what Transcendentalism gave us without also continuing to participate in old myths that conflict with our current beliefs?

Confined within the very assumptions about writing and art that Emerson's prose evades, Lawrence Buell wants to believe in Transcendentalism and locate it "between metaphor and metaphysics," assuming that there *is* space there into which Transcendentalism could fit. By combining critical categories, Buell wants to be precise, and to find just where Transcendentalism falls by looking at it from two angles at once, thought and art. This approach fails to consider that all seeing is binocular vision, viewing a single object from two positions, and that if simple seeing will not do the trick, increasing the angle will not help. As Melville points out, the real trick is seeing/saying two different things at once, like the whale. Metaphor is a way of doing that, conflating one thing with another and "seeing" the two at once. And metaphysics is the historical tradition of seeing the world as a metaphor for the ideal, that is, metaphysics is the great metaphor. There is no space *between* the two into which Transcendentalism could fit.

Bereft of ideal grounds, metaphysics is, as Emerson ruefully suggested, "the progressive introduction of apposite metaphors." Emerson's disappointment with that possibility simply reflects his nostalgia for what Nietzsche called "metaphysical comfort," the faith that conditions were grounded on some exoteric foundation. But dispensing with that nostalgia allows us to look at Emerson's own metaphors as productive rather than as "intellectually incoherent" or aesthetically embarrassing.[29] The nineteenth-century queasiness about Emerson's efforts to reshape thinking, requiring him as it did to revise the "usual" ways of talking, has already been preserved for too long in modern criticism.

In our own interests, then, interests markedly different both from Emerson's and from those of scholars trying to stake out an infant academic field, we no longer need to be disappointed by Emerson's "failure" to produce a coherent philosophy, or an organically unified text, or to discover an ultimate ground for all human experience. Instead we can see his writing as part of an ongoing project that he shared with writers in Europe and America to accommodate his inherited views to new conditions, a process of thinking *as* saying, a temporal enterprise floating on the current of time rather than a systematic one that hopelessly seeks completion. As this project was not peculiar to New England, so it is not confined to the nineteenth century. It is our business as much as it was Emerson's, the business of coming to terms again and again with a world that stubbornly refuses to indulge our yearnings for stable truths. In the absence of the "ground absolute and unconditioned" that Emerson sought, we must establish and reestablish our *inevitably* "original relation to the universe." Emerson's aspiration has become our fate. But what *is* that fate, and what its implications? If we are fated to continually reestablish our relationship with the world, if placing and replacing ourselves in history is our ongoing problem, how should we go about it? That question is the subject of the succeeding chapters.

Writing in/as History:
Thoreau's *Week*

> History has neither the venerableness of antiquity nor the freshness of the modern.
>
> **THOREAU**

I

How, the question remains, can scholars live and do their work in the history that, despite the apparently limitless potency of the myth of American renewal, we have been unable to escape? How can contemporary criticism establish a productive relationship with the past? And what is the role of texts, and of reading, in this practice? Narrative strategies for connecting the past and the present have preoccupied modern writing.[30] As Stanley Cavell puts it, "The essential fact of (what I refer to as) the modern lies in the relation between the present practice of our enterprise and the history of that enterprise, in the fact that this relation has become problematic."[31] Some of the most formative contemporary theoretical influences on recent American Literary Scholarship write in that tradition. Derrida's prose, for example, has been characterized in terms that might as easily apply to Thoreau or Emerson, as "one wherein repetition and change, iteration and alteration, occur together over (or as) time." The inability to accommodate such changes has been, as I have suggested, the persistent problem of American Literary Scholarship since the last quarter of the nineteenth century.[32]

Most generally, I want to argue the importance of embracing the historicity of our work in some more substantial way than we could by merely *recognizing* the conditionality of our subject, of the texts we study, or acknowledging (as many scholars now almost routinely do) the historical interests that found our own critical judgments. The history of Transcendentalist scholarship suggests the need for an approach that avoids the idealist assumptions that have dominated American Literary Scholarship for more than 100 years, one that builds on the work of nineteenth-century writers rather than recycling the problems they tried to resolve.

Just as the American Ideal has prevented its adherents from appropriating the most challenging elements of contemporary theory, it has also prevented them from reading historical texts as voices in contemporary conversations. In particular, it has obscured those texts' necessarily imperfect but suggestive efforts to produce narrative accounts that overcome the isolation of past from present. American literature scholars have failed to establish what Dominick LaCapra calls a "transferential" relationship with either the past they study or their own critical past. " 'Transference,' " LaCapra writes, "is bound up with a notion of time not as simple continuity or discontinuity but as repetition with variation or change—at times traumatically disruptive change."[33] The desirable ideal, as Freud indicates, is to work through the transferential relation without blindly replicating "debilitating aspects of the past." Rather than reflecting on their professional past, making it their subject, scholars have relived it, repeating its movements from one century to the next.[34] The problems historians have had with narrative accounts about things

American are analogous to those Thoreau is responding to. That is, historians have tried to write coherent stories and in order to do so have had to appeal to idealized notions of America. But, as we saw in the work of critics from Frothingham to Buell, that idealized coherence leaves out too many significant facts—the diversity of American facts, social changes over time—and produces incoherence in scholarly accounts.

Like contemporary scholars, Thoreau was struggling with questions about the relationship of the present to the past. Thoreau's journey in *A Week on the Concord and Merrimack Rivers,* like *Walden,* is an attempt to redefine for modern conditions inherited notions of spirit and world, absolute and conditional. But to do so is also to revise all the myriad associated terms that collectively constitute our cultural inheritance. Only by such a massive restructuring of the linguistic/conceptual field can Thoreau hope to reunite these opposed terms in a coherent human life. *A Week* is an experiment in living, an inquiry into the very possibility, in the face of historical instability, of meaningful life.[35] The central and continuing question posed by that writing is, ''how do we *live?*''—which means, among other things, how do we understand our lives, our selves, the works and world we read? How do we, in this sense, *live* in a world not divided into simple binary oppositions like those on which the project of American Literary Scholarship depends—Old World and New or material and spiritual—but confined within human history, a single historical world?

Thoreau's *Week* is preoccupied with the possibility for original experience in an autumnal age. ''A man's life,'' Thoreau says early on, ''should be constantly as fresh as this river. It should be the same channel but a new water every instant'' (p. 132). ''Constant'' but ''fresh,'' the ''same'' but ''new,'' inherited but original. Because a book, as Thoreau repeatedly insists, is the ''natural harvest'' of its author's life, these are also the modest requirements for Thoreau's account in *A Week.*[36] It explores the possibility of fresh experience in a historical world without origins. But if the first lesson of being in history is that one cannot ignore the formative circumstances of time and place, the next is that one also cannot abandon them. As Thoreau quickly discovers, attempts to evade precedent can never be free of their own narrative past. Each expression forecloses a possibility for future expression even as it points in a new direction.[37]

Thoreau's narrative explores the questions raised by dwelling, as we do, in history, where no fact, no insight, can possibly come unmediated to the observer. Everything comes, necessarily, secondhand. Under these conditions, the question Thoreau asks is "how can we *know* what we are *told* merely?" (p. 365). I take this to be a genuine rather than a rhetorical question. Thoreau is not denying that we can *"know* what we are *told* merely." The consequences of such a denial would be intolerable. He is asking "how" we can, since as historical and social beings, we are *"told* merely" *every*thing. How can this inevitable belatedness be squared with the imperatives to independence and individuality that insist that "knowledge is to be acquired only by a corresponding experience" (p. 365)? This is the question that Thoreau's narrative, particularly his *way* of narrating, tries to answer. Somehow, being *"told"* must also *be* a "corresponding experience." But what sort of experience is that?

I want to propose that Thoreau's narrative is not experience of the world, systematic convictions, concrete knowledge, an accumulation of facts but what might be called "descriptive experience." It is not an account of *an* experience that represents an external world, an "other." The account is itself the experience. This I take it is one of Thoreau's implications when he says, "Is not Nature, rightly read, that of which she is taken to be a symbol merely?" (p. 382). Is not *A Week,* rightly read, that of which it is taken to be the symbol merely, the symbol of Thoreau's "thought" or of his life? Thoreau's descriptions are experience insofar as they insist that the reader do the work required to make them meaningful. Like the river travelers, we have to "work our way" up the current of Thoreau's narrative, "gradually adjusting our thoughts to novelties" (p. 112).

The limitations of the more conventional narrative forms that Thoreau works his way out of are illustrated on "Wednesday" in Thoreau's "Emersonian" essay on "friendship," which articulates the whole of the quest for a relationship between the self and the "other" that is first mentioned as the cure for indebtedness in a poem in the introductory "Concord River" section. Thoreau pursues that quest throughout the text. The essay on "friendship" carries it to unsatisfactory conclusions. In a passage out of the heart of Melville, Thoreau describes the friend he seeks as an elusive landfall, ever receding, like Yillah before Taji. "Who would not sail through mutiny and storm, even over atlantic waves to reach the fabulous retreating shores of some continent man" (p. 262). Thoreau suggests here that, while any man might want to make this quest, the ideal goal of friendship, like Thoreau's distant mountains made meaningful by imagination, is "fabulous" and "retreating."

But the chances for a successful landfall, much less of making a dwelling there, are, even at the start of this essay, clearly slim. The lesson of his journey so far, as of this internal recapitulation of it, has been that epistemological models that require either identity or objectivity, closeness or distance, simply make relationship logically impossible. Identity obliterates the difference that makes relationship necessary and offers an ideal incompatible with real human relations, or with individuality. Objectivity denies the humanity of the other and offers no human intercourse. As a result, Thoreau's essay on "friendship" succeeds only in once more denying its possibility. Thus, though the essay reiterates his journey in other terms, it has also learned from it. It starts out with high aspirations but diminished expectations for achieving the perfect knowledge that requires identity with the other coincidentally with the perfect freedom that comes from isolation. Conflicting requirements for independence and identity (i.e., the division between two worlds, spirit and matter, and two sorts of knowledge, distance and immediacy) prevent Thoreau from describing a perfect relationship between selves in "Wednesday"'s "Emersonian" essay on "friendship." This unresolvable conflict throws Thoreau back on the implications of making such a journey without hope of success, or alternatively, of not making it. And that leads, in turn, to the need for a different model of relationship altogether, one that entails a different model of knowing and of the knower.

Just as the essay on "friendship" recapitulates the limits of analytical discourse, the first third of Thoreau's voyage tries out a radical break with the past. Thoreau's journey begins, as all journeys must, with what he has, the "Concord River," and his attempt to make sense of things begins, likewise, with an inherited language and the inherited strategies that necessarily accompany it. Just as Emerson covered old ground analytically in the first section of "The Transcendentalist" by reprising the Lockean tradition of epistemology, Thoreau begins his narrative journey in the traditional terms of the form. Thoreau must cover old ground before he can discover new, though as we shall see, his journey quickly instructs him that in history the goal of discovery must give way to recovery.

In *A Week,* descriptive narrative is a vehicle of transforming thought. Ultimately, this movement leads to an abandonment of established models of knowledge. Thoreau's search for originality in a world no longer "new" transfigures the travel narrative form that had been invented to comprehend new geographical worlds and the authority of the individual knower, producing new worlds of understanding, and pointing out the limitations of critical attempts to write history historically.[38] Thoreau's is narrative *as* time. Such discourse, like the river, is not only a route for exploration but a determining force, the flood of accumulated meanings "in the rear of us" that produces what is "current," constraining the freedom Thoreau seeks by determining possible future meanings (p. 7). If Thoreau's excursion is to take him anywhere worthwhile, it must be free to find its own way. Hence it is always in conflict with itself, pitting the necessity of transforming description against the fear of overdetermining specification.

Thoreau alternates, like Goddard or Parrington or Buell, between withdrawal from particular facts and intimacy with them in a rhythmic exploration of alternate ways of knowing, and producing, in these early stages, an epistemology of history and experience, of travel through time. Just as the critical debate has vacillated between positivist strategies faithful to particular facts and subjectivist ones that produce coherent wholes, the brief opening section on "Concord River" encapsulates the same problematical movement between fact and coherence. The *narrative* journey begins as soon as Thoreau moves from distant observation to particular description. Particular limited and limiting facts produce the dissatisfaction that drives Thoreau's narrative in search of alternatives. As soon as that narrative begins, it develops an agenda of its own that displaces the river trip Thoreau plans to describe. It starts with distance, distinctions effaced, change denied, all to assert harmonious unity. Its initial detached historical account of the river and its linguistic and geographical sources overcomes local categories, overlaying the "perennial" with "civilized history" represented respectively by the Indian name "Grass-ground" and the "other but kindred name of Concord" (p. 5). But by launching a description of the river, Thoreau's narrative immerses itself in immediate observations, seeking truth in accurate description, and as a result, it confronts fragmentation in the form of a conflict between the past and present. Where once "the white honeysuckle or clover" grew, water now stands all year round and farmers "look sadly round" (p. 6). Travel, in "Concord River," begins as a response to this sense of history as loss. It prompts an imaginary trip up the river to "see how much country there is in the rear of us," that mirrors and anticipates the longer narrative journey down the Concord and up the Merrimack toward "Unappropriated Land."

Thoreau's anticipatory narrative journey in "Concord River" evokes Thoreau's ambivalence about history, about cultivation and culture, and casts a shadow on the prospect of his own historical inquiry. "Concord River" produces a succession of unsatisfactory descriptions of Thoreau's native ground not unlike Emerson's series of incomplete metaphors in the first paragraph of "The Transcendentalist." For Thoreau, each repetition short-circuits constricting development. Each new beginning emancipates him from a narrative corner into which he has been inscribing himself. His second description of the Concord appropriates and recapitulates many of the features of his first: the history of its names, the list of trees on its banks, the description of its cranberries, and the homes of its inhabitants. But for his own earlier protests about dams, the civilized "improvements" that produced floods and lost lands in the first version, Thoreau substitutes a safer, because more neutral and abstract, numerical survey, the official "valuation of 1831" (p. 10). Yet, even this scrupulously sterile accounting cannot entirely escape the shadow of history, or ignore conflict between primitive nature and civilized degradation. "The meadow is not reclaimed so fast as the woods are cleared" (p. 10). And as if to distance himself from the unhappy contrasts apparent to a view from the narrative present, Thoreau gives up the narrative entirely to "Old Johnson," who delivers still a third description of the Concord, which, by going back 200 years, can find a pristine landscape untroubled by civil progress. In seventeenth-century Concord, the cattle still live on "wild fother," and if, "when the summer proves wet they lose part of their hay," at least the floods are natural rather than dammade (p. 11).

A description of agricultural circumstances develops into a complaint about creative circumstances, the limited prospects for a writer, like Thoreau, who "put pen to paper" at this late date. Farmers become an emblem of that cultural past and the literary legacy Thoreau must overcome. "What have they not written on the face of the earth already, clearing and burning, and scratching, and harrowing, and plowing, and subsoiling" (p. 8)? Although this passage has recently been treated as indicating Thoreau's ambivalence about the "violence" of writing, Thoreau is not so much troubled by violence here as frustrated with the constraints of his own meager plot in a farmed-out literary landscape that has been, as he says, worked "in and in, and out and out, and over and over, again and again" for all it was worth.[39] This frustration with secondhand material—which embraces not only Thoreau's writing but

all the possibilities of a life now self-conscious about its place at the end
of a long history—motivates the larger river journey and the project of
accounting for it.

Striking out for the new with the start of his narrative in "Saturday,"
Thoreau seeks first to abandon his place at the tail end of history.[40] In this
act he tests out the potential of a traditional escape from civil constraints
and his own past that is characteristic of the rhetoric about America and
its literature and explores the possibility of originality as it is conventionally understood. On the last day of the summer months in the last year
of the decade, Thoreau and his brother begin their journey by floating
through a landscape in which every detail bespeaks meanings already
established, of revolutionary zeal now merely historical, of natural
beauty "faded." Early in this "Saturday" journey, still surrounded by
the familiar, the wild and the civil, originality and tradition, are irrecon-
cilably hostile; their opposition can be resolved only by sacrificing one or
the other. These are the conditions that prompt escape and make distance
appealing, and the travelers predictably find that "the land seemed to
grow fairer as we withdrew from it . . . and addressed ourselves to new
scenes and adventures" (p. 22). As Thoreau drifts away from his
Concord origins, he distances himself as well from the familiar sort of
description that represents outward experience. The facts he describes
figure the anxieties that generate his account. Like the farmers in the
fields in "Concord River," fishermen incarnate independent inquiry and
writing. And the omnipresence of fishing poles "sticking up to mark the
place where some fisherman had enjoyed unusual luck" (p. 22) remind
Thoreau that this part of the stream has been fished "over and over, again
and again."

When surrounding circumstances insistently remind him of his cultural
indebtedness, Thoreau retreats inward, as Emerson had, to the mind and
the imagination. But that escape simply raises all the problems associated
with subjectivity that had been submerged as long as the meaning of
experience had been tied to a "place." "Sunday" examines the transitory quality of "uncommon sight" and raises anxiety about the validity
and permanence of subjective experience. It shows that the discovery of
"a nature behind the common" is a fleeting experience to which the
traveler must return, if he can, again and again, as Thoreau's headnote
from Channing suggests. The "auroral rosy" prelapsarian quality of
Sunday morning must "vanish with its dews," reminding Thoreau that
"the impressions which the morning makes," original impressions, if

they are to color this latter day, must somehow be renewed because "not even the most 'persevering mortal' can preserve the memory of [their] freshness" even to "midday," much less into the "afternoon" of the world that Thoreau inhabits. Innocence, freshness of insight, the products of imagination as a term in the traditional referential structure of knowing, cannot be protected from history (pp. 43–44).

Yet, the more substantial forward-looking alternative of a genuinely new territory so essential to the American Ideal seems simply unreachable, an ideal or idyll that casts their explorations in an ironic light. The "leafy wilderness" to which their "long pull" takes them is remote enough from civilization. It evidences "no recognition of human life . . . no human breathing." But it is not a real location outside civilization. It is a mythic matter of "fauns and satyrs" concocted, as Thoreau makes explicit later on, by poets (p. 38). The whole project of escape can only be ironic in nineteenth-century Massachusetts. And that is the appeal of art and the imagination. It is a historical condition of Thoreau's narrative that there *are* no new *places*. Yet, it is impossible, in a thoroughly historical world, to stay in the old ones, hence the journey, hence the life in history of which it is a model and an experimental revision. If retreat into the imagination is temporary and not altogether trustworthy, retreat into Nature is no more permanent. Civilization is always waiting around the next bend in the river, and all Thoreau's questing just enforces the impossibility of escape.[41]

When Billerica, a town that was a good enough representative of civilization for his "intents and purposes" (p. 49), interrupts Thoreau's pastoral vision, the opposition it dramatizes between civilization and wilderness fails of a simple resolution. Thoreau's narrative discovers that it cannot simply pursue the original and primitive, cannot even simply prefer them to civilization. The difficulty is not just that the wild and primitive are no longer available, indeed, have always been more an ideal than a feature of human experience, but that the notion of civilization itself includes elements too valuable to sacrifice. "Neither can displace the other without loss" (p. 54). Not only can civilization not be abandoned but we would not really want to abandon it if we could. The early part of Thoreau's narrative makes it clear that there is no world into which Thoreau can escape from this world and this life. Any complete story must locate itself there. "There are various tough problems yet to solve, and we must make shift to live, betwixt spirit and matter, such a human life as we can" (pp. 73–74).

II

Frustrated in his efforts to escape from the customary world by abandoning it for new territory, Thoreau begins to reconceive the problem in social terms and to develop new strategies for solution. Rather than a new experience in a strange new land, or an other world, revealed like the phantom tree reflected on the surface of the stream, through a "separate intention of the eye" (p. 48), Thoreau must now reach for experience that unites travel and stasis, providing experience simultaneously new and familiar, "so aptly fitted to our organization that the eye wanders and reposes at the same time" (p. 159). As long as Thoreau's model of knowledge depends on alternating visions applied to alternate worlds, rather than alternative descriptions of *this* world, he is trapped in an unending series of oppositions.[42] The subsequent account of the new territory of the Merrimack necessarily carries over the terms that described the old and continues the debate between distance and directness, imagination and fact, that had been raised as the day began but in new terms that reflect what he has learned from his travels. Now, *A Week* looks forward rather than back and is concerned more with the production of the self and of writing in the historical and social context than with isolation from the common world.

Confinement within history and society create new conditions for narrative and knowledge. The entry onto the Merrimack, the scene of human living, with its bustling commerce, represents the shift from an opposition between civilization and nature to one between society and individuals. There, men in the common world go about their common business. Their routine life depends on routine understandings, and expresses itself in routine language—the "standard English" of "standard men." From his position on the moving margin of this social mainstream, Thoreau argues that we are impeded in our quest for knowledge not by our inability to "know" material objects, obscure thoughts, foreign customs, past facts but by our failure to make sense of what we do know, of the present and local world of which all things, including the past, are part. The experience the world of contingent historical fact offers, one in which "all things pass in review," suggests the constraints that being in history places on the freedom of experience Thoreau is seeking (p. 124). A "re-view" is the only possible view in and of the historical world, so Thoreau has to ask what sort of experience can make a "re-view" new? In what sense is it possible to truly know anything for yourself when it all comes in "re-view" secondhand, in a world whose "realness" *is* its routine, its necessary repetition of the past. Under these conditions, Thoreau's narrative becomes not so much a search for knowledge as an inquiry into the possibility of any knowledge that comes inevitably secondhand and what sort of narrative can offer a true account of such experience without being merely redundant.

To this point, Thoreau's narrative journey has stubbornly returned him to the constraints from which he fled. Still at the center of Thoreau's narrative reflections is the question of the possibilities for freedom, for originality, and thus for a self under the pressure of the cultural constraints that "this [*Week*]'s commerce" more and more clearly identifies as inescapable. Efforts to domesticate those constraints, to imagine the possibility of relationship between self and world by "naturalizing" culture and "using" nature repeatedly break down and prompt a renewed oscillation between the poles of mind and nature, inside and outside, that have always defined the realist/idealist debate in which Thoreau has, so far, participated. "There is need," he says, "of a physician who shall minister to both soul and body at once, that is, to man. Now he falls between two stools" (p. 257). Facing the inadequacy of more traditional narrative explorations, Thoreau's account begins to "pleasantly reflect upon itself" in good earnest, twisting customary meanings to wrest new relationships out of old circumstances. Thoreau calls this self-reflection a "waking dream" (p. 158), thus opposing it on one hand to "sleeping awake," the routine life of customary labor on the shore, and associating it on the other hand with the privileged experience he describes as the outward journey comes to an end on "Wednesday" evening. "Our truest life," he says there, "is when we are in dreams awake" (p. 297). A transforming experience, distinct but not divided from the world of common fact and more profound, is central to Thoreau's effort to redefine the relation between past and present and thus appropriate the confining authority of a cultural inheritance that he has learned cannot be abandoned.

Such "waking dreams" preoccupy the end of "Monday" and the first half of "Tuesday," which evade cultural authority in what Thoreau would call "remarkable" moments, moments that overcome time, distance, and habitual categories. The second of these epiphanies, the ascent of Saddleback that occupies the first half of "Tuesday," is a modern day *Pilgrim's Progress* that Thoreau has already called the "best sermon which has been preached" on the Scriptures (p. 71). But Thoreau has also said that all great books are Scripture and the new *Pilgrim's*

Progress he writes is a new revelation even as it reflects on the original. As in his version of Antigone's story in "Monday," the meaning of the experience is as much in its difference from its literary antecedents as in its similarity. And this case is typical of Thoreau's treatment of the literary tradition and of the past in general. In each case, Thoreau adapts inherited material to his own needs, making the past more fully expose the conditions and possibilities of the present.

Thoreau's allegorical satire on journeys out of the world begins uncertainly. At the end of "Monday" and the start of "Tuesday," Thoreau "redundantly" (as some critics would have it) repeats an entire phrase, twice asserting that the travelers "were ready to pursue our voyage as usual" (pp. 178, 179). Though this repetition might feed critical complaints about Thoreau's sloppy writing or editing, it can more usefully be seen as insistently questioning what that "usual" way of voyaging is. And that question is compounded when, in the next sentence, the fact that the voyagers are "enveloped in mist as usual" recasts our sense of their entire intellectual voyage, linking it to misty obscurities rather than the achievement of new clarity, and making those obscurities the immediate occasion, as well as the frame, for the story of Thoreau's far from "usual" climb up Saddleback.

As Thoreau examines and exceeds the "usual" in that tale, his critique predictably takes in conformity to "usual" behavior (he is undeterred when the occupant of the "last house" warns him "that nobody ever went this way; there was no path" (p. 182), but it also extends to "usual" morality. Though this latter-day Christian remains undistracted from his summit journey by the attractions of the "young woman . . . in a dishabille" (p. 182), unlike Bunyan's Christian, Thoreau knows, as he turns aside from temptation (and, more especially, as he writes about it), that he will be coming back *down* the hill and pass this way again, "perhaps remaining a week there [a week that would no doubt produce an account very different from *A Week*], if I could have entertainment" (p. 182). Thoreau's parody of conventional understanding lampoons even the "usual" alternatives to convention, not excluding the "self-reliance" for which he and Transcendentalism are so famous. Once on the mountain, Thoreau is more than merely a model of self-sufficiency; he is a caricature of it, an entire society unto himself, engineering public works ("ingenious aqueducts on a small scale," a well) that supply his own wants in concert with nature rather than by despoiling it. He not only produces his own meal but even manufactures the utensils he eats it with.

One might say that in this tale Thoreau is telling a joke about other worlds and the escape from this one that is purportedly required to get there. Even though the way up Saddleback "seemed a road for the pilgrim to enter upon who would climb to the gates of heaven" (p. 181), it only "seemed" that way. Thoreau's is not a climb to the eternal haven of the "Heavenly City." It is a temporary sojourn in a real world of heavenly beauty. The world above the clouds into which he awakens the next morning, with its echoes of Mt. Snowdon, is no merely "other world" of transcendent truth. Above the mists, he is "a dweller in the dazzling halls of Aurora . . . drifting amid the saffron-colored clouds and playing with the rosy fingers of the Dawn, in the very path of the Sun's chariot, and sprinkled with its dewy dust" (p. 189). Thoreau's inflated rhetoric, his parodic string of poetic cliches, all elements of the "usual" poetry, ought to keep us from taking this vision too seriously as an insight into some transcendent realm. This language reminds us that Thoreau's vision is of a real world that "required no aid from the imagination to render it impressive" (p. 188).

But Thoreau's *account* of it depends heavily for its significance on the imaginative interweaving of elements from the earlier narrative. He finds himself floating on an "ocean of mist" as on the "ocean stream" of the Merrimack, riding on a "carved plank, in cloudland" (p. 187), the proof that, as he said of his carved boat earlier, "wood alone will rudely serve the purpose of a ship" (p. 16) carrying him into "the new world." This "new" world, however, is also the "pure world" of "eternal day" that Thoreau has elsewhere associated with the Orient, with nooning and slumber, and declared impractical for autumnal times, however replete "with all the delights of paradise" (p. 188). It is a "vision" from which "inhabitants of earth" must inevitably return into the " 'forlorn world' " of common experience, though at least Thoreau knows better than the rest of those inhabitants, who affirm that it had "been a cloudy and drizzling day wholly" (p. 190).

As a "digression" from which Thoreau returns to the misty business of his journey "before the fog disperses" (p. 190), the Saddleback episode suggests that such visions do not resolve the problems that produced that journey but are gestures within it. Thoreau's parodic escape from the world is only an interlude, bounded by the conditions it "abandoned." The shores that confine and direct his excursion are the same as those from which he sets out. Any complete story must locate itself there. "There are various tough problems yet to solve, and we must make shift to live, betwixt spirit and matter, such a human life as we can.''[43] When Thoreau returns from Saddleback, none of the problems that produced the voyage have been resolved, and it begins to look as though such resolution is not only beyond the power but beside the point of the narrative. He returns into the same world he left, to consider once again the same issues he has already raised, though his narrative experience (as opposed to that of the river journey) has complicated the terms he has available for that reconsideration.

These pivotal tales raises questions about where knowledge or experience is produced. The events the narrative describes are increasingly interwoven with the events of the narrative itself, or with the narrative as event. Both of the tales that make up the first half of "Tuesday" substitute accounts of earlier journeys for an account of the journey itself and narrative time for the historical time of the events Thoreau describes. The irony of the tales, their misappropriation of inherited language, and stories, and ideals, prevents us from finding comfortable morals there, and their intertwining with other images from the journey turns us back into the text of which they are part for all the meaning we are to find in them.

This self-referential narrative hints at another sort of experience than the common that becomes central in the last part of the narrative, a "speculative experience" that erases the traditional epistemological distinctions between descriptions and the reality to which they are supposed to correspond. It is a gesture toward a model of experience indistinguishable from descriptions, of language as a changing historical medium of social intercourse rather than on accurate representation of empirical fact. Such narrative necessarily violates the expectations created by more referential forms. As if anticipating our discomfort with the "novelties" of his own prose, reading our thoughts as we are reading his, Thoreau gives us advice about reading that anticipates the "Reading" chapter of *Walden*. True books, Thoreau asserts, must be the "natural harvest of their authors' lives" (p. 98). "A man's whole life," he remarks, "is taxed for the least thing well done. It is its net result. Every sentence [for reader as for writer] is the result of a long probation" (p. 105). He urges, not particularly sympathetically, that "we should consider that the flow of thought is more like a tidal wave than a prone river" and that "the reader . . . may well complain of nauseating swells and choppings . . . when his frail shore craft gets amidst the billows of the ocean stream" (pp. 102–3) (as we and Thoreau have been since leaving the canal for the Merrimack and the "ocean stream of our voyage"). As readers, we, like Thoreau, have to adjust our thoughts to novelties, and again like Thoreau, we have to *work* our way up the stream of his narrative to do it.

Thoreau's model for establishing meaning under these conditions is "fronting" facts, which may mean, as Eric Sundquist has said, "frontiering" them, though I don't take this to be a search for a purity unstained by civilization, a return trip to Eden. After all, what would be the point, much less the possibility, of that? Thoreau insists that it is *human* life we need to make sense of. We need a doctor for the body and the soul *together*. The frontiering Thoreau recommends is not a retreat from life's problems (or America's sins). It is a process of *making* frontiers, not of discovering them, one that makes facts new by going beyond their customary, or surface, meanings as a result of long and intimate relationship. It is not experience of the new but making experience anew, original descriptions of familiar objects that re-create the past.

Thoreau first suggests the conditions of an alternative to "friendship" (one which, by "Thursday" and "Friday" dominates Thoreau's account) in the most unlikely of places, the story of his encounter with Rice, a civil/uncivil man. Just before his entry into the Merrimack, while the travelers are still locked in the dogmatic constraints of the canal, Thoreau encounters the isolated Rice, whom he conceives as a natural object. Thoreau comes to Rice not for society or a sympathetic heart but to find novelty and adventure, to "see what nature had produced" (p. 207). What nature had produced, as it turns out, was a rough-mannered wood-dweller. As a natural phenomenon, Rice provides an interesting experience, the material for a good story rather than a lasting relationship that might keep Thoreau from going his own way the next morning in scrupulous solitude "before my host, or his men, or even his dogs, were awake" (p. 219). But amidst this apparent reaffirmation of individual isolation, Thoreau sketches the model for another sort of experience than he has, so far, described, one that reconceives knowledge as relationship-over-time and becomes central to his narrative:

> A true politeness does not result from any hasty and artificial polishing . . . but grows naturally in characters of the right grain and quality, through a long *fronting* of men and events, and rubbing on good and bad fortune (p. 201).

The possibilities of this alternative are more fully and successfully represented in another unlikely way throughout the narrative by Thoreau's insistence on eliding his own identity with that of his brother. Throughout the narrative, the two are so stubbornly identified that telling them apart is seldom possible. This strategy might be read as a stubborn denial of the reality of his brother's death, but it seems at least as much an example of the particular *way* the textual experience Thoreau offers preserves the past. The loss of a brother with whom he so completely identifies raises questions about what of him*self* is lost, just as it raises the issue of what of the brother remains.[44] Thoreau's narrative identification with his brother does not make the textual brother an adequate substitute for the real one. It does not regain, or preserve in any concrete sense something lost. Descriptions do not represent the travelers and their reality; rather, the travelers are produced in the narrative reflections of *A Week*. In Thoreau's hands, narrative produces not only the "self" but a self that overcomes the contradictions of the essay on "friendship," a self *constituted by and as a narrative relationship*.[45]

For a reader, the long fronting and familiarity that Thoreau recommends also discloses new relationships between the elements of Thoreau's narrative. Those relationships depend, as his response to Rice suggests, on transforming passing time from an enemy into an ally, from the agent of belatedness into the precondition of rubbing, wear, and mutual familiarity. Like the ideal friend (his brother/self), the resulting experience elides perfect identity and perfect distance, immediate knowledge and shaping (re)vision. It extends over the whole narrative process, begun in momentary epiphanies in "Monday" and "Tuesday," in which narrative increasingly expands upon itself, reiterating its earlier elements in new contexts that create a transforming resonance between them. In "Concord River," rehearsing previous elements of the narrative had meant what then seemed a series of new beginnings that put off prematurely determining meanings so as to permit new possibilities.

In the rest of the account, however, reiterations also become a recollection or recuperation not so much of a historical past as of Thoreau's narrative past, by which it is repeatedly reexamined and redefined to remedy, rather than to escape, the fear of belatedness and restrictive routine that has haunted this autumnal journey from the first. Like the echoing sounds that press Thoreau into the epiphany that ends "Monday," moments in the narrative seem more and more to echo other moments, the narrative increasingly to refer to itself not in a self-enclosed, aesthetically autonomous way but as a series of variations on the themes and images it has introduced and developed. In this sense, it is an attempt to overcome its own relentless temporality, an effort to present a historical account that is also a coherent one. This coherence is not a matter either of river travel or of mountain-top vistas between which Thoreau's journey alternates. It unites fragmentary understandings into meaning-full relationships rather than plunging toward the ideal origins of perception in an unknowable because transcendent "other" world of which America has always been the worldly figure.

Understanding is also, as Thoreau makes explicit, a matter of time. A "long probation" with *A Week* leads to an increasing awareness of the way the initially apparently fragmentary pieces of the narrative—Thoreau's tendentious soliloquies and whimsical observations—turn out to be "somewhat better than whim at last," resolving into an ever more complex web of relationship. His sentences, so viewed, are not merely linear, our eyes passing over them like the linear movement of time itself, one sentence following another as a series of truth statements, connected by a logic. They also operate like individual words and relate to each other in a radiating web of meaning like that of words in a unique language, and we have to make sense of them by learning their interrelations, as we would an unfamiliar grammar. "The expressions of the poet cannot be analyzed; His sentence is one word, whose syllables are words" (p. 328). The "making" of those grammatical relationships by the reader reiterates Thoreau's meaning-making in writing and rowing *A Week*, and that order, rather than a secondhand tour of nineteenth-century New England streams, is the experience the text offers.

The instability of historical experience turns Thoreau to a revaluation of conventional experience and ultimately to a speculative or descriptive experience that "has metaphysical ingredients." If Pound insisted that true vision requires immediacy, that the world and the *Cantos* were best perceived "not as land looks on a map / but as sea bord seen by men sailing," Thoreau seems to suggest that the traveler who will undergo sufficient "probation" with him in *A Week* will find that world and book must be seen *both* ways. Mapping and seeing, distance and immediacy, coherence and facts are mutually transforming activities, so that the map is never either complete or accurate and the sights never familiar.[46] This view of experience, and the narrative that embodies it, is a rebuke to the optimism of the scientific revolution, that all knowledge would yield itself up to sufficiently accurate observations of a material world, that all phenomena would succumb to rational analysis.

In this rewriting, Thoreau is not merely expanding on continuing themes. His repetitions do not *develop* his images as a revision might wring additional meaning out of an earlier draft. His prose collectively creates a web of references that connects and cross-connects individual terms and expands the meaning of each. The resulting verbal connections turn the linear movement of the narrative back upon itself, in a telling "over and over" that is also a telling anew, a re-freshment of old material that is essential to Thoreau's effort to redeem the inevitable belatedness of experience and make use of his own past. Rather than knowledge about Thoreau's travels, it offers the reader the experience of the narrative. That offer demands, as Thoreau makes explicit, a long and deep engagement to turn conventional reading, a mere recounting of facts and events, into a complex interweaving of reiterated terms that modifies the implications of each description by overlaying it with other related descriptions.

III

I've tried to draw a close analogy between Thoreau's inquiry and current critical debates about the status of narrative orders: the relative authorities of material conditions and subjective response or interpretation. Reading *A Week* feels to me very much like working through that debate between realism and idealism to the point where Thoreau's solution becomes possible. This text points out a route for abandoning old ground in favor of a territory of thought in which knowledge sheds its veridical claims, its reach for authority, its promises of mastery. Writing (and life), Thoreau would urge, does not supply, step by step, the information required to possess its meaning. It is not "mastered"; it is pondered. With such living writing, as with living persons, understanding is more a matter of increasingly intimate acquaintance, rubbing and wear, than of "following a demonstration," or possession of a fact, or mastery of material.[47]

The experience one gets from Thoreau's narrative is not that described in the account. It is the account. Neither writer nor reader takes back some special knowledge distinct from *A Week*. Both perform the process of making sense by "fronting" narrative facts. Thoreau does this time and again in passages as short as the few lines that redescribe the entire week's journey up to Agiocochook on "Thursday" or as long as the whole of the return to Concord on "Thursday" and "Friday." At the start, Thoreau captured the paradox of living in history. "A man's life," he said, "should be constantly as fresh as this river. It should be the same channel but a new water every instant" (p. 132). By recapitulating earlier narrative elements that are indistinguishable from his self-as-narrative, Thoreau uses, usurps, and replaces his earlier selves, his own past, making himself "fresh" like the waters of the river, newly "current" at every moment.

This descriptive process provides a more fully rhetorical view of facts that is also a more fully historicist one. It abandons the debate between real and ideal, facts and coherent order, that has shaped scholarly study of American literature and Thoreau's own earlier narrative. It offers a model of experience that depends on descriptions, on accounts, on language as a changing historical medium of social intercourse rather than on accurate representation of empirical fact. Facts are not known or perceived apart from accounts. Paul Feyerabend has shown that Galileo's triumphant demonstration of Copernican astronomy did not depend on accurate observation of empirical fact, the persuasive testimony of the senses, because there was, in fact, no agreement about those observations. That is, observation did not precede the theory that turned the universe inside out. Copernicus had no telescope. Observation *succeeded* a compelling argument that displaced empirical evidence. Copernicus's account, and Galileo's elaboration of it, like Einstein's theory, preceded and helped to produce the observations that ultimately confirmed them. Thoreau picks out the same example. "Copernicus, reasoning long and patiently about the matter, predicted confidently concerning it, before yet the telescope had been invented, that if ever men came to see it more clearly than they did then, they would discover that it had phases like our moon, and that within a century after his death the telescope was invented, and that prediction verified, by Galileo" (p. 385).

Facts are the essential material for an account, the precondition for narrative rather than its object. When Thoreau asserts that "we can never safely exceed the actual facts," he expresses not so much a fidelity to facts as their inescapability (p. 325). On this view, both the objective and the subjective threats have been overstated. Although our histories will inevitably be projections of present interests, that does not make them "merely" invented, or unconnected to reality. Such antinomian fantasy is not a threat because, as Thoreau says, "of pure invention, such as some suppose, there is no instance'' (p. 325). On the other hand, Cartesian skepticism evades the facts of life and denies the social context of all meaning. To deny the facts of the world is simply to remove oneself from the human community, the only scene of life. "It is true," Thoreau writes, that "we may come to a perpendicular precipice, but we need not jump off, nor run our heads against it. A man may jump down his own cellar stairs, or dash his brains out against his chimney, if he is mad" (p. 183). Yet, facts, though intransigent, are also not the point, and so do not determine accounts. Accounts do not simply reflect or re-present facts. Such slavish mimicry is the product of "common sense," which "always takes a hasty and superficial view." Facts in isolation lack the "discipline" (p. 388) of a "view of the universe" (p. 387) that shapes narrative. Facts are tools for producing the accounts that overcome the superficiality of "mere facts." "I have no respect for facts," Thoreau says, "except when I would use them, and for the most part I am independent of those which I hear, and can afford to be inaccurate, or, in other words, to substitute more *present* and pressing facts in their place" (p. 363).

As Thoreau suggests here, using facts in accounts is a way of making the past present, while the mere accumulation of facts only incurs the indebtedness to and domination by the past that Thoreau's narrative tries first to escape and then transforms. "Facts," Thoreau complains, "are being so rapidly added to the sum of human experience, that it appears as if the theorizer would always be in arrears, and were doomed forever to arrive at imperfect conclusions" (p. 364). The force of these accumulating facts inspired Thoreau's first speculative journey in "Concord River" "to see how much country there is in the rear of us" (p. 7). But Thoreau's actual, as well as his narrative, journey was not toward the "rear" but toward the "Unappropriated Land" he reconstructs as his own history. Freeing himself from the obligation to run stride for stride with the rush of historical change, he aims instead to make sense of his experience. "The power to perceive a law," he says, "depends but little on the number of facts observed" (p. 364). And as Thoreau first hinted in "Saturday," "the fruit of . . . observations is not in new genera or species, but in new contemplations" (p. 23). "The one great rule of composition," he wrote, "is, to *speak the truth.*"[48] The trick is getting it right. "A true account," he says with typically doubled meaning, "is the rarest poetry" (p. 325), so rare because it is not simply a faithful rendering of the facts but a rendering that is faithful to itself as well, one that does not betray its own conclusions in the telling.

The solution to the epistemological problem that Thoreau launched on "Concord River" is rhetorical. In this sense, Thoreau's narrative fulfills the promise of Emerson's performative prose.[49] If traditional narrative might be described as the record of the autonomous self's experience of an external world, Thoreau's narrative produces both self and world, present and past. It does not refer. It does not reflect, either a prior interpretation or a world. This process is not *governed* by an autonomous self; it is *true* to itself. Like Emerson's rigorous narrative explanations, it is directed by its own movements, by the drift of its own previous thoughts.

In the context, the refusal to supplement a summary meaning for that of the text itself in a "true account," the "undescribed" trek to the top of Mt. Washington (Agiocochook) is not, as critics have claimed, a quest into the ultimate and unnameable source, the heart of American darkness. The notion of the Agiocochook vignette as a search for the "concealed" source, the "end-point" of Thoreau's quest conflicts with the often reinforced notion that this journey is not seeking an "end" at all, that at best it comes to an end, falls, as Thoreau says, into silence, like "Sunday," "without regard to any unities which we mortals prize" (p. 114). This latest account is sketchy partly because, by this point in the narrative, there is no need to return to that particular summit again. In fact, this pointedly cryptic passage *acquires* its significance from those earlier narratives. Its power depends on its evocation of previous summit experiences that *are* described in detail and lend to it their significance as it does to them. In this sense, it is a model of Thoreau's developing intrareferential narrative style.

By leaving the view from Agiocochook undescribed, Thoreau refuses to trivialize his own narrative path, the historical process of working one's way up his narrative stream, by providing a "general" assessment of it, a metanarrative, that would displace the language that surrounds it. Such usurpation would short-circuit a central function of the particular understanding of writing to which Thoreau's own narrative has brought him.[50] By leaving the trek to Agiocochook undescribed, unused in his own narrative, he makes it a placeholder for his own previous descriptions and redirects his reader back to them. Thus Thoreau both preserves the possibility of the new, and makes capital out of the secondhandedness of experience that he originally set out to escape. After Agiocochook, the world and Thoreau's narrative seem to have been transformed, but the absence of any description of Thoreau's experience on Agiocochook short-circuits readerly impulses to explain this transformation as a product of a single revelatory experience, the capstone of Thoreau's quest. It prevents us from treating his account as the sort of travel narrative in which a traveler—the Ancient Mariner, Ishmael, Ethan Brand, Robinson Crusoe—penetrates the unknown and returns transformed and bearing mysterious and transforming truth. The empty place represented by the ominous word *AGIOCOCHOOK* drives readers back to their own encounter with the text, rather than to any experience Thoreau had, for explanations of the changes that shape "Thursday" and "Friday."

And after Agiocochook, Thoreau's narrative is profoundly changed. It plays a transforming variation on the inherited division between the two worlds of spirit and matter that has troubled him from the start. Thoreau no longer wants to trade one world for another, the artificial for the natural, the material for the spiritual. There is no world other than this one. "Here or nowhere," he says, "is our heaven" (p. 380). Rather than alternating between two incompatible but equally essential worlds, a world of fact and a world of value, Thoreau wants to unite them, and he takes a giant step in that direction by focusing on accounts rather than on perception. Thoreau's notion of transcendence does not point through the physical world to a separate spiritual one, of which the physical is merely an emblem, as critics of Transcendentalism have always assumed, placing him in a theological rather than a rhetorical tradition. It points toward a re-seeing or "right reading" that he associates with a redescription of the natural world so as to reveal its divine nature (where "divine" is more an adjective, a metaphor, than a label for godhead). "Is not Nature, rightly read, that of which she is taken to be a symbol merely?" (p. 382).

Thoreau's narrative recycles the past. The return trip makes autumn *new*, rather than the unavoidable and pervasive reminder of Thoreau's belatedness. As the "true harvest of the year," it is the seasonal manifestation of writing, which he has called the "true harvest of the author's life," and the description of the return trip to Concord is the "true harvest" of Thoreau's narrative. The very conditions of the return journey seem to reverse the terms and values of the outward trip by reversing directions. The world into which Thoreau returns from Agiocochook, and in which he returns to Concord does operate on different principles than governed his outward trip. He has not resolved the oppositions that generated his labors, but his repeated reworking of those terms has revised their implications and altered their contexts so as to dissolve their old incompatibilities. Sailing now with the help of both current and breeze, Thoreau's boat is no longer the "dull water fowl" of "Saturday." Its progress "was very near flying." Its reversed direction reverses time as well, taking the narrative back over its own experience and making that experience historical, as "many upward days voyaging were unraveled in this rapid downward passage," and "the places where we had stopped or spent the night in our way up the river had already acquired a slight historical interest for us" (p. 353).

This narrative is Thoreau's version of a redefinition of the "usual" understandings that overcomes the conflict between art and life that troubled "Concord River" and has dominated the critical debate from O. B. Frothingham to Walter Benn Michaels. "Art," Thoreau proposes, "is not tame, and nature is not wild, in the ordinary sense. A perfect work of man's art would also be natural or wild in a good sense" (p. 316). It is communication both wild and domestic, "from our home and solitude" (p. 341), and the ripples of their wake image, at once, the union of earth and heaven, their progress and that of birds, and the alternating close and distant perspectives on the world that have framed the narrative and figured in the book's epiphanic visions. This harmonic motion, and the accompanying concentration of images that recapitulate narrative events, redeems time ("who hears the rippling of rivers in these degenerate days will not utterly despair" [p. 334]). Thoreau's incessant elisions, this alloy of elements that seemed incompatible at the start, the repetitions, the sameness in change in this rippling narrative, give him an alternative to the redundancy that frustrated him on "Saturday" with an intellectual landscape that had been worked "in and in, and out and out, and over and over, again and again" (p. 8). The revealing conjunction of terms that made for *momentary* epiphany in "Monday" and "Tuesday" becomes identical with description in Thoreau's "Friday" account. Thoreau's account makes conditional facts both new and timeless, returning Thoreau to his Concord past, made part of his own meaningful history.

On "Friday," the beginning of this narrative journey recurs as its end, or the mark of its endlessness. Returning to the Concord necessarily returns us to the "Concord River," the place where the reading and writing, as well as the rowing, began. That "Concord," too, is transformed. It has, at length, become the product as well as the premise of the reflections that produced the whole. By the time Thoreau returns the reader to them, both Concord and "Concord River" are different, his previous existence and experience there evidenced by marks and memorials no less historical than those that punctuate the riverside and his reflections on it as he passes by. The "spring freshets" to which the narrative's final words recall us are the very ones that swelled the stream in "Concord River," where they pulled at the boat chain, marking the wild apple tree that spreads its mixed pre- and postlapsarian associations throughout the narrative and human history. The force at work, in the beginning as at the end, is the urgency of the lapsing stream, the propelling past and the potent present, the movement of the narrative itself, for as Thoreau puns, "The story is current" (p. 9), and "There is," he says, "something even in the lapse of time by which time recovers itself" (p. 351).

For all his immersion in old books and historical detail, Thoreau's interests were not antiquarian. His motives were not very different from those that drive contemporary critical debate. Time and again in *A Week* he asks the same question that hangs menacingly over the head of contemporary literary studies, one that appeals to historical context do not answer persuasively, that is, Why does the past, why do old texts, continue to interest us? Coming out of an idealist tradition, Thoreau often assumes a posture that rejects the particular differences that divide past and present. We want not the pastness of the past, he says, but its presentness, "not its *then,* but its *now*" (p. 154).

Thoreau complicates what might appear to be a simplistically idealist view by making it clear that the present, the "now," is equally problematic. The "now," as Thoreau's formidable learning and his obsessive attention to histories, monuments, remains, and artifacts throughout the book make clear, is largely that *part* of the past that has come down to us as our inheritance.[51] Not everything comes down to us. Much is simply lost, like the buried corpse, marked, after rising water, by the vacancy its decay has left in the grave and then, with the next flood, all signs erased, lost forever. Much, like the story of Hannah Dustan, has been reduced to little more than an object of wonder by subsequent changes in the world. In its strangeness, her story measures the distance and the similarity between her Concord and Thoreau's. Our relation to her story has become a matter of analogy or metaphor. Though the wild Indians no longer lurk along Thoreau's river bank, "we have need to be as sturdy pioneers . . . we are to follow another trail, it is true, but one as convenient for ambushes'' (p. 120). Reading Thoreau's book exemplifies the relation with the past he describes. *A Week* itself is an analog of the lake that keeps appearing in it as a metaphor for the continuing (even if obscured, forgotten, or ignored) significance of the past. Seeing our relationship to both the book and the past is a matter of clearing away impediments to reveal the old in a new light. Like a lake revealed through a clearing made by woodcutters, ''so are these old sentences like serene lakes in the southwest, at length revealed to us, which have so long been reflecting our own sky in their bosom'' (p. 151). This is the power of texts, however, that they can, at least sometimes, preserve, with a complexity that amounts to an articulated world, something that we can adapt to our own uses, something of identity, of life, from the past into the present.

That projection gives relevance to inherited artifacts, but it also gives substance to the present, which would otherwise be nothing but pointless change. The present, after all, is no time at all. It has significance only in relation to the past and the future that it divides. Thoreau asks, ''Do we live but in the present? How broad a line is that?'' (p. 153). Having repudiated empirical history and absorbed past and future into the merely theoretical thin line of the present, Thoreau redescribes the ''past'' as a projection of and by the present—''memories,'' as Dewey said, ''re called for a purpose.''

In this chapter, I have described Thoreau's style as a strategy for relating past and present in a coherent interreferential narrative web. Using the conceptual tools at hand, Thoreau, like modern critics, tried to explain the continuing uses of the past without ignoring either historical fact or contemporary interests. That prose makes his account an exemplar of historical relationships, one that Thoreau develops and elaborates as he goes along. Thoreau's narrative of ''speculative experience'' abandons the debate between real and ideal that shaped scholarly study of American literature and Thoreau's own first narrative intentions. Epistemology, he suggests, does not apply to thoroughly historical accounts. To *know* the past is impossible. ''The past,'' he argues, ''cannot be presented, we cannot know what we are not'' (p. 155). As Thoreau performs it in *A Week,* the abandonment of epistemology is not simply a change in the way people ''view'' the world, it is a change (with the largest implications) in narrative style, in the way people talk about their experience.[52] That change developed as nineteenth-century writers ''fronted'' the limitations of their inherited language and of the forms of thought and life it could describe. What that change produced is not a radical uncertainty, nor, I believe, is it a rhetorical battleground in which persuasion is all that counts and anything goes. For, as Thoreau discovers, there is no escaping the constraints of the socially conditioned relations among the terms we use and criticize with.

This writing redefines experience itself as a matter of accounts, and as such, it is an extension and amalgamation of the postmedieval turn from prevenient authority to individual experience of the world, from static security to change, from heaven to history. Such speculative experience is not a product of life in the New World. Newness, in fact, has nothing to do with it. Instead it requires a "long probation." It "grows naturally . . . through a long fronting of men and events, and rubbing on good and bad fortune." It is a temporal process of self-development, an encounter with alternate vocabularies out of which we might construct new accounts, an education. As Thoreau says in *Walden,* to "front a fact" is the true wilderness. This experience does not require a "separate intention of the eye." It is not an altered state, a "flash-of-lightning faith," that interrupts normal experience and from which we return to the overcast common world. It is not a momentary elevation into a spiritual world outside time and life but living fully itself. In Thoreau's writing, it is also "work" or "labor," the daily unavoidable "re-view" that yields the "flower" and "monument" of thought, a human act that persists through time and so can speak to us of/as the past.

« 4 »

American Literary Scholarship for the Twentieth Century

I am not wise enough for a national criticism.

EMERSON

It is a principle that shines impartially on the just and on the unjust that once you have a point of view all history will back you up.

VAN WYCK BROOKS

I

Although it may seem a bit late in the day to be looking forward to an American Literary Scholarship for the twentieth century, our persisting need for that project reflects the degree to which scholarship still works within the nineteenth-century vocabularies that writers like Emerson and Thoreau revised. As I have tried to show, the problem with the way American Literary Scholarship is generally practiced is not, as recent critiques have claimed, merely that its canon is erected on prejudice. On the contrary, the whole project of describing a peculiarly "American" literature, including its recent Neohistoricist revisions, depends on the language of Romantic idealism that dominated cultural discourse when the profession of American literary studies was being invented. Scholarship needs to catch up by abandoning the old rhythmic swing between literature and culture before it can jump ahead.

As long as Americanists defend traditional disciplinary boundaries and lean on the myth of American literary studies that even revisionists continue to present, they will misconstrue nearly 500 years of writing in and about America as well as the scholarship that has been dedicated since the 1870s to the peculiar task of distinguishing that writing from other writing in English. As parts of the effort to establish a new scholarly field, the arguments that have constituted American Literary Scholarship amounted to justifications for reading more American books. Now we *do* read more American books and, partly because of this success, most of the polemical arguments for doing so have lost their point and could safely be discarded but for their ties to the institutional forms they mandated. In terms of professional practice rather than political ideology, a radical approach to American Literary Scholarship would not, as Tompkins would have it, center on the "struggle" to determine "the picture America draws of itself." That struggle has been the meat and potatoes of scholarly debate since the Civil War. The radical position for which, I believe, a thoroughgoing and reconceptualized historicism prepares would assert, among other things, that, like all once-powerful idealist categories, the discourse that assumes an "American" literature and the accompanying quest for a "coherent story" about American writing belies the convictions of a posttheological age and ought to be retired. It makes no practical sense for criticism in the late twentieth century to be dominated by a cultural paranoia—an insecurity about the status of America and American writing—that was inherited from Revolutionary times and is, by now, an increasingly obvious anachronism. The point of historicist criticism for American Literary Scholarship, one that has not been turned aside, skewers the sustaining narrative strategies of establishment work, leaving the field groping for something else to *do*.

Alternatives do not depend simply on a choice between politics and aesthetics. As the scholarly history makes clear, the American Ideal is as much a feature of political as of aesthetic formulations of "American" writing. If American literary studies is to escape the dead end created by its repeated substitution of art for culture and culture for art, Americanists need to learn how to describe both literature and society without sacrificing one to the other. An idealized literature has not afforded literary scholars safe harbor, nor has an hypostatized culture provided a solid ground to which they could moor their conclusions. Imagining a useful articulation of literature and culture means reconceiving *both* terms, and that job will be difficult enough without the extra baggage of an a priori professional obligation to the word *America*.

A reading of the *full* history of American Literary Scholarship suggests that the "fall" into fragmentation that has revisionists at once dismayed and delighted is not the fortunate one they suppose but fatal to the traditional project of American Literary Scholarship. It is figured not by Adam's fall but by Humpty-Dumpty's, and the broken fragments of American literary studies show no inclination to cooperate in revisionist efforts to put them back together again into the "coherent narrative" Bercovitch, Tompkins, Kolodny, and others are waiting for.[1] Their patience, in the meantime, with the current disarray simply amounts to the determination that because they cannot reconstruct Humpty, they will collect the scattered debris into a pile and continue the ritual as before, though most of the life has long ago seeped out of the fractured body.

It has become increasingly clear that we cannot continue to talk as we have about things "American" without violating other fundamental beliefs, the very anti-foundationalist convictions that have supported revisionist claims. This remark amounts, as Richard Rorty might say, to the claim that we should stop using the word *America* so often and see what other changes that entails in our scholarly accounts. Having lost the benefit of that authoritative word, it is time for Americanists to straighten out their arguments and stop re-retelling what has been an excessively simple story, even if that means telling less reaffirming ones. Being "in history" has presented literary studies with a crisis of purpose. If we no longer study literature to get as close to God as we can on earth, or to initiate ourselves into a cultural elite, or to improve our characters, the intellectual and emotional energy driving the call for revision makes it clear that we need some more substantial worldly and historical reason for doing it. An understandable desire for security in these troubled times has made a "radical" political position attractive as a litmus test for relevance. That may be the wrong test for the time.

The open question, then, for American Literary Scholarship is, What will critics have to say about American texts when they no longer say simply (or elaborately) that texts are "American"? My (designedly) undramatic reply to that question is that it is the wrong question. Casting off the old forms of American Literary Scholarship will not open the door to still another brave new world—American Literary Scholarship *redivivus*—and my critique of American Literary Scholarship does not open a new perspective on the field. In advocating that scholars abandon the "peculiar project" of American literature studies, that is, the effort to use the word *America* as an unexamined a priori source of coherence about which a particular professional field can be organized, I am not *prescribing* a new critical practice, since such prescriptions are bound to prove embarrasing in the face of later developments. At most, I am trying to *proscribe* one particular critical practice by urging that Americanists stop trying to do what they have been unable to do for more than a century and, moreover, no longer have much reason for doing. The views I am proposing do not aim to refute the arguments of scholars in the field that their findings have helped us to understand American literature and culture better. They suggest that, as a review of Transcendentalist scholarship discloses, such justificatory appeals to either "American literature" or "American culture" are precisely the sort of propositions American literary studies has been unable to defend coherently for 100 years. Their regular appearances prefatory to arguments about an American literature do not so much rationalize the project as identify the whole debate as a pseudoproblem, one that *cannot* be resolved even in its own terms.

American Literary Scholarship was created (with still less substantial justification than most academic fields) out of political and professional motives. Now that all but the most narrow professional justifications have pretty much disappeared, the field, in its current form, should disappear as well. An alternative approach would make the word *America* just another national category, shorthand for all the disparate activities that occur in America rather than the name of a unique and coherent literary heritage or the defining subject of a distinct sort of professional scholarly discourse. If we did not use the word *America* so often and to such grand effect, if we stopped thinking of it as a categorical rug under which we can sweep our narrative problems, we would change the subject in the conversation about American literary studies, dissolving the ideal glue that has always held the field together *as a distinct field*. While there is obviously no reason we cannot continue to talk about American texts, we will have to do so in ways that do not appeal for our interest in them to some uniquely American character or to their status as expressions of the experience of the New World. This insight produces no startlingly new things to say about American texts, except insofar as new insights might be produced by talking about them in a broader textual field. The only sense in which this may be startling is that it means the dismantling of a powerful, if not exactly venerable, academic institution.

Yet, the fate of the American Ideal has a deeper resonance. If

American Literary Scholarship can be taken as a synecdoche for the problems that have inspired revision in literary history in general, its 100-year war between art and culture suggests that the recent turn to cultural criticism will not, of itself, solve our professional problems. More important for the ambitions of literary scholars to cultural and political influence, by taking the New Criticism as its defining "other," cultural criticism helplessly mirrors the New Critical mistake, though from the opposite direction. If formalist polemic against the "old" historicism went too far, defusing the political implications of texts by denying their connection to social contexts and conflicts, cultural criticism, even as it insists on the political force of texts in the context of their historical production, actually defuses their threatening implications for the present by confining them to the past as markers for the historical conditions in which they first appeared.[2] As an antidote to fears of professional marginalization, I do not see how this approach can do the job. That is, it will not tell our students or the rest of the world why literary work is important. Students are unlikely to be convinced that old books are worth reading as windows into what they see as a remote and irrelevant past. That claim confirms rather than overcomes the indifference to texts and to history (among students and the culture at large) that keeps them from reading at all, and thus makes moot any transforming or subversive power texts might have.

If the profession *has* been mistaken in its focus over the past forty years, as recent historicist critics have frequently declared, the mistake has not been in concentrating on universal literary value rather than the more substantial concerns of cultural practice. It has not been the failure to connect literary works firmly to the social context in which they were produced. Texts are not the gossamer offspring of untrustworthy (because inner and thus untestable) mental processes. Nor is culture the more substantial original of aesthetic expression and therefore an appropriate object for the scholarly quest after ever more fundamental truths. Such oppositions just leave criticism worrying the old dualistic bone—literature at one end, life at the other. By repudiating the traditional canon and formalist standards, revisionists imagine they have cleansed American literary studies in much the same way the people of Boston fancied they had expelled sin by banishing Hester to the edge of the wilderness. But like Hawthorne's Bostonians, they are only banishing the error that they have learned to define as "other" while enacting error in another more contemporary form. Both of these complementary assumptions reflect what Sartre called "the urge to be rid of one's freedom to erect alternate vocabularies." They are efforts to evade the burden of choice.

The failure of the profession (and a cause of its marginalization in our culture) could more usefully be seen as its inability to develop a critical vocabulary independent of foundationalist assumptions that could explain the relation between the past and the present and show *how* it can be said that to concentrate on literature *is* to concentrate on life. And in view of the circumstances that surrounded the emergence of professional literary studies, even this was not so much a mistake as a strategy in the debates of the time, a strategy that contemporary critics have the hindsight to regret. It is instructive, and not a little ironic, that American Literary Scholarship is moving back once again toward culture just as many professional historians are moving toward texts.[3] Historians have begun to recognize, as Emerson and Thoreau did explicitly 150 years ago, that the historicity of experience, the resigned acceptance of conditional human action as the only arena of life, has also changed and confused our notions of history itself. Relinquishing ideal standards does not somehow automatically *make* things historical. It means that we have to decide all over again, or perhaps for the first time, what being historical *means*. In "putting the text back into history," as Edward Pechter says, we need to be "certain we know what history means and what the practical consequences of such a program are."[4]

Uncertain as we are about where that questioning might lead, it ought to be clear that orthodoxies of any kind, with their firm formulations and reassuring rhetoric can only stifle inquiry. Like the rest of the profession, American literary studies has only just begun to question the assumptions and methods that have supplied its intellectual and institutional foundations. We should not rush to establish new stabilities before we have exorcised the pervasive and still potent ghosts of the old. The critical impulse to describe texts simply as cultural productions reflects the need to maintain the conventional causalities that generate a familiar narrative about disturbingly unfamiliar and unmanageable phenomena, much as the U.S. Air Force insists on describing UFOs as heat lightning and weather balloons. In contemporary discourse, the traditional mission of scholarship to press back the boundaries of knowledge too often disguises the effort not merely to "normalize" the unfamiliar or abnormal but to deny its abnormality or treat apparent strangeness as a sign of imperfection. As Bernard Bledstein points out, professionalism arose in America (about the time American Literary Scholarship was invented) to impose expertise as a control on the mysteries of a life that had been cut loose from theological orders. Sherlock Holmes billed himself as the first "professional consulting detective," reassuring clients and readers alike that life's mysteries were no mysteries to him. Our own investigations could very well clarify our historical understandings, but they need *not* confirm the ideological assumptions and aspirations that inspired them in the first place. Like Emerson and Thoreau, contemporary revisionists are struggling against the persistent implications of their own inherited and ahistoricist rhetoric. Emerson and Thoreau did not submit.

II

A crucial determinant of our ability to write productive literary history will be the sort of relation we establish with our own professional history. As cultural practices go, academic literary scholarship is still relatively new, and therefore, we ought to expect, primitive. Grounded in Biblical interpretation, it is still breaking away from exegetical models and trying to decide what textual interpretation is for and how it should proceed if its end is merely historical, a human activity, rather than the timeless and absolute truth of God. Especially while we are so uncertain, old models should not be treated as undesirable baggage, the garbage of the past, any more than old books should be, but as reservoirs of potential strategies for solving continuing or as yet inadequately formulated problems. If we treat the manifestos of literary "schools" anti-foundationally as necessarily imperfect attempts to articulate intuitions about literary study, then we ought to respect even those attempts that disagree with our own on the assumption that they may contain, however disguised, legitimate contributions toward an improved approach. Like Emerson's effort amidst the fragments of idealism to describe a coherent human life, a scholarly strategy like the New Criticism might be viewed as a flawed but powerful early formulation of a brilliant hunch about how to overcome the historical distance between reader and texts.[5] If its contemporary reputation has suffered, that is because its practitioners as well as its critics often failed to distinguish its methodological attention to enlightening linguistic relationships from its polemical insistence on aesthetic autonomy and universality. The latter reflected its nostalgia for scriptural origins as well as its ambitions for professional exclusivity. But there is no reason for us to abandon the useful insights of New Criticism for fear of continuing its "mistakes."[6]

In our tentative gestures to revise literary history, the point is not to abandon the tradition but to recuperate it in terms that speak to contemporary beliefs. Rather than simply repudiating critical approaches that have in large part *produced* the profession and generated a huge body of fascinating criticism over the past fifty years, contemporary scholars could be looking for what Dewey called a ''constructive synthesis'' of competing models. That posture would make especially good sense because the effort to defend one position against the other only produces incoherence and a self-destructive denial of the repressed ''other'' in whichever model (historical or aesthetic) happens to be popular at the moment. I'd argue that we should see questions about the connection between texts and politics, society and history, as more complicated than has been acknowledged. They ask how we can describe such relationships without sacrificing other important, perhaps essential, features of literary study.

As we seek answers to these questions, the work of a critic like Matthiessen might serve us better as a provocative example than as a whipping boy.[7] Without slighting its own passionate commitment to social issues, to moral values and political justice, Matthiessen's generation was the first that could inject art into the discourse about American writing and culture without having to apologize for it. The question that generation was able to ask, really for the first time in American scholarship, was what literary art *in particular* has to do with the inescapable human social problems that have preoccupied Americanists in every generation. That question has certainly not lost its point in the context of late-twentieth-century commercialsm, and I do not see how we can answer it by denying its relevance and simply swinging back yet again into a modernized version of the cultural criticism from which an earlier generation of Americanists dissented. To do so would be to deny rather than to learn from our professional past, and to reduce generational change to a mindless mechanical process of action and reaction.

The professional priority given to the supposed split between text and context has been magnified by the influence of New Critical polemic, which was itself partly shaped by dissatisfaction with the inability of the old historicism to account for the interest of the present in the past. But the attack on formalism currently under way seems to me a case of unwitting self-mutilation. Apart from some totalizing authority, the vehement scapegoating of past critical models, whatever its polemical force, only conceals the empty place where the foundations of a new order ought to be. However refreshing it may be as a corrective to the more extreme versions of formalist polemic, the lean toward culture in contemporary historicist criticism, especially when colored, as it so often is in American Literary Scholarship, with claims to ethico-political superiority, belies its own most fundamental (and productive) principle, the insistence on the conditionality of all practice.[8] Historicist arguments "may become dubious," as Dominick LaCapra argues, "when [as, I would assert, in American Literary Scholarship] they engender dogmatic socio-centrism, methodological populism, the refusal to recognize the historical significance of exceptional aspects of culture."[9]

One point I want to reach along this line of thinking is that it will be fruitless to institutionalize any "New Historicism" that is not also and at the same time a "New Formalism."[10] Formalist assumptions go deep, and for good reason. The fact that they have a long history in our thinking should, as I argued in Part I, suggest to us that they cannot and should not be discarded lightly.[11] We cannot simply ignore the real work they have done, and continue to do for us. The notion of intrinsic meaning or value that historicists attack was a modern redaction of the Romantic effort to locate the ideal in the world. It expresses the same impulse that idealized America, made American Literary Scholarship an academic institution, and not incidentally, inspired the "sentimental" fiction that some revisionist critics wish to revalue. The fact that critics interested in (re)historicizing texts (among whom I count myself) now find some of these notions unsuitable should not obscure the fact that they express aims we continue to hold.[12] They succeeded by providing a rationale for valuing books and the professional study of books, and by giving critics a way of generating new things to say about them. Any alternative must prove itself comparably useful in analyzing where criticism is now, where it is going, and how it can get there.

The historicity of discourse is not a good reason for displacing the close study of exceptional language use with the study of culture. It would be a particularly egregious mistake to let an anti-formalist bias tempt us into simplistic descriptions of texts that carry on complex historical debates because those texts exceed and thus critique the terms that prevailed in their own time and often in ours. More to the point, in the context of the current developing consensus in favor of a "New Historicism" in some form, would be an explanation of literary work that preserves what we need in *mimesis* (principally reassurance that interpretation is not a matter of whim and that texts are not unrelated to life), but in a way that responds

to our modern distrust of determinate meaning. Rather than abandoning
the New Critical idea of aesthetic value over its claims to intrinsicality
(the model of abandonment, as Thoreau discerned, is, after all, the flip
side of the ahistorical myth of the "radically new"), we should try to
reconceive that aestheticism in intellectually respectable historicist
terms.

Writing like Emerson's and Thoreau's contributes to this project by
demonstrating, among other things, that moving language into the place
vacated by "the failure of the various candidates for the position of
starting point" does not mean retreating once again into a (this time
linguistic) idealism.[13] It does not condemn our work to isolation and
irrelevance or to an ivory-tower political quietism. It does not isolate us
from the real world. Emerson and Thoreau do not turn to language for the
resolution of all their problems but as the only tool available for exploring
those problems. In the course of that exploration, they discover that the
limits on inquiry are the limits language (rather than God or nature)
imposes. Using language is an act, a material gesture. The language we
use does not constitute phenomena; it embodies our current attempts to
make sense of phenomena, attempts that are as bound by history and
society as language itself.

Abandoning a correspondence model of language makes language
material and meaning historical. For critics, to say that meaning is
relative to language is not an idealist claim that language makes objects in
the world; it is only an observation that, like Thoreau, we are unable to
carry out a quest into unfamiliar territory in any but our own existing
terms, although as Thoreau also demonstrates, the quest can modify
those terms as it goes along. This notion does not make the truth language
provides less objective any more than it makes it less formative. A view
of language as social rather than subjective does away with both the fear
that particular convictions are groundless and the possibility of easily
dispensing with existing ones.[14] Historicism and the kind of prose we
saw in "The Transcendentalist" and *A Week* imply (or ought to) that
what we call meaning is always a matter of specific linguistic acts, never
of abstractions behind them separable from and determining those
particular acts. This, rather than an immersion in a particular ideological
perspective, is the sense in which meaning is a matter of time and place
rather than a timeless essence.

Thus, insofar as concentrating on culture has seemed to critics the
natural alternative to aesthetic isolation, the significance of the formal has

been misrepresented both in modernism and in recent critiques of it.[15] Style and form are themselves essential features of historical and social change. A more productive literary scholarship will treat the forms of texts as both cognitively and culturally significant. Scrapping the distinction between two separate and incompatible worlds, inner and outer, and the correspondence model of meaning they entail, also dissolves the historically persistent distinction between language and reality, literature and culture, that has stigmatized literary interests as abstraction, escapism, or mere entertainment.

III

Thoreau's prose plots an alternative direction for the central debates about the meaning and uses of texts that have generated the revisionist impulse in literary studies. Those debates dramatize a continuing uncertainty about the nature of interpretation by shuffling the location of textual meaning between reader and text. The effort, in the relatively narrow arena of American literary studies, to overcome an uneasiness with aesthetic detachment by making what I have described as oversimplified connections between texts and culture is only the most recent swing in a debate that is older than the profession. Contemporary criticism preserves the subjective and objective options Emerson exhausted in "The Transcendentalist."[16] Where is meaning located? Is it discovered or made by the reader? Are reading and writing processes of communication or do readers construct texts out of their own assumptions or those of one of the communities to which they belong? These alternatives have generated corollary disputes over interpretive validity and the posture of the interpreter toward the text.[17] Perhaps the relative uncertainty and insecurity of this situation can explain why scholarship has clung so tenaciously to assumptions that preserve the illusion of fixed meanings produced by the intentions of an author and possessed by a detached and stable critic. But the apparent stability of this position is belied by the dissatisfaction that drives the impulse to revision itself.

I have said that New Historicist accounts in American literary studies cling despite themselves to elements of ahistoricist vocabularies. While historicist versions of the traditional interpretive positions acknowledge the historicity of the text and of the reader in respect to their contexts (the conditions of textual production, and the local interests behind readerly interpretation), they fail to account adequately for the temporality of reading and writing themselves. That is, they still implicitly adhere to a "scheme/content" model of language and treat texts as embodying or disclosing a content distinct from the language of the text, a content governed by authorial intention, or interpretive assumptions, or ideological matrices, or cultural moments—all distinct from particular instances of language use. Such reading discounts writing and reading as historical understanding by portraying it as a fixed object of knowledge that has its significance apart from the language used.

Other critical approaches have come at the problems history poses for criticism from the other side of the subject/object fence. The Reader Response Criticism that came to prominence in the 1970s can be seen as an alternative response to ahistorical constraints of this kind. It focused on the temporality of reading as a process, an activity that produces meaning as readerly experience, the unfolding of the text for a reader over the time of the reading. But insofar as Reader Response Criticism stressed the experience of an imagined reader "in" whom the reading occurred, it preserved the myth of presence, of a reading self that constituted interpretations and to whom they should be traceable. The potential for unconstrained subjectivism and for undecidable conflicts over interpretive authority in this position led critics like Stanley Fish to displace the interpretive self into interpretive assumptions and relocate those assumptions as the defining features of an "interpretive community." The still more socially contextualized views of reading and meaning proposed by New Historicism counteract the potential for passivity and static apoliticism in this critical move, but only by sacrificing what was prescient about Reader Response Criticism: its productive engagement with the temporality of textuality itself. This is just the element that Emerson and Thoreau add to the textual equation, and just the element they demand of the reader who would really contend with their texts.

Thoreau's account suggests that this problem and its solution are both largely matters of narrative. The movements I have described in Emerson's and Thoreau's prose enact a complex effort to make sense of the world. Insofar as that world is still ours (and the consistent terms of the critical debate over literature and culture, past and present, suggest that it is), I believe we can learn from the details of those movements, the performative qualities of their writing, and should attend closely to them. Reiterating and revising his own earlier descriptions, Thoreau both reviews and revises the experience they presented and by doing so, he appropriates and adapts the surrounding terms that supply their context as he *makes* them present. Past and present are not confused or blurred in this prose; they are related, or rather, Thoreau articulates a relationship for them as they shape and reshape each other. But past and present so articulated are not distinct from accounts. In his writing, language and narrative *are* history. Describing and transforming the past is one act with establishing the same sort of relationship toward Thoreau's own developing account of it, his *narrative* past, and he forces us, if we are to follow him, into a similar posture toward our reading, one that, in its continuous self-revision, insists on the temporality of our own critical accounts.

The resulting narrative not only identifies truth with experience, as travel narrative had done since Columbus, but identifies experience with narrative itself, reversing the foundationalist priority of the thing over the word. If knowledge is conceived as description rather than as perception, it connects to reality not *by way of* representation but *as* activity, the attempt to make sense of the world in coherent and useful accounts so as to live in it.[18] In this respect, their prose speaks to the plight of contemporary literary historians for whom chronological fragments can no longer be ordered by reference to some external authority, a divine plan, or an evolutionary model of progress, or even the overarching order of a consistent narrative persona. If scholars want to avoid false causality or the easy allegorizing of our own interests in the texts we read, we have to face the same question that troubled H. C. Goddard in 1908. "Into the wilderness [of particulars] how will it be possible to bring any meaning?"[19] Whatever response we offer to this question will have to acknowledge the historicity of critical accounts not merely as reflecting a local interest but as themselves enacting a historical process. That process does not simply reflect the point of view of some self located in a particular historical moment, since such selves and moments are among the categories called into question by the historicist critique of foundationalism. On the contrary, a critical account unfolds a historical self enacted *as* thinking about its subject. Consideration of the historicist conditionality of a text must include the way its features are conditional upon surrounding linguistic acts, most crucially its own.

Although Emerson and Thoreau faced problems analogous to those that trouble contemporary critics, their writing places them in a different posture toward history than subsequent scholars have managed to assume. The approach to these questions performed in their prose replaces the traditional divisive "scheme/content" model of language with one that makes *description* the arena of historical understanding and the object of critical attention. Specifically, Emerson performs the temporality or historicity of thinking by producing an analysis in which words cannot be counted on to retain fixed meanings from one usage to another. Emerson's prose interrogates the implications of textuality for historical knowing, the implications of *thinking* historically. Thoreau takes things one step further, enacting historicity in historical narrative itself. Thoreau interrogates the implications of textuality for the place of the self in the world, for *living* historically. In *A Week,* Thoreau alters conventional narrative to acknowledge both the temporality of his own writing and its "reality," by which I mean its internal coherence and its effective implications as a possible alternative way of ordering our own experience.

Thoreau's writing is in history because it enacts the temporality, which is to say the textuality, of the self in relation to its own history. It performs historical understanding as a thing always *being* written through time. Similarly, the experience it offers a reader is in history because rather than communicating information in a process modeled on the possession and transfer of a discrete object (knowledge), it provokes an ongoing and open-ended process of relationship, the "long familiarity" that "redeemed the time" in *A Week* and that is necessary to what Thoreau calls "right reading." In that activity, experience of an other becomes part of an always changing self by becoming part of the vocabulary with which each individual produces the accounts that are indistinguishable from his or her understanding of the world.

Like Emerson, scholars must find words with which to think about historical texts, words to characterize them and to articulate them with their own beliefs and interests, a process of descriptive "translation" that preserves, and even concentrates on, the particularity of individual forms of expression rather than reduces them to a common denominator or deep meaning. To say that a scholar's writing expresses an understanding of historical material is to say that it negotiates the differences between the text's language and its own. A scholar's implicit subject is the relationship between his or her own use of words and the usages in texts. The ability to recognize and respond to such differences is what we mean by *reading.* Not atomistic words, arbitrary and empty forms apart from world, a thing we would not even recognize as language, but world-making words, our unavoidable production of the coherence that we live with.[20] Detached from its aspirations to eternal, certifiable meaning, history becomes another field of conditional human actions, taking shape as history only in the stories that historians tell to satisfy the curiosities of their own time and place. The value of such historical accounts, like the value of Emerson's or Thoreau's, does not lie in their approximation to real historical fact, or in any claim to reveal, for the first time, the Truth about their subject. Their value lies, for the inquiring scholar, in their ability to satisfy the impulses and interests that inspired the study in the first place, and then for others, in their ability to offer new and revealing vocabularies for talking about their subjects.

I would argue that scholars create unnecessary chasms for themselves to leap when they tie texts to the particular historical ''moment'' of their production and thus overstate the ''other''-ness of the past. The relationship between historian and subject bridges no Cartesian chasm. It is not something that needs to be made and thus accounted for. It is an unavoidable linguistic relationship. The historian cannot stand apart from it any more than Emerson could detach himself from Transcendentalism, for there is no way to divide ourselves from the objects of our interest. Our interests inspire our studies in the first place. Our studies alter and expand our language and our language shapes our interests. So, we have a circle in which history and historian spin in mutual formation and transformation. There is no place to step outside to, no place to catch our breath or get our bearings. Our subjects shape the language with which we would describe them, at once changing the implications of that language and their own natures. As Thoreau makes clear, all texts are historical texts, but also present voices, and the assumption that older ones are necessarily more distant from us in anything but time overlooks the ways those texts teach us about the pastness of the present—our own practices—by instructing us in the persistent presentness of the past.

Using the conceptual tools at hand, Thoreau, like modern critics, tried to explain the continuing uses of the past. And like him, our interest is (or ought to be, if we want out of the cultural dustbin) the past in the present, the past that is present to us both as artifact and as life—something that has survived and something that continues to interest us. This strategy gives perspective on the present by defamiliarizing it, by translating present issues into a different context. At the same time, it connects us sympathetically to the past by recuperating its foreign vocabularies, applying them to descriptions of the present and so making them potentially useful tools for living with. Writing like Emerson's and Thoreau's may not help much in the quest for a coherent American literary tradition. It may not impart theoretical coherence to the disparate practices of nineteenth-century poetry and fiction by American writers. But it explores, as we continue to explore, consequences of losing foundational authority that, taken together, might be called the historicizing of discourse.

Seen in this way, Emerson and Thoreau were among the numerous participants, along with writers like Coleridge and Melville, Wordsworth and Nietzsche, in the change from a situation in which descriptions claimed to represent reality to one in which descriptions are the reality of human experience. As transitional from foundational to postfoundational culture, this nineteenth-century writing participated in a long process of which we are still part. We are still working within and working out its implications. And we are not, strictly speaking, further along some imaginary time line of progress than were Emerson or Thoreau. We are interested in what Emerson and Thoreau have to say about textuality and history because, by offering us new vocabularies for dealing with persistent problems, they are, in a sense, more advanced than we. They are our future, not our past.

IV

Amidst this rigorous acknowledgment of temporality, it is still both essential and inevitable that critical claims be assessed, though that assessment will not aim for validity. On one hand, the historicist recognition that literary judgments reflect values deeply embedded in social agreement rather than in incontrovertible inner inclinations or absolute truth certainly deprives literary judgments of their subjective immunity from question. It is no longer *de gustibus non est disputandum*. On the other hand, it is no more difficult or controversial to say that one book is better than another (for particular purposes) than to say that one basketball player is better than another. That is just to say that it *is* controversial and difficult (though not theoretically impossible), a matter of reasons, arguments, and justifications rather than either universal value or indisputable (but trivial and condemnable) tastes. If, in their teaching and writing, scholars chose works not *from* a canon (understood to mean something like "the best works") but *for* something more like a syllabus comprised of "works that suit current purposes," then they would not be impeded from using particular texts by doubts about their value ("professional status"), and such distinctions as they did make between texts would refer simply to the various uses to which those texts were being put. Apart from absolute standards, the value of texts is a matter of use. They are good in different ways for different things. Thus, it is insufficient merely to attack established literary judgment. Historicist criticism should also clarify the broader implications of trying to change those judgments.

Far from removing values from our choices, historicist criticism insists that we interrogate our values for their sources and implications, not as a preliminary step to discarding them but to assess which ones we need to retain and which we can afford to give up in the face of new and incompatible circumstances. Emerson's writing and Thoreau's engage the reader in a discourse the validity (or usefulness) of which is testable by its coherence and its articulation with experiences offered and embodied in other accounts. As Wittgenstein points out, "Nothing we do can be defended absolutely and finally. But only by reference to something else that is not questioned. I.e. no reason can be given why you should act (or should have acted) *like this,* except that by doing so you bring about such and such a situation, which again has to be an aim you *accept.*"[21] In the place of objective truth, historicist criticism offers ways of structuring life, possible orders that must be judged by existing desires and ideals for their usefulness in forwarding some essential aims without sacrificing too many others. It involves an endless, and circular, process of practical choices. *"A rule is amended,"* Nelson Goodman says, *"if it yields an inference we are unwilling to accept; an inference is rejected it if violates a rule we are unwilling to amend."*[22]

If truth and the good are historical, if the former is more like "justified belief" than like "unclouded perception of the world" and the latter more like "the useful" than like "divine decree," then proposed changes must serve our purposes without violating other crucial beliefs and practices. Our beliefs can be assessed (indeed, are continuously being assessed) for their own internal coherence, for their coherence with our other beliefs and aims, and for their capacity to make sense, *in terms we are willing to accept,* of their subject so as to enable us to go on in our inquiry.[23] That interrogation is no simple chore, however, since it requires us rigorously to ask ourselves what we really *need* to hold onto among our most cherished notions, notions that are so cherished that we are inclined to see them as intuitions, as natural, despite the difficulties our allegiance causes us. If one of the points of historicism for art is that there is no clinching argument, that there is only a series of arguments

making claims and counterclaims, that fact only emphasizes the importance of continuous and detailed discussion, a critical give-and-take in
which arguments are called upon to justify themselves.[24] Rather than a
New World consistent with our ethico-political ideals, such inquiries
may produce simply a new and revisionary description of the existing
one.

Reading could be described as entering a projected or alternative
world. But it could also be described as learning the grammar of what
amounts to a foreign language, and thus giving oneself new tools for
making sense of things. The patterns we see in the language we study are
not either independent objects or our own whimsical creations. They do
not wait for us in an objective world, nor do we narcissistically paint our
own self-portraits. They *are* real, nonetheless, in the only sense that
counts because we see, use, and understand them, just as we gladly take
paper dollars for coin of the realm. They slice experience into digestible
chunks, fitting and refitting it to our needs and us to our experience. Our
job is not to determine whether or not those chunks represent objective
reality with specifiable origins and traceable influences. Such relationships, as Emerson demonstrates, are metaphorical too and only lead us
on. Our job is to use them to make still more chunks.

This line of thinking brings us back to the desire for social change so
important to the revisionist impulse in literary studies. Can that desire be
consistent with historicist convictions? An implication of what I have
been saying is that although change occurs constantly, it is certainly not a
rapid process. "Change can occur," William Cain sensibly remarks,
"and it is our responsibility to strive for it, but it is a slow and steady
process and demands daily work" (p. xv). Yet, even Cain's responsible
position may be optimistic in its implication that we can control the
consequences of proposed reforms. Whatever changes do occur may not
follow reliably from particular programs. "Nor, it would seem, can the
new be consciously prepared," Fredric Jameson says, "any more than
those dissatisfied with the old paradigm can, by taking thought, simply
devise some new one out of whole cloth."[25] Change can, indeed, must
inevitably, occur, but it may have little to do with any guidance we may
try to give it. What we are slowly changing as we adapt our understandings (which is to say our critical accounts) to our historical circumstances
is the way we use words like *knowledge,* our understandings of what we
mean by acquiring it, and its relations not to some fixed collection of facts
but to ever-changing motives and practices. Those revisions also neces-

sarily revise, as I have been suggesting such changes must, surrounding related terms that collectively shape our understanding of reading and writing, of notions about the meaning and uses of history, of the self that writes and reads historically, and of the relationship between readers and historical texts. Those changes amount to steps in a very long process of accommodating our critical vocabularies to the consequences of being in history.

To commit oneself to historicist criticism is to invest in a process of inquiry and its consequences rather than a set of existing ideals. Rigorous inquiry of that kind is implicit in the coherence of exceptional texts. Their conflict between two potentials—the articulation of imagined conditions and the historical constraints imposed by working with existing language—enables them to change language (by using it to create a new context) and thus to change the potentials for understanding that shape the world. From this point of view there is no contradiction in imagining texts as ''interrogating'' culture from within because the inside/outside cultural model oversimplifies the problematic relationship between a text and the surrounding vocabularies from which it springs and diverges. Like Thoreau on the Concord and Merrimack rivers, texts can never free themselves from their cultural circumstances, but their explorations can reshape those surroundings by working out the implications of particular beliefs for the forms of life they might produce.[26] They can project possibilities for life even as they memorialize previous understandings by appropriating past rhetorical strategies.[27] Such possible descriptions are as formative of our understandings and thus our actions as are real experiences.

Emerson and Thoreau instruct us that there are no grounds for distinguishing between changing descriptions, changing beliefs, and changing the world, or as Emerson would have it, between metaphor and metaphysics, life and art.[28] If this is so, then what contemporary criticism *ought* to be doing with the help of work in a number of fields that unsettles our sense of a one-way relation between descriptions and the world is inventing a way of doing historical work, of making sense of past texts (and of the past) that will justify our interest in them by accounting for their current value. As texts work with their own conflicting intuitions, they are also articulating alternate paradigms for understanding in order to comprehend altered and altering conditions. To use them as an occasion for thematizing our own values is to oversimplify our understandings of the problem rather than ''fronting'' its complexity in an encounter with the complexity of the text. And simple understandings, I would propose, do not generate useful solutions. The particular future we seek will depend on our understanding of the present, which is to say that the solutions or social goals we choose to pursue will depend on the stories we tell about our current state of affairs.

Though the texts we choose to read will always and necessarily be part of our conversations (otherwise why would we choose them), we disarm them, defuse their transforming power, and prevent them from being genuine voices in that conversation when we insist that they conform to our professional categories or support our political views, especially when the texts in question put such categories and the conceptual and institutional structures they support on trial. Richard Rorty describes writing like Emerson's or Thoreau's as "the reverse of hermeneutics: the attempt to reinterpret our familiar surroundings in the unfamiliar terms of our new inventions."[29] This seems to me a good description of the posture criticism could take in "fronting" the facts of writing like Emerson's or Thoreau's. As George Steiner says of reading Heidegger, the reader has to "accept entry into an alternative order or space of meaning and being."[30] In this work, I have been arguing that criticism can bring the monuments of the past to bear on contemporary debates by treating them as participants in our conversations. But to do so, it needs to "front" the challenging complexity of their *intra*textuality *as well as* their *inter*textuality, so as to avoid merely self-delusively impressing them into our service.

This approach would value texts not as autonomous aesthetic objects but as brilliant attempts to frame new understandings out of old ones. Such attempts, insofar as they involve twisting existing terms into new and unfamiliar shapes, necessarily appear awkward, even to the writer who produced them. But Thoreau proposed that such experimentation, with all its imperfection, is the proper activity of writing. "A book should contain pure discoveries, glimpses of *Terra Firma,* though by ship-wrecked mariners" (p. 98). With Kuhn and Derrida, we might make problematic passages the focus of our inquiries. The question in reading authors of historical texts, as Rorty says, is "how to translate them without making them sound like fools."[31] If, in looking at prose like Emerson's, we were to ask how a brilliant and innovative (and even sensible) person could have meant such apparently absurd, or naive, or reactionary things, we would be challenging ourselves to question not only the text before us but the assumptions we bring to our reading of it.

To "front" the peculiarities of those texts, scholars must be willing to labor as Thoreau did through conflicts among our own immensely deeply rooted foundationalist intuitions and face up to our own dismay, in the absence of handy alternatives, at the inadequacy of our beliefs. Too often, the inherited impulse to scholarly mastery has led critics to apply hegemonic standards of judgment to texts that were trying to escape them, and reject the experimental *ad hoc-ness* essential to that escape. By insisting on familiar forms and reasoned arguments, criticism has forced Emerson and Thoreau onto just the ground they are most unwilling to occupy.[32] Plato defined the philosopher as one who could give reasons, and by that measure, as Part III showed, Emerson and Thoreau would happily exclude themselves from the philosophical pantheon. "Some minds," Thoreau said, "are as little logical or argumentative as nature; they can offer no reason or 'guess,' but they exhibit the solemn and incontrovertible fact" (p. 250). If we accept Sellars's view that to "know" is to place in a space of reasons, of justifying and being able to justify, then this is the sense in which Emerson and Thoreau step out of the "knowledge game" of traditional metaphysics and into "saying things." The style or textual form they developed was not a measure of their aesthetic or intellectual deficiencies; it reflected their recognition of the limitations of the atemporal claims in conventional argument.

Academics, on the other hand, dwell—will-they nil-they—in the space of reasons and face imposing problems as they try to produce historical narratives that acknowledge the descriptive complexity of exceptional texts.[33] How can we apply the lessons of Emerson's and Thoreau's writing about the relations of textuality and temporality, of descriptions and experience, to our own situations as producers of critical texts in history? On one hand, the history of American Literary Scholarship tells us that we cannot continue to waffle, that we must be rigorously historical, avoiding both the objective and the subjective sides of the traditional foundationalist debate. On the other hand, the examples of Emerson and Thoreau instruct us in the wisdom of directing our attention to the features of accounts—literary or critical—and insist that what we are trading in (in both senses of that phrase) are not so much idealist or realist *points of view,* as idealist or realist *descriptions*. In their place, we need to develop, as Thoreau does, coherent accounts that enact in ways appropriate to their genres, their own historicity.

In this light, I hope it is clear that my critique of new historicist revision in American Literary Scholarship is not so much a complaint about

theoretical assumptions as about the troubled accounts revisionists produce even as they try to adapt criticism to the requirements of historical
inquiry. While contextual criticism may disclose those elements of texts
that operate within the conventional terms and narrative methods of their
times, it consistently shortchanges the features of texts that interrogate
and complicate those terms and explore alternative ways of describing
and understanding experience. The language in which such conceptual
revision occurs contends by definition with the accepted concepts, the
forms of understanding, of its own time rather than simply illustrating or
exemplifying them. Exceptional texts are particularly interesting (exceptional) partly *because* they are more complex than surrounding ideological accounts, perform conflicts among them, and thus, at least sometimes, produce new narrative forms to negotiate the gaps between
conflicting ideological stories. This is a key to the connection between
what has been called (aesthetic) form and the particular stories that we
call ideology.[34] In this context, the problem with cultural criticism,
amidst contemporary interpretive doubts, is not that it effaces the
beauties of literature. It is that it gives us a ready-made security, one that
oversimplifies our readings and thus prevents us from learning something
really new from our study, something that could materially change not
just *what* we think but *how* we think.

Books that exceed our customary uses of language can teach us not just
new facts—something we did not already know—but new forms of life:
something we did not necessarily know we wanted or needed to know.
Emerson's and Thoreau's writings grope toward alternatives to the
established assumptions of their time and of ours. In this sense, reading
works like *A Week* or "The Transcendentalist" is an *education.* They do
not change the world. They are changes *in* the world that prompt change
in the reader who will "front" *as unfamiliar* the facts of the text.[35] As
readers of such works, our job is not to master their meaning. It is to
assimilate them, to learn their grammar, to get acquainted with them, as
one does with a new language, by trying it out until it flows trippingly
from the tongue so that it can become a productive part of our own
accounts. Whitman claimed we do not have much choice. "My words
itch at your ears," he said, "until you understand them."[36]

At the heart of my reading is the belief that the inquiry into issues that
are often called cultural carried on in a text like "The Transcendentalist"
or *A Week* is more complex, more problematized, and more self-critical
than any supplementary story I could have concocted out of selected

historical facts that I would, necessarily, be treating metaphorically as textual. Reading does not produce an experience *in* the reader, not in the sense of a merely subjective feeling, a vague affective stimulus. It is a highly complex engagement with an alternate world projected through extraordinarily complex linguistic relationships. Exceptional texts perform a grammar so complex and yet coherent that it likens to another world. Grounded, as it is, in a shared language, that world is not an idealist escape from the real one. Like Thoreau's narrative journey, it both diverges from and returns to it in ways that are particularly instructive and provoking. In this sense, exceptional texts can be seen not as mere "fictions" but as particularly complex descriptions of *our* world that are better in the sense that they are more complex and coherent versions of our own cultural accounts. This is the resonance for literary history of Thoreau's claim that "the truest life is when we are in dreams awake." We are "in dreams awake" when we are reading so as to "front" the facts of such texts. And those texts are valuable because they are "true accounts" of life—as it is lived and as it might be lived.[37] Yet, even if these texts are more complex than the accounts critics produce, my talk in this work about exceptional texts and the difficulty of accounting for them, and about the limitations of cultural accounts is not intended as a claim that such texts are somehow more complex than what we call culture itself. On the contrary, obviously, they are less so. In fact, the unspeakable complexity of culture is just the reason for examining accounts that claim to describe it with close attention and a healthy dose of skepticism.[38]

Criticism, like the texts it examines, is an experiment in redescribing the world, in adapting old terms to new conditions and altering both in the process. "The perceiving of what is known," Heidegger says, "is not a process of returning with one's booty to the 'cabinet' of consciousness."[39] It is the work of constantly changing and adapting our understandings and (which may be the same thing) our descriptions, to the new historical circumstances Thoreau called "novelties" and figured in the bends of the river. Thoreau so closely associated "labor" with both art and knowledge not because it takes effort to produce both but because both are themselves unceasing activities of working against the prevailing current rather than states of being or possessed essences. This is precisely why criticism might give up the effort to unlock the meaning of texts in order to contend with them, testing the critics' own values and ways of understanding against theirs. The resulting accounts may not transform the world, or even the world of criticism, from one day to the next, but in the context of our "bondage" within history and the immersion of all our practices in a social and linguistic web, the project of constructing radically new orders may itself be still another Romantic fantasy. Though it is tempting to think of social change as leading to utopia, that notion of utopia and change and society itself seems inconsistent with the historicity of discourse. Such aspirations are vestiges of the old opposition (preserved in the word *America* and the academic study that enshrined it) between real and ideal worlds of experience and so carry the seeds of the old defeats. As Thoreau says in full recognition of the unavoidable limits of daily life, "With our music we would fain challenge *transiently* another and finer sort of intercourse than our daily toil permits" (p. 381; my emphasis).

To be historicist in this sense is not to resign ourselves to political pacifism. On the contrary, to change our views is to change life *as we know it,* and this is precisely the province of those complex texts that exceed our relatively simple critical stories. The cultural work that texts do is often the slow and deliberate work of revising culture by revising our vocabularies, and thus our ways of thinking. They pursue this revision (as they necessarily must) from the inside, using and misusing culture's own tools as the only ones available, rather than trying hopelessly to journey outside of it, as to a New World. Writers of literary histories can abet that process by producing accounts that engage rather than edit the complexity of texts. In light of the 100-year history of literary studies, that too is a very long-term project, a goal toward which writers of historical accounts may labor, like Thoreau at his oars, by working their way backward into new territory.

Notes

Introduction

1. Perhaps it does not need saying that the idealist narrative strategies that have characterized the discourse about "America" alienate the justifying spirit of "America" from any particular acts. "America" is of good character, so its particular actions must be either good by definition or irrelevant. Only the motives behind them or the spirit in which they are carried out matter.

2. Stanley Cavell, *The Claim of Reason* (New York: Oxford University Press, 1979), p. 3.

3. There is nothing new about this exclusivity either. Richard Hofstadter quotes Charles Sumner, who accounts for the lack of popularity of the excellent historian Richard Hildreth by saying that "his unsympathizing account of the pilgrim Fathers has prevented his History from being as popular here as otherwise it might have been." *The Progressive Historians* (New York: Knopf, 1969), p. 22.

Part 1

1. Terry Eagleton, *Literary Theory: An Introduction* (Minneapolis: University of Minnesota Press, 1983), p. 198.

2. Stanley Fish, "Pragmatism and Literary Theory," *Critical Inquiry* 11 (March 1985): 433–58.

3. Ibid., p. 437.

4. Steven Mailloux, "Rhetorical Hermeneutics," *Critical Inquiry* 11 (June 1985): 621.

5. Richard Rorty, *Philosophy and the Mirror of Nature* (Princeton: Princeton University Press, 1979), p. 306.

6. For early invocations of the American Ideal, see Benjamin T. Spencer, *The Quest for Nationality* (Syracuse: Syracuse University Press, 1957), and Richard Ruland, *The Native Muse: Theories of American Literature*, Vol. 1 (New York: Dutton, 1972), For discussions of this notion as applied in academic study of

American literature, see Richard Ruland, *The Rediscovery of American Literature* (Cambridge: Harvard University Press, 1967), and "The Mission of an American Literary History," in *The American Identity,* ed. Rob Kroes (Amsterdam: American Institute of the University of Amsterdam, 1980), pp. 46–64; Michael Colacurcio, "Does American Literature Have a History?" *Early American Literature* 13 (1978): 110–31; and a series of essays by William Spengemann: "What Is American Literature?" *Centennial Review* 22 (1978): 119–38; "Puritan Influences in American Literature," *Early American Literature* 16 (1981): 175–86; "Three Blind Men and an Elephant: The Problem of Nineteenth-Century English," *New Literary History* 14 (1982–83): 155–73; "Discovering the Literature of British America," *Early American Literature* 18 (1983): 3–16; "The Earliest American Novel: Aphra Behn's *Oroonoko,*" *Nineteenth-Century Fiction* 38 (1984): 384–414; "American Writers and English Literature," *ELH* 52 (1985): 209–38; and "American Things/Literary Things: The Problem of American Literary History," *American Literature* 57 (October 1985): 456–81. Spengemann's essays have recently been collected in *A Mirror for Americanists: Reflections on the Idea of American Literature* (Hanover, N.H.: University Press of New England, 1989). For an extremely interesting analysis by a European scholar of the theoretical assumptions behind various approaches to American Literary Scholarship, see Winfried Fluck, "Theories of American Literature: Double Structures and Sources of Instability in American Literature," *Actas X Congreso Nacional, A. E. D. E. A. N.* (Zaragoza, 1988), pp. 115–36.

7. Leo Marx, "Thoughts on the Origin and Character of the American Studies Movement," *American Quarterly* 31, 2 (1979): 399–400.

8. Frank Lentricchia, "On the Ideologies of Poetic Modernism, 1890–1913: The Example of William James," in *Reconstructing American Literary History,* ed. Sacvan Bercovitch (Cambridge: Harvard University Press, 1986), p. 244.

9. Robert A. Ferguson, " 'We Hold These Truths': Strategies of Control in the Literature of the Founders," in *Reconstructing American Literary History,* pp. 1–28.

10. Myra Jehlen, "Introduction: Beyond Transcendence," in *Ideology and Classic American Literature,* ed. Sacvan Bercovitch and Myra Jehlen (Cambridge: Harvard University Press, 1986), p. 14. That Jehlen and others make such statements amidst critiques of the nationalist critical tradition only shows the centrality of these assumptions for American Literary Scholarship. Toril Moi argues the conservatism of Jehlen's feminist critique in *Sexual/Textual Politics: Feminist Literary Theory* (New York: Methuen, 1985), pp. 80–86.

11. Sacvan Bercovitch offered this term in "America as Canon and Context: Literary History in a Time of Dissensus," *American Literature* 58 (1986): 99–108. This now nearly ubiquitous portrait of the problems facing contemporary criticism is, as Dominick LaCapra observes, less a description than a way of making still more intransigent problems disappear. LaCapra's point is so relevant to the subject at hand, that I quote it at length.

The problem for the historian of criticism would seem obvious: how does one write a history of a radically heterogeneous and internally dialogized "object"? One way to simplify one's task is to simplify one's story. A traditional plot may serve here as it has served throughout Western history. The present "time of troubles" may be perceived as an aberrant, babble-like era of confusion—a time of transition from a purer past to a repurified future. [Such narratives share] not only a convenient reduction of the complexities of the current critical scene, but an avoidance of inquiry into the *sociocultural and political conditions that may actually be common to heterogeneous modes of criticism* [my emphasis]. (*History and Criticism* [Ithaca: Cornell University Press, 1985], p. 99)

For a critique of this term as essentially conservative, see Donald Pease, "New Americanists: Revisionist Interventions into the Canon," *boundary 2*, 17, 1 (Spring 1990): 20.

On the role of mythic narratives in legitimating social institutions, see Francois Lyotard, *The Postmodern Condition: A Report on Knowledge,* trans. Geoff Bennington and Brian Massumi (Minneapolis: University of Minnesota Press, 1984), especially pp. 18–20.

12. As the variety of opinion offered in the works of its proponents—scholars like Paul Lauter, Annette Kolodny, Emory Elliott, Myra Jehlen, Jane Tompkins, and Sacvan Bercovitch—makes clear, this New Orthodoxy is constituted not so much by programmatic agreement as by an implicit loyalty to the disciplinary assumptions that define professional scholars of American literature. See Paul Lauter, ed., *Reconstructing American Literature: Courses, Syllabi, Issues* (Old Westbury, N.Y.: Feminist Press, 1983); Annette Kolodny, "The Integrity of Memory: Creating a New Literary History of the United States," *American Literature* 57, 2 (May 1985): 291–307; Emory Elliott, "New Literary History: Past and Present," *American Literature* 57, 4 (December 1985): 611–21; Sacvan Bercovitch, "America as Canon and Context" and "The Problem of Ideology in American Literary History," *Critical Inquiry* 12 (Summer 1986): 631–53; Bercovitch and Jehlen, *Ideology and Classic American Literature;* Jane Tompkins, *Sensational Designs: The Cultural Work of American Fiction, 1790–1860* (New York: Oxford University Press, 1985).

13. Work in this area is proliferating faster than bibliography can record. What might be called the early volleys in the debate can be seen in the works by Mailloux and Fish cited above and in such works as Steven Knapp and Walter Michaels, "Against Theory," *Critical Inquiry* 8 (Summer 1982): 732–42; the series of articles in *Critical Inquiry* 9 by E. D. Hirsch, Jr., Mailloux, Adena Rosmarin, and Knapp and Michaels; Richard Rorty, *Consequences of Pragmatism: Essays, 1972–1980* (Minneapolis: University of Minnesota, 1982), particularly "Philosophy as a Kind of Writing," and "Nineteenth-Century Idealism and Twentieth-Century Textualism"; and William Cain, *The Crisis in Criticism: Theory, Literature, and Reform in English Studies* (Baltimore: Johns Hopkins University Press, 1984).

14. On the tendency of marginalized intellectual groups to produce self-justifying idealist ideologies, see Antonio Gramsci, *The Prison Notebooks*, ed. Q. Hoare and G. Nowell-Smith (London: International Publishing Co., 1971). And on the complicity of academics in their own marginalization, see Gerald Graff, *Literature Against Itself: Literary Ideas in Modern Society* (Chicago: University of Chicago Press, 1979), pp. 28–29.

15. Nor is the effort to point out a new direction for American literary studies governed by exclusively intellectual considerations. Academic producers and products are as much subject to market conditions as any other. Like professionals in other fields, they must shape their work to fit professionally prescribed criteria. Despite their recommendations for changes in American Literary Scholarship (and in fact, the most of it amounts to little more than still another round in the almost continous expansion of the canon that has characterized American literary history from the first), Americanists simply cannot afford to let go of the established faith that, regardless of current confusion, criticism can produce a "coherent and integrated story about our literary past." Even the work of revision is supported (or, in the case of the new American literary histories, made possible) by publishers whose commitment to intellectual exploration must necessarily vie with their commercial interest in supplying what an audience already knows it wants. It should not be surprising, therefore, that, amidst all its prescriptions for the ills of the field, the New Orthodoxy leaves the enabling project of American Literary Scholarship inviolate.

16. See Spengemann, *Mirror*.

17. Tompkins, *Sensational Designs*, p. xi. Subsequent page citations to this work in the text appear in parentheses.

18. The history of the American Studies movement, which was quickly absorbed, in its essentials, by the more established field of American literary studies, provides a useful analog that illustrates just how central the motives and strategies espoused by revisionist critics have been for earlier Americanists. Gene Wise points out that, like the New Historicist critics, the founders of the American Studies movement viewed themselves as having been "left out" by the traditional English and History departments and seemed to enjoy their "embattled" status *vis-à-vis* "entrenched" forces. "'Paradigm Dramas' in American Studies: A Cultural and Institutional History of the Movement," *American Quarterly* 31, 2 (1979): 292. In "Thoughts on the Origin and Character of the American Studies Movement," Marx asserts that American Studies was founded in part to allow entry into the profession of excluded minorities, but complains that it has not fulfilled this aim. And S. Barlis associates American Studies with a Whitmanian impulse to be "always beginning" and "excluding nothing" (quoted in Wise, "Paradigm Dramas," p. 293). Like the current revisionism, American Studies, too, was introduced as an alternative to New Critical work by scholars who felt that the New Criticism left out too much of life (Wise,

"Paradigm Dramas," p. 292). American Studies shares a number of significant features with the revisionist cultural criticism, including its moralism, its desire to expand the canon, its opposition to formalist aesthetics, and its interest in the "representative" features of culture. Motivated by social and professional aims very much like those of the New Historicist critics, it sought to make literary criticism ethical and to overcome its isolation from the culture at large (Marx, "Thoughts on the Origins," p. 399; Wise, "Paradigm Dramas," p. 293). Revisionist forces within American literary studies have, so far, taken advantage of historicist trend in theoretical discourse to give new force to those established critical aims. They have extended the tradition rather than dissented from it. The instruments have changed, but they are playing a familiar tune.

19. Following Harold Bloom, Kolodny points out that "most of us are so much *inside of* or *held by* well established categories of thought" that "only enormous effort can make us aware of how reluctant we are to know our incarceration" ("Integrity of Memory," p. 295). Subsequent page citations to this work in the text appear in parentheses. In the context of Kolodny's hopes for a radically new criticism, this imprisonment metaphor appeals as much by its optimism as by its drama. The notion of prison has no meaning apart from the possibility of freedom. If you are in prison, you can get out. Though our tastes limit us, this view promises, they are themselves limited and artifical. But this model seems to me self-deceptive. What Bloom describes as imprisonment is an inevitable fact of life, a simple condition of being in history. While some particular "prisons" may indeed be preferred to others, the inmates do not necessarily get to choose, and if they *could,* the choice ought to be based on a practical weighing of particular advantages and disadvantages rather than a specious distinction between slavery and freedom.

20. Kolodny, "Integrity of Memory," p. 293. The ethical stance at the moment is the one Bercovitch assumes for the contributors to his proposed *Cambridge History:* suspicious of certainties, tolerant of dissent, skeptical of the "formulae." Of course, this is itself a powerful formula. Bercovitch's description is indistinguishable, so far as that goes, from scholarly ideals at any time in this century. It would be hard to imagine Spiller, for example, bragging that his contributors were remarkable for their mediocrity, adherence to critical dogma, and closed-mindedness.

21. J. Hector St. John de Crèvecoeur, *Letters from an American Farmer* (London: Thomas Davies, 1782; reprint, New York: Dutton, 1957), p. 41.

22. Her myth of the origins of the "new historical criticism" in sixties radicalism distorts both the history of American Literary Scholarship and the genesis of the New Historicist criticism. In the first case, Kolodny ignores the extent to which, as Gerald Graff points out (*Professing Literature: An Institutional History* [Chicago: University of Chicago Press, 1987], p. 13), the *whole project* of American literary studies is relatively "new," the allegedly "stan-

dard'' canon is not and never has been fixed but has been repeatedly revised over the past 100 years. And by characterizing American literary studies as the ''concepts with which we confidently taught American literature twenty years ago'' (p. 300), she erects a straw man to be knocked down by her critique. American literary studies has never been so monolithic and ''confident'' as she suggests. Always aware of its status as a ''minority report'' within English departments, American Literary Scholarship has been obsessively self-conscious and self-critical about its project. And as I suggest in my discussion of American Studies, the theoretical impulse to reform that Kolodny links to the ''spirit'' of the sixties is rooted at least two decades deeper in American Literary Scholarship. The work of Continental theorists actually made its way into American critical practice through the internationalist interests of New Critics and Comparatist scholars of the 1940s.

23. Tompkins, *Sensational Designs,* p. 127. Tompkins's critique of the tradition often sounds like a conspiracy theory. ''It is hard to overestimate the importance of Hawthorne's connections,'' she asserts. To weave her historicist theory into this programmatic attack on the canon via Hawthorne, Tompkins waffles back and forth between the wrongheaded but pointed political assertion that Hawthorne's reputation derived from his connections, and the defensible but flat assertion that becoming and remaining famous is, in part, a matter of luck— between, that is, a historicist denial of absolute grounds for our choices and a rejection of those choices themselves. As Tompkins would have it, failure to single Hawthorne out shows his lack of value, recognition shows his ''connections,'' and prolonged reputation shows the power of institutionalized assumptions (*Sensational Designs,* pp. 27–28). Hawthorne can't win.

24. For a more balanced but no less politically critical reading, see James Cox, *Nineteenth-Century Fiction* 38, 4 (March 1984): 444–66. Cox argues, like Tompkins, for the effect of the novel and shares, in less polemical terms, her feelings about standards of ''imaginative literature.'' But he firmly fixes the novel in its cultural and literary circumstances, explains its impact and its demise, and, most important, offers a persuasive and detailed account that explains why the novel is worth reading even for those who do not share a particular political view.

25 For a useful alternative from a feminist perspective to Tompkins's feminist critique of New Criticism, see Joan E. Hartman, ''Reflections on 'The Philosophical Bases of Feminist Literary Criticism,' '' *New Literary History* 19, 1 (1988): 105–16.

26. Henry David Thoreau, *A Week on the Concord and Merrimack Rivers,* ed. Carl F. Hovde et al. (Princeton: Princeton University Press, 1980), p. 79.

27. To distinguish themselves from this tradition, Kolodny and Tompkins distort it. For example, the problem of explaining the ''representativeness'' of American literature that revisionists describe as the discovery of a modern criticism more alert than earlier scholarship to social injustice has been a key issue

in the 200-year-old conversation about American writing. What the New Orthodoxy describes as consensus was actually a heated, if decorous, debate between
competing strategies for making this connection. Aesthetic formalism was
adopted, in part, as one such strategy, designed to correct deficiencies in existing
critical practice. One of the reasons the previous generation of American scholars
introduced formalist concerns into the discussion of American writing was their
recognition that the cultural bias pervading American literary studies in the
twenties and thirties would make literature representative by making it redundant,
one more item in the catalog of cultural artifacts.

28. This demand for coherence has moved some revisionists toward an
alternate version of ideology that abandons conflict for mediation. *This* ideology
is inclusive rather than divisive. It encompasses all of the vast web of values and
assumptions that constitute culture. In Sacvan Bercovitch's terms, it "enact[s]
the purposes of a society in its totality." Compelling as this all-embracing
ideology sounds, it begs all the questions that inspired revision in American
literary studies in the first place. Like the "myth" criticism of the sixties, it is a
stand-in for the "National Spirit" of nineteenth-century criticism. It tames the
complex *diversity* of texts by tying them to the complex *unity* of the surrounding
culture rather than to the motives of a dominant social group. For many revisionist
critics of American literature, ideology is the "Holy Ghost" that unites the
cultural "Father" to the textual "Son." Even as proponents of the New
Orthodoxy deny that they want to mean by *America* anything so simplistic or
naive as an idealized national identity, they go on treating their ideologically
saturated "America" in the same old way, assuming, as Americanists have
always assumed, that whatever innovations appeared during the turmoil of the
mid-nineteenth century (or the revolution, or the Puritan migration) they were
somehow "American." See Bercovitch, "The Problems of Ideology," pp. 642–
43. Any brief excerpt, such as this one, does an injustice to the sophistication and
complexity of Bercovitch's rhetoric, which responds more fully than I can
describe here to the limitations on the American Ideal raised by both theory and
his own knowledge, both vast and intimate, of the literature. His rhetorical
sophistication, however, does not alter the fact that to justify his project at all,
Bercovitch must repeatedly return to reiterations of the American Ideal that
contradict dissenting voices. The familiar terms of these discussions illustrate the
continuing involvement of the New Orthodoxy in the mission that has characterized American literary studies from the first: the effort to reveal what is *truly*
American in American writing.

29. This critique should not be misconstrued as an attack either on feminist
criticism *per se* or on the possibility of change. Feminist criticism is to be praised
for helping (abetted by professional hard times) to break up what had become a
professional logjam. But when it tries to be programmatic about American
Literary Scholarship, it inadvertently extends the system it is attacking. Its

allegiance to the idealist assumptions of American Literary Scholarship substitutes for the overall theoretical justification of feminist programs that critics like Elaine Showalter and Barbara Hernnstein Smith have lamented the lack of. It gives them a way of gathering texts together in bundles that extends beyond gender and is more uniformly respectable in the profession.

30. Fish, "Pragmatism," p. 441. Subsequent page references to this work in the text appear in parentheses.

31. Rorty, *Philosophy*, p. 284.

32. On the idealist tradition in nineteenth-century literary attitudes, see Ann Douglas, *The Feminization of American Culture* (New York: Knopf, 1977), especially p. 419, n11. Eagleton discusses this tradition in more international terms in *Literary Theory*, pp. 27–28. The introduction of literary studies into the academy is surveyed in Lionel Gossman, "Literature and Education," *New Literary History* 13 (1982): 341–71.

33. Ludwig Wittgenstein, *Culture and Value*, ed. G. H. Von Wright in collaboration with Heikki Nyman, trans. Peter Winch (Chicago: University of Chicago Press, 1980), p. 83e.

34. One cannot avoid the feeling that for some revisionist scholars, the appeal of historicism is less a matter of methodology than polemical strategy. Tompkins, for example, changes sides in the foundationalist debate as her argument requires. Interpretive strategies that she wants to displace she describes as "prejudices" (subjective); those she favors are described as "historical" (hence concrete or "real").

35. I do not mean the need to make large claims. Greater timidity is not a crying need in scholarship. I mean the need to make claims that are incoherent or fly in the face of evidence.

36. Philip Fisher, *Hard Facts: Setting and Form in the American Novel* (New York: Oxford University Press, 1985).

37. Fisher talks about "culture" much as Goddard talks about "history" (see Part 2). It is an active agent busily shaping history in much the way he claims texts also do. "Within the present," Fisher says, "culture stabilizes and incorporates nearly ungraspable and widely various . . . experience. It changes again and again what the census of the human world looks like" (ibid., p. 3).

38. Cain says of Lentricchia, but I say of ideological historicists, that their position "is founded less on logic and reasoned exposition than on a desire for a certain, preferred state of affairs." Cain, *Crisis in Criticism*, p. 224.

39. Walter Benn Michaels, *The Gold Standard and the Logic of Naturalism* (Berkeley: University of California Press, 1987), p. 14, n16. See also p. 240. Subsequent page references to this work in the text appear in parentheses.

40. Brook Thomas, "Review of *The Gold Standard*," *American Literature* 60, 2 (May 1988): 301. Thomas has expressed reservations about the totalizing effect of Michaels's use of "the logic" of naturalism or of capitalism, and I want

to carry his questions further. Thomas suggests that Michaels might better have acknowledged the "differences within history" by describing "competing logics" (p. 302). This recommendation, sensible, even modest, as it is, over-looks Michaels's strategic use for his formulation. Michaels uses "logic" as he does other totalizing concepts to help him overcome the epistemological gap between subject and object that has mired criticism in fruitless disputes about the location of meaning. To take Thomas's critique one step further, I would say that capitalism does not have *a* logic, or even competing logics. *Texts* may, but capitalism does not. Similarly, the appeal to a cultural "moment," apart from simply being too exclusive—as Michaels applies it to American phenomena while ignoring concurrent voices in the larger Euro/American context—also disguises a textual account as objective history, a definable place in time. "A certain moment," we might ask after Thoreau, "how broad a line is that?"

41. Fredric Jameson, *The Prison-House of Language: A Critical Account of Structuralism and Russian Formalism* (Princeton: Princeton University Press, 1972), pp. 213–14.

42. I am not, of course, criticizing Michaels for making metaphorical connections. That may be the only kind available to us. But if so, that fact confronts us with the task of testing the particular metaphors we use for their aptness as organizing figures for the particulars to which we apply them.

43. This point applies as well to the "risk" Michaels claims Lily takes in considering attaching herself to Selden. This is what Michaels characterizes as a "love of risk": "She leaned on him for a moment, as if with a drop of tired wings: he felt as though her heart were beating rather with the stress of a long flight than the thrill of new distances." Their momentary union seems less the "height" of "erotic excitement" that Michaels asserts to support his model of "risk" than a passive and gentle capitulation in inexorable natural forces, those "influences of the hour" that "drew them to each other as the loosened leaves were drawn to the earth." Edith Wharton, *The House of Mirth,* ed. Cynthia Griffin Wolff (New York: Viking Penguin, 1985), p. 73. And indeed, the very first intrusion of the real world, a passing autobus, reminds Lily of the risk to her prospects of merely being there with Selden, and her *fear of that risk* brings her, and Selden with her, back to earth and their habitual mutual misunderstanding, "their flight over." Subsequent page references to this edition in the text appear in parentheses.

44. For a parallel argument, see Steven Mailloux, "Truth or Consequences: On Being Against Theory," *Critical Inquiry* 9, 4 (1983): 760–66.

45. Critiques of the New Historicism have come from all sides. Some, like Lee Patterson in *Negotiating the Past: The Historical Understanding of Medieval Literature* (Madison: University of Wisconsin Press, 1987), seem to complain about New Historicist political quietism. Yet Patterson's own critique has not escaped either what amounts to political sentimentalism embodied in the conviction that criticism must affirm current political values or the foundational

assumptions that have divided word from thing, literature from life. Patterson clings to the distinction between subject and object because he conflates the idea of the "subject" with that of the "individual." Unwilling to give up the latter, he has to defend the former. One crucial consequence of this decision is an ambivalent oscillation between a methodological commitment to textualism and a philosophical attachment to "historical reality" as "object." For a view of the New Historicism similar to my own in its skepticism about political claims, see Edward Pechter, "The New Historicism and Its Discontents: Politicizing Renaissance Drama," *PMLA* 102, 3 (1987): 292–303.

46. In this context, however, "world" should not be mistaken for some concrete *ding-an-sich* at which all descriptions ideally aim. The world to which texts might be connected is simply that reality about which there is general agreement, the collection of noncontroversial descriptions that enable us to live together.

47. In its (quite justified) attempt to remember the historicity of its subject and its own interpretations, it is important that criticism avoid confusing temporal coincidence—the fact that disparate events happened at around the same time— with the idea of a coherent historical moment, and therefore investing it with too much explanatory force. Our attraction to such explanations identifies once again the seductive link between contextualism and an idealized or Platonist notion of a full or essential meaning that permeates and joins particular appearances. As Paul Armstrong has pointed out, we do not escape "epistemological" problems by appealing to history. Though I don't share his allegiance to the term *epistemology*, I believe he's right in declaring that historicist programs that try to connect texts to contexts end up making questionable claims. This does not mean we should stop trying, but it may caution us against building elaborate programs on this shaky ground.

48. Bercovitch, *Reconstructing American Literary History*, p. viii.

49. Bercovitch, "The Problem of Ideology," p. 647.

50. If, in their teaching and writing, scholars chose works not *from* a canon (understood to mean something like "the best works") but *for* something more like a syllabus comprising "works that suit current purposes," then they would not be impeded from using particular texts by doubts about their value (status), and such distinctions as they did make between texts would refer simply to the various uses to which those texts were being put. The value, such as it is, of texts is a matter of the uses to which they are fruitfully put. They are good in different ways for different things.

51. David McLellan, *Ideology* (Minneapolis: University of Minnesota Press, 1986), p. 59.

52. I do not see losing sight of that fact as an invitation to the imposition of power but as a lost opportunity to shape our projects according to our needs.

Part 2

1. Jay Hubbell writes:

It had been resolved unanimously that we must and would have a national literature. England, France, Spain, Italy, each already had one. Germany was getting one as fast as possible, and Ireland vowed that she once had one far surpassing them all. To be respectable, we must have one also, and that speedily. . . . Surely never was a young nation setting forth jauntily to seek its fortune so dumbfounded as Brother Jonathan when John Bull cried gruffly from the roadside, "Stand and deliver a national literature!" After fumbling in his pockets, he was obliged to confess that he hadn't one about him at the moment, but vowed he had left a first-rate one at home which he would have fetched along—only it was so everlasting heavy. (*Who Are the Major American Writers? A Study of the Changing Literary Canon* [Durham: Duke University Press, 1972], p. 5)

2. Richard Ruland, *The Native Muse: Theories of American Literature* (New York: Dutton, 1972), p. 146.

3. See Michael Colacurcio, "Does American Literature Have a History?" *Early American Literature* 13, 1 (1978): 110–22. For an explanation of the critical preference for the Puritans over the Southern colonies as founders of the American Ideal, see W. F. Craven, *The Legend of the Founding Fathers* (New York: NYU Press, 1956), p. 5. *Transcendent Reason* (Tallahassee: Florida State University Press, 1982) records my own earlier ambivalent adherence to this model.

4. In the context of nineteenth-century efforts to discover national origins, American scholars were at a disadvantage. To adapt the established scholarly project to their own national conditions, would-be Americanists had to discover an American historical origin of their own. In practice, they discovered two: Puritanism as a cultural origin, and Transcendentalism as a literary one. See H. M. Jones, *The Theory of American Literature* (Ithaca: Cornell University Press, 1948), p. 94.

5. For an interesting discussion of Lincoln's use of Christian idealism in a rhetoric of national unity, see Gary Wills, *Inventing America: Jefferson's Declaration of Independence* (New York: Vintage, 1978), pp. xiv–xxii.

6. One of the oddities of Transcendentalist criticism has been that some of the most instructive observations about Transcendentalism have come from its opponents—Francis Bowen, or Andrews Norton, or Paul Elmer Moore, or Yvor Winters—who, disapproving of it, had no need to make it acceptable and so could content themselves with describing its various conflicting forms.

7. Richard Rorty, *Philosophy and the Mirror of Nature* (Princeton: Princeton University Press, 1979), p. 34. Among the recent works that have begun to provide histories of the profession are, William Cain, *Crisis in Criticism: Theory, Literature, and Reform in English Studies* (Baltimore: Johns Hopkins University

Press, 1984); Gerald Graff, *Professing Literature: An Institutional History* (Chicago: University of Chicago Press, 1987); Kermit Vanderbilt, *American Literature and the Academy* (Philadelphia: University of Pennsylvania Press, 1986).

8. O. B. Frothingham, *Transcendentalism in New England*, ed. Sydney Ahlstrom (1876; reprint, Philadelphia: University of Pennsylvania Press, 1959). Subsequent page citations to this work in the text appear in parentheses.

9. Frothingham's work shows, among other things, how easy it is to turn Emerson to conservative social purposes, especially if one ignores his texts in favor of his "thought." By 1876, what Frothingham called the "spiritual philosophy" was no longer a dangerous new entry into the cultural debate about social and religious authority. It had been appropriated to shore up established orders by plugging weak spots—principally the poverty of a spirituality predicated on Scottish Common Sense moralism and the loss of personal spiritual authority—that had been apparent earlier and had in effect given impetus to alternative models of faith from Dunkers and Comeouters to evangelists like Charles Grandison Finney. For an account of the limitations of established theological positions in the early nineteenth century that inspired writers like Emerson, see my *Transcendent Reason*, Chap. 1.

10. For the best discussions of distinctions among the factions that collectively constituted Orthodoxy, see Sydney E. Ahlstrom, *A Religious History of the American People* (New Haven: Yale University Press, 1972), and "Theology in America: An Historical Survey," in *Religion in American Life*, 3 vols., ed. James W. Smith and A. Leland Jamison (Princeton: Princeton University Press, 1961), 1:232–322; and not to be missed, Frank H. Foster, *A Genetic History of New England Theology* (New York: Russel & Russel, 1907).

11. H. C. Goddard, *Studies in New England Transcendentalism* (New York: Columbia University Press, 1908). Subsequent page citations to this work in the text appear in parentheses.

12. Vanderbilt, *American Literature and the Academy*, p. 150.

13. For less substantial early academic efforts to describe Transcendentalism, see Walter L. Leighton, "French Philosophers and New England Transcendentalism" (Ph. D. diss., University of Virginia, 1908; New York: Greenwood Press, 1968), and Henry David Gray, "Emerson: A Statement of New England Transcendentalism as Expressed in the Philosophy of its Chief Exponent" (Ph. D. diss. Columbia University; New York: Frederick Ungar, 1917).

14. Charles A. Beard summarizes the implications of scientific history in "That Noble Dream," *American Historical Review* 41 (October 1935): 74–87.

Scholarly agreement is both Goddard's foundation and his aim, so it is not surprising that even his own dissenting voices are banished into the footnotes, which might be described as the subconscious of Goddard's work, the place where both his sources and his unacknowledged conflicts reside. It is there that we learn that even the Transcendentalists themselves used the word *Transcendentalism* in the popular sense that Goddard says is responsible for their low esteem. It is also there that he reveals that the choices for the scope of his project that had supposedly been "imposed" from without by "common consent" were actually a product of his own interpretations. Thoreau, Goddard tells us in small print, is not included, although "the passing of time" has placed him second only to Emerson among the Transcendentalists. Goddard rationalizes this by appealing both to his own scholarly focus on "sources" (Thoreau was too young to be in at the start) and, where that argument does not work, to the obviousness of Thoreau's relation to the issues he will discuss. This latter explanation is particularly odd since it is presumably just such clarity that accounts for the consensus that, according to Goddard, dictates the inclusion of Emerson, Alcott, Parker, and Fuller.

15. On the limitations of German philology as a model for American historical scholarship, see W. Stull Holt, *Historical Scholarship in the United States* (Seattle: University of Washington Press, 1967), pp. 19–20. A. N. Applebee says that "the prestige of philology served to justify English studies without necessarily limiting them" (quoted in Graff, *Professing Literature,* p. 56). Goddard's appeal to scholarship is vitiated by the same bias against abstruse metaphysics that moved Frothingham to distinguish the genteel culture of America from European formalism. This bias survives in Goddard's writing as an incongruous intellectual's anti-intellectualism, a dismissive taking-for-granted of learning. An understanding of Transcendentalism, he allows, requires that the student must have "sojourned for a time in the kingdoms" of Kant, have "at least a bowing acquaintance with the formidable inhabitants of these realms (*Studies in New England Transcendentalism,* pp. 1–2). This modest depreciation of his own scholarly expertise also serves, of course, to distinguish him from the masses. But it makes it clear that even scholarly Americans were still as ambivalent about technical metaphysics in 1908 as they had been in 1876 or, for that matter, in 1836, a reluctant erudition that complicates the place of the scholar in American society. Scholarship was applied by writers like Goddard as a tool for confirming received truth, and was not permitted to delve so deeply into things as to leave common understandings behind.

16. Van Wyck Brooks, "America's Coming of Age," in *America's Coming of Age* (1916; reprint, Garden City, N.Y.: Doubleday, 1958). Subsequent page citations to this work in the text appear in parentheses. On the development and lingering influence of what Santayana called the "Genteel Tradition," see John Tomsich, *A Genteel Endeavor: American Culture and Politics in the Gilded Age* (Stanford: Stanford University Press, 1971); Werner Berthoff, *The Ferment of Realism* (Cambridge: Cambridge University Press, 1965); Henry F. May, *The*

End of American Innocence: A Study of the First Years of Our Own Time. 1912–1917 (New York: Knopf, 1959); and Graff, *Professing Literature,* especially chap. 2.

17. For an evenhanded discussion of Sherman, More, and Babbitt, see Richard Ruland, *The Rediscovery of American Literature* (Cambridge: Harvard University Press, 1967), pp. 15–90.

18. For Brooks's protest against the criticism of his day, see Vanderbilt, *American Literature and the Academy,* pp. 197–201. Vanderbilt describes "America's Coming of Age" as the *Democratic Vistas* of its time. My argument is that Brooks's rhetoric is, finally, not all that different from the *Democratic Vistas* of Whitman's time, and that the similarity reflects the constraints on any attempt to tell the sort of story about America that Brooks finally embraces.

19. Brooks, "America's Coming of Age," p. 44. Brooks cannot too often identify Emerson as the son of a culture that never escaped the abstraction from life typical of the "calvinist temper." Emerson is the model of all "highbrows," imcapable of personal relations, caring little for "experience or emotions, possessing so little himself," and fleeing from particular facts to the "refuge" of "capital letters." In part, this portrait simply appropriates the old complaint about Transcendentalist aloofness from the world that Transcendentalist sympathizers had been arguing against from 1840 on. But Brooks is upset not so much because Transcendentalism is too "metaphysical," by which early critics meant unintelligible. He is complaining that Emerson is not sensual enough, not planted firmly enough in the common American soil. "He never lingers in the bodily world, he is always busy to be off again; and if he takes two or three paces on the earth they only serve to warm him for a fresh aerial adventure" (p. 41).

Paradoxically, however, the prototypical American "highbrow" is also the father of all "lowbrows." This paradox seems no paradox to Brooks because he sees "Idealism" at the source of both and abstraction from life as their common end. The key to aligning these commonly opposed terms is a blurring of the boundary between spirit and life that troubled earlier writers. Later critics would find the essence of American writing in its portrayal of the clash between the heroic individual and repressive society. But for Brooks, "individualism" joins the spiritual and material lives on the ground of personal ambition. Emerson's idealism, Brooks argues was "double-edged"; it was concerned not merely with the spiritual life of the individual, but also with "the individual in society" (p. 42). "For if the logical result of a thorough-going, self-reliant individualism in the world of the spirit is to become a saint, it is no less true that the logical result of a thorough-going, self-reliant individualism in the world of the flesh is to become a millionaire" (p. 43).

20. Peter Uwe Hohendahl describes the consequences of idealist oppositions for early twentieth-century criticism. "The relationship between the literary and the political public sphere was severed by the middle-class public as it set itself

apart more distinctly from the masses. The educated elite withdrew to a 'sacral' reception of art which sought to shelter the work of art from a vulgarized world of reality in order to preserve the human potentials which though repressed by society, were preserved in the work.'' *The Institution of Criticism* (Ithaca: Cornell University Press, 1982), p. 73. Though Hohendahl's terms are nearly as stark as Brooks's, it is clear that Brooks's split between "high" and "low" pushes him into the frankly idealist view of literature with which he concludes.

21. Brooks, "America's Coming of Age," p. 86. Americans, particularly American intellectuals, have been looking for a national savior longer than the nation has existed. In 1839, for example, in reaction to the radical new philosophies invading New England from Europe, the three leading lights of the Princeton Theological Seminary complained that "it might have been better for us if the proposal for change had come *ab intra,* if one of our own productive minds had been led to forsake the beaten track and point out a higher path." J. W. Alexander, Albert Dod, and Charles Hodge, "Transcendentalism of the Germans and of Cousin and Its Influence on Opinion in This Country," *Biblical Repertory and Princeton Review,* January 1839.

22. It is of more than passing interest that Brooks elides the divisions within American values with the difference between the sexes. That parallel distinction was, of course, pervasive in nineteenth-century writing. Alan Trachtenburg quotes Horace Bushnell, for example, as distinguishing between the "beauty principle" in women and the "force principle" in men in *The Incorporation of America: Culture and Society in the Gilded Age* (New York: Hill & Wang, 1982), p. 145. By associating learning with women, Brooks figures his own feelings of its emasculation as a cultural force.

23. Lewis Mumford, *The Golden Day* (New York: Dover, 1926), p. 140. Subsequent page citations to this work in the text appear in parentheses.

24. Vernon L. Parrington, *Main Currents in American Thought,* 3 vols. (New York: Harcourt, Brace, 1927–1930). Subsequent page citations to this work in the text appear in parentheses. Earlier scholars had looked at things more narrowly. Barrett Wendell's *A Literary History of America* (1900) was really, as Richard Ruland has remarked, little more than a history of writing at Harvard. Tyler's work was a model of nineteenth-century scholarship but did not include the whole scope of American culture, as Parrington tried to do. For the response of Parrington's contemporaries to *Main Currents* see Richard Hofstadter, *The Progressive Historians* (New York: Knopf, 1969), pp. 484–85. See also the interesting review by Charles A. Beard, "Fresh Air in American Letters," *The Nation* 124 (18 May 1927): 560, for a characterization of Parrington's work that fits it neatly into the values associated with the American Ideal. Parrington complained that earlier critics had "an exaggerated regard for esthetic values. Our literary historians have labored under too heavy a handicap of the genteel tradition. . . . They have sought daintier fare than polemics" vol. 1: vi).

Hofstadter discusses the relationship between Parrington's ethics and his methodology in *The Progressive Historians,* pp. 398–99. And for a detailed discussion of Parrington's method, see H. Lark Hall, "Vernon Louis Parrington: The Genesis and Design of *Main Currents in American Thought*" (Ph. D. diss., Case Western Reserve, 1979), especially chap. 3.

25. This quotation from Parrington's review of Waldo Frank's *The Rediscovery of America,* published in the month of Parrington's death, is quoted in Hall, "Vernon Louis Parrington," p. 178.

26. As should become increasingly clear, I see this as the formula for success in American Literary Scholarship. Works that have translated the American Ideal into a vocabulary coming into critical dominance, especially when ballasted by heavy scholarship, have dominated the field. Parrington, Matthiessen, Miller, and Bercovitch could all be described in these terms.

27. That Parrington's elision of real and ideal has become such a powerful tool in subsequent scholarship speaks to the force of the drive for cultural coherence and the power of what is still an essentially spiritual model as a tool for achieving it.

28. From the perspective Parrington provides, we can see the move to formalism that has been so much lamented (and to which, in an earlier form, Parrington responded) as a measure of critics' frustration with their inability to find their social and moral values embodied anywhere in the real American world. That is, it is an extension of the desire for a better social order rather than simply an elitist withdrawal from the world.

29. *American Renaissance: Arts and Expression in the Age of Emerson and Whitman* (New York: Oxford University Press, 1941). On Matthiessen's life and career, see Richard Ruland, *The Rediscovery of American Literature* (Cambridge: Harvard University Press), pp. 216ff.; Giles Gunn, *F. O. Matthiessen: The Critical Achievement* (Seattle: University of Washington Press, 1975). For more recent and critical views, see Jonathan Arac, *Critical Genealogies: Historical Situations for Postmodern Literary Studies* (New York: Columbia University Press, 1987), pp. 157–75; Donald Pease, *Visionary Compacts: American Renaissance Writings in Cultural Context* (Madison: University of Wisconsin Press, 1987), pp. 248–70, and "F. O. Matthiessen," in *Modern American Critics,* vol. 1, ed. Gregory S. Jay (Detroit: Gale Research Co., 1988), pp. 138–49; William E. Cain, in two essays, "F. O. Matthiessen's Labor of Translation: From Sarah Orne Jewett to T. S. Eliot," *South Atlantic Quarterly* 87, 2 (1988): 355–84, and "Criticism and Politics: F. O. Matthiessen and the Making of Henry James," *New England Quarterly* 60 (June 1987): 163–86; and Vanderbilt, *American Literature and the Academy,* pp. 469–81. For a critique of the accounts by Arac and Pease, see Frederick Crews, "Whose American Renaissance?" *New York Review of Books,* 27 October 1988, pp. 68–81.

30. The vagueness of "the possibilities of democracy" makes it the place-

holder for varied resonant terms. Most significantly, it gives him a single umbrella to cover both the individual and society at large, artist and audience. In the course of Matthiessen's long discussion, he elides "democracy" with the "common people," with "nationalism," with "the human race," and even with "life" itself.

31. When critics complain about Matthiessen's formalist isolation from life in such quotations as this, they may be tying him more tightly than they should to the spiritual vocabulary from which he was, admittedly, still emerging. Efforts like this one (and like Emerson's or Thoreau's) toward connecting the "simpliest" and the "universal" might justly be seen as tentative gestures toward Wittgenstein's focus on the "common" as a route to the truth about human experience.

32. Lawrence Buell, *Literary Transcendentalism: Style and Vision in the American Renaissance* (Ithaca: Cornell University Press, 1973). Subsequent page citations to this work in the text appear in parentheses. I do not mean to diminish Buell's considerable achievement in this work, but one of the startling facts of Transcendentalist scholarship is that so central a field has generated so few general studies. Buell's is surely the best since Goddard, and it is, by any standard, an outstanding piece of scholarship. Still, the works that have been published on the subject could be held, much less counted, with the fingers of one hand.

33. See Clarence Gohdes, *The Periodicals of American Transcendentalism* (Durham: Duke University Press, 1931), pp. 3–10. Gohdes uses all the same strategies Buell uses, just as Goddard did before them. Such accounts of the difficulties involved in Transcendentalist studies amount to a ritual among the initiated, an incantation to exorcise impossible questions. One of the most troubling features of Transcendentalist scholarship is that despite all the changes in scholarly practice over the past century and a half, the description of the "object" has been carved in stone. As companions to recurrent protestations about the evasive definition of the subject, criticism features recurrent confident descriptions of it. The historical sketch Lawrence Buell offers (see below) can also be found in Frothingham, Goddard, Parrington, and literally hundreds of other works. Alexander Kern (*Transitions in American Literary History,* ed. H. H. Clark [Durham: Duke University Press, 1955], p. 292) explains the varied types of Transcendentalism with the same generalized motives that J. F. Clarke used in 1838; see Perry Miller, *The Transcendentalists* (Cambridge: Harvard University Press, 1950), p. 44. These motives obviously apply to many of the non-Transcendentalists as well. But that does not prevent them from being reiterated in contemporary work. Moreover, the features of Transcendentalism are treated as simple fact in numberless accounts of American writing that lean on it. They are preserved because the field needs them. One might say that one function of scholarly "authority" within academic society is to turn strategic interpretations into acknowledged fact.

34. For an account of the transformations in the word *Reason* from Neoplato-
nism to Romanticism and from Europe to America as it was adapted to different
uses, see Carafiol, *Transcendent Reason,* pp. 34–84. Thomas McFarland,
Coleridge and the Pantheist Tradition (London: Oxford University Press, 1969),
offers a brilliant description of the combat between materialist and spiritual
philosophies that the notion of "Reason" was designed to resolve.

35. Referring to the countless papers debating whether one figure or another
deserves to be called a Transcendentalist, Wright ruefully observes that "if many
more such articles are written, there will be no Transcendentalists left." *The
Beginnings of Unitarianism in America* (Boston: Starr King Press, 1955), pp. 34–
35.

Part 3

1. Even Emerson's modern editors seem uncertain about how to evaluate him.
They praise his earlier writing on the ground of its "absolute literary merit" but
seem uncomfortable with the "excesses" of its "irrational eloquence." They
apparently prefer the "dispassionate depth and balance" of the later work. For an
interesting summary of the responses Emerson's essays evoked in his nineteenth-
century readers, see Ralph Waldo Emerson, *The Collected Works of Ralph Waldo
Emerson,* ed. Alfred Ferguson et al. (Cambridge: Harvard University Press,
1971–), 2: xxxiv–xxxv.

2. See "Reading Emerson for the Structures: The Coherence of the Essays,"
Quarterly Journal of Speech 58 (1972): 58–69.

3. Julie Ellison, *Emerson's Romantic Style* (Princeton: Princeton University
Press, 1984), p. 2. Subsequent page citations to this work in the text appear in
parentheses.

4. Ibid., p. 3.

5. As another example, what Ellison calls "Emerson's theory of intertex-
tuality" is really his notion that great books have a significance that has nothing to
do with the individual author. Surely this is misleading translation.

6. The imposition of power that Ellison discovers is still more insidious for the
fact that it is secret power. "Power," she says, "keeps quite another road than the
turnpikes of choice and will; namely the subterranean and invisible tunnels and
channels of life." This is the somewhat excessive but popular rhetoric of power
and conspiracy that fits so well with the traditional talk about Transcendentalist
writing, evident in Buell, that stresses the obscurity of the principle of coherence
in Emerson's prose. That obscurity justifies the expert critic's work, just as New
Criticism appealed to the critic of taste and sensibility. As an example of the way
Ellison's theory inclines her to impose on Emerson, consider the following:
"Emerson never abandons the position that the rule of thought is 'to reduce the
most diverse to one form'—*to one's own form*" (p. 95; my emphasis). Without
warrant or discussion, Ellison turns a remark about the organizing power of

thought into an assertion of the power of the self to transform the world into its own image.

7. Admirable as the work of these critics is, and influential as it has been on my own, I believe all three overemphasize the doctrinal character of Emerson's writing. In the very act of redeeming Emerson as a really important thinker, they produce a portrait of his thought rather than explain how he is "man thinking." For example, I strongly share Pease's sense of Emerson's conservatism as a corrective to the revolutionary ethos that American Literary Scholarship has kept discovering in American writers to its own repeated surprise. I also concur in his dissatisfaction with a critical tradition that thematizes Romantic models of the self as literary forms and political values. It should, however, be clear from what I say elsewhere in this book that I don't share Pease's sense that Emerson was speaking for a rebirth of particularly American values. Emerson wants to establish a sort of compact, but the ones he favors do not seem to me peculiarly American, or even designed to encompass the whole of a society. They are efforts to establish relationships between people and the things (or people) that are obviously important to those people. The desire to establish such relationships is exactly what I am focusing on here, and it includes the desire to establish them in narrative and not just between selves but with one's self. I would argue that it's the very effort to bring "America" into this equation that has brought so much trouble for criticism, even as the rhetoric of "America" has been one of the most important examples of the difficulties of the problem of uniting particulars into a whole.

8. Emerson's innovative prose follows Coleridge and prefigures writers like Nietzsche, William James, Dewey, Heidegger, Wittgenstein, and Derrida, who were led to abandon traditional discourse by their attempts to adapt it to modern circumstances. Of Emerson, Nietzsche wrote, "Never have I felt so much at home in a book, and in *my* home, as—I may not praise it, it is too close to me." For a discussion of Emerson and Nietzsche, see Friedric Nietzsche, *The Gay Science,* trans., with commentary, Walter Kaufmann (New York: Random House, 1974). On the other hand, countless scholars have either lamented the lack of system in Emerson's thought or struggled to find a system there, and so, as I would argue, miss the point. As two of many possible examples, see Henry Pochmann, *New England Transcendentalism and St. Louis Hegelianism: Phases in the History of American Idealism* (Philadelphia; Carl Shurz Memorial Foundation, 1948), p. 58, and a more recent work by David Van Leer, *Emerson's Epistemology: The Argument of the Essays* (New York: Cambridge University Press, 1986). Van Leer's dense and interesting work makes points parallel in many ways to those I offer here. But he insists on the "systematic" in Emerson's thought in ways that constrain his readings of the essays, as for example, his reading of "The Transcendentalist," pp. 3, 5, 55–56, where he joins the long line criticizing Emerson for his inexact appropriation of Kant.

9. Emerson, *Works,* 1: 201. Subsequent page citations to the collected works

in the text appear in parentheses. Van Leer calls this a "direct statement of purpose." I do not want to belie my admiration for the scholarly rigor of Van Leer's work, but his treatment of the first paragraph of this essay represents the limitations of his systematic approach. It leads him, as it has many other intelligent critics, to overlook the complexities of Emerson's writing that are its difficulty and its interest, reducing Emerson to something clear-cut and installing him comfortably in a tradition. "His concerns," Van Leer writes, "can be . . . translated into . . . the terminology of traditional epistemology" (*Emerson's Epistemology*, p. 15).

10. Lawrence Buell, *Literary Transcendentalism: Style and Vision in the American Renaissance* (Ithaca: Cornell University Press, 1973), p. 15. As Part II shows, Transcendentalist critics have been trying to balance these and related terms for 100 years with no equilibrium in sight. But this failure should not be surprising. Making sense of such oppositions was the very stuff of Romantic writing. They are precisely the oppositions Emerson's writing breaks down. For criticism to resurrect them so uncritically as a methodological framework for explaining that writing is, at best, self-defeating. For an interesting application of this notion to English Romanticism, see Jerome J. McGann, *The Romantic Ideology* (Chicago: University of Chicago Press, 1983), pp. 3, 40–49.

11. In her interesting work on Thoreau's journals, Sharon Cameron astutely analyzes the way the meanings of passages are changed when they are excerpted from their context. *Writing Nature: Henry Thoreau's Journal* (New York: Oxford University Press, 1985), p. 9.

12. Emerson's aim here is similar to the one Richard Rorty ascribes to Heidegger in "Overcoming the Tradition: Heidegger and Dewey," *Consequences of Pragmatism: Essays, 1972–1980* (Minneapolis: University of Minnesota Press, 1982), p. 39. Emerson is not trying to provide a true description of persisting reality in order to correct false old descriptions; he is just trying to say something that makes sense in its own linguistic and historical context.

13. Hayden White implies a similar movement when he eschews the word *dialectic* as suggesting a transcendent subject above contending interpretations. He offers *discourse* instead to refer to a back-and-forth movement, "the actions of consciousness trying to come to terms with the unfamiliar." *Tropics of Discourse: Essays in Cultural Criticism* (Baltimore: Johns Hopkins University Press, 1978), p. 5.

14. See Meyer Abrams, *The Mirror and the Lamp* (New York: Oxford University Press, 1953), pp. 67–69, and for the sources of this figure in Locke, see Ernest L. Tuveson, *The Imagination as a Means of Grace* (Berkeley: University of California Press, 1960), pp. 133–63.

15. Here, Emerson gestures toward the purity of the ideal, resurrecting in altered form his original opposition between contingent and therefore knowable facts and an ideal but inaccessible "Fact"—"that Fact which cannot be spoken,

or defined, nor even thought'' (1:204). As contingency invades even the mind, he removes the ideal to a safe haven in an ''Unknown Center'' of the self, leaving the rest—world and all—behind in consciousness, where it is accessible but once again cut off from its ideal foundations (1:203), which are now still more remote, outside the mind, and beyond all knowing. What began as a split between mind and world becomes a division within the mind itself. With this step, Emerson clearly gives up as much as he gains, and he immediately moves on to an alternate position. Yet the qualities that criticism has generally viewed as the pervasive message of Emerson's writing—its mysticism, its cosmic optimism—are associated with such momentary and ineffectual strategies, and thus reflect only one side of Emerson's ongoing inquiry.

16. Emerson's language here marks the story of the inquirer as an extrapolation from the story of the ideal coherence that he seeks to know. Like all of Emerson's formulations, this is not so much a statement of belief as a statement in transition. It is a stage in the movement between two traditional views of an autonomous self that Emerson can neither mediate nor resolve: one as foundational consciousness shaping the universe, and the other as itself founded on some transcendent fact that cannot be spoken, known, or thought. These alternating notions of the self are Siamese twins, mirror images, analogous to what Coleridge calls a ''Polar Unity,'' distinct but not divided, with the essay moving back and forth between them, unable to rest with either extreme.

Owen Barfield describes Coleridge's concept of polarity in terms that are suggestive for the long history of scholarly dissatisfaction with Emerson's prose. They also reveal its association with notions about linguistic meaning developed further by Wittgenstein and others. ''Polar contraries,'' Barfield writes, ''exist by virtue of each other *as well as* at each other's expense. For that very reason the concept of polarity cannot be subsumed under the logical principle of identity; in fact, it is not really a logical concept at all, but one which requires a leap of imagination to grasp it. . . . Unlike the logical principles of identity and contradiction, it is not only a form of thought, but also a form of life.'' *Speaker's Meaning* (Middletown, Conn.: Wesleyan University Press, 1967), pp. 38–39.

17. Robert Frost, ''The Figure a Poem Makes,'' in *Complete Poems of Robert Frost* (New York: Holt, Rinehart & Winston, 1949), p. vi.

18. Ferdinand de Saussure, *Course in General Linguistics,* ed. Charles Bally and Albert Sechehaye, in collaboration with Albert Riedlinger; trans. Wade Baskin (New York: McGraw-Hill, 1966), p. 120. Earlier Saussure says, ''When [words] are said to correspond to concepts, it is understood that the concepts are purely differential and defined not by their positive content but negatively by their relations with other terms of the system. Their most precise characteristic is in being what the others are not.'' This formulation is particularly resonant as a gloss on Emerson's prose.

19. For the cultural background of this linguistic turn, see Philip Gura, *The*

Wisdom of Words (Middletown, Conn.: Wesleyan University Press, 1981). Gura's notion is that a more complex age required a more complex form of expression and that the writers of the New England Renaissance succeeded in producing it. I would argue that the writers of the earlier nineteenth century did not establish linguistic meaning on new ground but that they began to confront the consequences of a loss of all foundations.

20. Emerson, *Works*, 2: 3.

21. Emerson, *Works*, 2: 113.

22. Emerson, *Works*, 2: 14.

23. Paul K. Feyerabend, *Against Method: Outline of an Anarchistic Theory of Knowledge* (London: NLB, 1975), pp. 24, 84.

24. Ibid., p. 27.

25. Cornelius Castoriadis says, *"Tout langage est abus de language,"* a view that could describe the constant transformations of Emerson's prose, if that constant and inevitable change did not sap the word *abus* of its force. *Institute Imaginaire de la Societe* (Paris: Seuil, 1975), p. 469, published in the United States as *The Imaginary Institution of Society,* trans. Kathleen Blamey (Cambridge: MIT Press, 1987).

26. Letter to Henry Ware, Jr., 8 October 1838. Quoted in Stephen E. Whicher, ed., *Selections from Ralph Waldo Emerson* (Boston: Riverside, 1957), pp. 116–17.

27. Ezra Pound, *The Cantos* (New York: New Directions, 1956), Canto 59, p. 70.

28. This has been the moral imperative behind calls for revision, even when the particular answers that have been offered remain in practice within the tradition they reject theoretically. Dewey enforces the importance of this moral consideration in intellectual work even as he reminds us of the difficulty of understanding our historical situation with a sufficient complexity.

> Until we know the conditions which have helped form the characters we approve and disapprove, our efforts to create the one and do away with the other will be blind and halting. . . . To content ourselves with pronouncing judgments of merit and demerit without reference to the fact that our judgments are themselves facts which have consequences and that their value depends upon *their* consequences, is . . . to indulge ourselves in pleasurable passion. (John Dewey, *Human Nature and Conduct: An Introduction to Social Psychology* [New York: Holt, 1922], p. 19)

29. Van Leer, *Emerson's Epistemology,* p. 22. See Jacques Derrida, "White Mythology: Metaphor in the Text of Philosophy," trans. F. C. Moore, *New Literary History* (1974), 6, pp. 5–74, on the displacement of philosophical discourse by metaphor. Apart from demands for conformity to standards of intellectual coherence or aesthetic form, Emerson's famous "transparent eyeball" metaphor looks like a straightforward, even brilliant, effort to describe consciousness without recourse to a model of identity that denies the historicity of

the self. However bizarre the images it may have evoked for Christopher Cranch, in the context of subsequent efforts in the same direction, it looks more than respectable. Consider Wittgenstein in the *Tractatus:* "The subject does not belong to the world: rather, it is a limit of the world. Where *in* the world is a metaphysical subject to be found? You will say that this is exactly like the case of the eye and the visual field. But really you do *not* see the eye. And nothing *in the visual field* allows you to infer that it is seen by an eye." Quoted in Saul Kripke, *Wittgenstein on Rules and Private Language* (Cambridge: Harvard University Press, 1982), p. 122.

30. Lee Patterson argues that this common definition of the "modern" ignores much earlier manifestations of the same impulse. But he also finds it particularly characteristic of modern criticism, linking such divergent critical types as Meyer Abrams and Harold Bloom. See *Negotiating the Past: The Historical Understanding of Medieval Literature* (Madison: University of Wisconsin Press, 1987), p. 32.

31. Stanley Cavell, *Must We Mean What We Say?* (Cambridge: Cambridge University Press, 1976), p. xix.

32. Nineteenth-century literary history assumed, as Jauss says, that "national identity" was an "invisible part of every fact," thus providing coherence to a sequence of literary works. "To the extent that this conviction disappeared," he continues, "the thread connecting events had to disappear as well, past and present literature fall apart into separate spheres of judgment." American Literary Scholarship held on tight for a long time largely because of its need to establish itself in the profession, but it too is finally giving way. Hans Robert Jauss, *Toward an Aesthetic of Reception,* trans. Timothy Bahti (Minneapolis: University of Minnesota Press, 1982), p. 8.

33. Dominick LaCapra, *History and Criticism* (Ithaca: Cornell University Press, 1985), p. 72. "Transference implies that the considerations at issue in the object of study are always repeated with variations—or find their displaced analogues—in one's account of it, and transference is as much denied by an assertion of the total difference of the past as by its total identification with one's own 'self' or 'culture.'"

34. Worried over a growing gap between literature and the popular culture, eighteenth-century analogs of contemporary revisionists sought criteria for assessing texts that would bridge the gap, including the "standard" of popularity (Peter Uwe Hohendal, *The Institution of Criticism* [Ithaca: Cornell University Press, 1982], p. 156). In the nineteenth century, American scholars marshaled terms very like E. D. Hirsch's or Alan Bloom's as they tussled at Harvard, Yale, Penn, and Virginia over early avatars of the elective system following the Yale Report of 1827. One hundred years later, American scholars raised these issues again, in what Richard Hofstadter calls "a major difference of opinion over the kind of mind and personality that higher education was expected to produce," a difference between seeing knowledge as "mere utility" or as "somehow a part of

the innermost character of man," that is, as a privileged inner experience or as merely phenomenal or "objective." Hofstadter attributes this debate in part to the "moral crisis" brought on by the depression (Hofstadter, *The Progressive Historians* [New York: Knopf, 1969], p. 54). And now, decades later, as universities increasingly buy-in to the bottom-line mentality of corporate culture, and we work our way out of the apoliticism that marked the postwar decade, scholars reiterate this debate yet again, reenacting their own professional history. Apparently unaware of the familiarity of their arguments, their *replication* of the past, they preserve the illusion that they are enacting the true mission of scholarship by doing something *new* and thus making progress in the quest for knowledge.

35. Henry David Thoreau, *A Week on the Concord and Merrimack Rivers*, ed. Carl F. Hovde et al. (Princeton: Princeton University Press, 1980). Subsequent page citations to this work in the text appear in parentheses.

36. To portray Thoreau as an "artist" in more conventionally respectable terms, Linck C. Johnson describes different focuses of the book (on the city, on pastoral, on the wild) as "layers" of meaning, that is, as synchronous meanings held in a consistent aesthetic vision. By doing so, however, he overlooks both the internal debate in the book and its status as a temporal act. This omission is particularly striking in a work devoted to studying the "process" of composition. Johnson must assume that such a process leads to or toward a perfect form that, when reached, stops the process and steps outside time, as Thoreau explicitly refuses to do in his narrative. This view of the artistic "process" becomes particularly overt when Johnson compares the "flawed" work of *A Week* to the presumably perfected masterpiece of *Walden*. *Walden: Thoreau's Complex Weave* (Charlottesville: University of Virginia Press, 1986), p. 4.

Stanley Cavell has taken the most essential step toward an alternative reading by insisting in such sophisticated and persuasive terms on taking Thoreau's writing seriously, by asserting that he means what he says, in the most rigorous and demanding way. *Walden,* Cavell says, "is perfectly complete . . . it means in every word it says" (*Senses of Walden: An Expanded Edition* [San Francisco: North Point Press, 1981], p. 4). In my most ambitious moments, I see this essay as both an extension of Cavell's work on Thoreau and Emerson and a preparation for it. It is an extension because Cavell has said better so many of the things I have thought and wanted to say here, and by doing so has spurred me onward to think still harder about the implications of this writing. And it is a preparation because *A Week* is a preparation, Thoreau's and his readers', for *Walden.* Not that *Walden* deserves priority as a greater book, but since the journey in *A Week* was largely written there, its composition is the background, the "country in the rear," of that book. It is what Thoreau was doing at Walden, and its writing carried Thoreau to the place where he could write *Walden.* Cavell's work has made it easier to say that *A Week* is more about Thoreau's writing, and about the largest implications of writing, than about a river journey, that it is designed to teach the student willing to undergo the necessary probation how to read it.

Thoreau uses familiar terms in ways that alter their significance, upsetting conventional understandings without endorsing a particular new one. Like any experiment, Thoreau's writing feels its way along, learning from its own progress as it discovers the limitations of the strategies it tests. As Sharon Cameron says, it "can find no model . . . because he is constructing a model." *Writing Nature,* p. 47.

37. In her recent book, *Thoreau's Alternative History* (Philadelphia: University of Pennsylvania Press, 1987), Joan Burbick offers a discussion of *A Week* that is admirable for its rhetorical emphasis and its focus on the transforming power of Thoreau's descriptions. For Burbick, however, to be "uncivil" is to oppose civilization represented by commercial culture. Like Poirier on Emerson, she paints Thoreau in the rebellious American tradition, and like Sharon Cameron, she champions the "natural" in a way that seems an overreaction against attempts to squeeze Thoreau into a formalist aesthetic. Like a number of earlier scholars, Burbick finds the coherence of Thoreau's work in his alleged appropriation of a cyclical model of history rather than in coherent narrative relations.

38. The most suggestive discussion of Thoreau in relation to the traditional epistemological model of knowledge is Cavell, pp. 106–07. See also Stanley Bates "Self and World in *Walden,*" and Stanley J. Scoot, "Neighboring Reality: Stanley Cavell and the Experience of *Walden,* both in *Thoreau Quarterly* 14, 3 and 4 (Summer and Fall 1982): 124–32 and 141–50. For the relationship between travel narrative and a Romantic poetics in fiction, see Spengemann, *The Adventurous Muse* (New Haven: Yale University Press, 1976).

39. Eric Sundquist claims in " 'Plowing Homeward': Cultivation and Grafting in Thoreau and the *Week,*" in *Henry David Thoreau,* ed. Harold Bloom (New York: Chelsea House, 1987), p. 103, that "writing . . . is figured as a violent scarring of the land, and . . . made to form a . . . despoiling force that perpetuates itself by adding continually to the profane load of both thought and commodities with which a presumably once virgin land is encumbered." Sundquist seems to assume that he is siding with Thoreau in what Sundquist takes to be Thoreau's conflict between pristine nature and despoiling civilization. Actually, Sundquist clings to an opposition that Thoreau's narrative dispenses with.

40. Thus, this early part of the narrative fits neatly into standard interpretations of American protagonists striking out into the territory, but as James Cox pointed out in regard to the civilized world Twain (and Thoreau) occupied, the "territory" was more an imagined place than a real one. See James Cox, *Mark Twain: The Fate of Humor* (Princeton: Princeton University Press, 1966). As I suggest below, Thoreau's travels demonstrate not only that civilization is inescapable

but, more important, that he (and we) would not *want* to escape it if we could.

41. This, as I argue in Part 1, is precisely the lesson that many politically motivated New Historicists have not learned.

42. Richard Rorty makes the parallel point that as long as we think of language as a medium between "the self and the nonhuman reality with which the self seeks to be in touch," we will end up in "seesaw battles between romanticism and moralism, between idealism and realism." *Contingency, Irony, and Solidarity* (New York: Cambridge University Press, 1989), p. 11.

43. Yet, material circumstances, the lapse of history, inspire a punning longing for books that unite particulars into a timeless order, revealing "not the *annals* of the country, but the natural facts, or *perennials,* which are ever without date" (p. 231). Like the other-worldly observatory on Saddleback, books are a "platform" from which "life seems as still and serene as if it were very far off." Literature is *"the flower of the mind"* where "we can converse . . . without reserve or personality" because our counterpart is "bodiless." This spirit triumphs only by denying the flesh, and as long as he juggles these familiar oppositions, Thoreau is not the physician he calls for.

44. For a discussion of similar issues in both English Romanticism and contemporary theory, see Jonathan Arac, *Critical Genealogies: Historical Situations for Postmodern Literary Studies* (New York: Columbia University Press, 1987), pp. 53–55.

45. See Richard Bridgeman, *The Dark Thoreau* (Lincoln: University of Nebraska Press, 1982), pp. 27–74. I disagree with John Carlos Rowe's assertion, typical of treatments of this issue, that "the importance of John's [Thoreau's brother's] death as a controlling concern cannot be overemphasized." I think it has almost always been overemphasized. But, on the other hand, Rowe's reading of the essay on friendship, especially as it relates to Thoreau's poetics as a project in time rather than an escape from it seems to strike the right note. John Carlos Rowe, "The Being of Language: The Language of Being," in Bloom, *Henry David Thoreau,* pp. 168–70. Jonathan Bishop has observed that Thoreau's brother "disappears into the 'we' who together constitute the anonymous sensibility of the narrator," in "The Experience of the Sacred in Thoreau's *Week,*" *ELH* 33 (1966): 89–90. See also Steven Fink, "Variations on the Self: Thoreau's Personae in *A Week on the Concord and Merrimack Rivers,*" *ESQ* 28 (1982): 24–35.

46. Feyerabend, *Against Method,* pp. 89ff.

47. Richard Rorty, *Philosophy and the Mirror of Nature* (Princeton: Princeton University Press, 1979), p. 319. Thoreau makes this process still more imposing with one of his most problematical metaphors, calling into question the very possibility of understanding and of being understood. "The front aspect of great thoughts," he says, "can only be enjoyed by those who stand on the side whence they arrive."

48. Quoted in Wendell Glick, ed., *The Recognition of Henry David Thoreau: Selected Criticism Since 1848* (Ann Arbor: University of Michigan Press, 1969), p. 350.

49. For an interesting discussion of the role of performatives in reading Faulkner (another writer whose style has been a source of critical discomfort), see Warwick Wadlington, *Reading Faulknerian Tragedy* (Ithaca: Cornell University Press, 1987), pp. 13–49. Wadlington describes the reader's responsibility for what he calls a "consummation by performance." Wadlington's model applies reasonably well to the reading of Thoreau's text as well, with the added necessity of overcoming, through a "long probation," the conventions of reading that Thoreau's text both invites and undermines. See also Dominick LaCapra, *Rethinking Intellectual History* (Ithaca: Cornell University Press, 1983), p. 62.

50. In this section, Thoreau is disrupting the sort of methodical narrative that would allow us to draw simple equivalencies between parts of his narrative experience. In this sense, like Emerson, he does not offer accounts that can be reduced to their gist. Thoreau's writing denies the ideal of commensurable discourses that is so central to scholarly study. See Hans-Georg Gadamer, *Truth and Method* (New York: Seabury Press, 1975), p. ix.

51. This observation suggests the importance of projects like that of feminist criticism, which recover parts of the past that have been "lost" and so change the nature of the present.

52. The word *epistemology* has become a separate battleground among theorists. Some like Richard Rorty, insist that it be or has been abandoned, and others, like Paul Armstrong say that it has only been revised or redefined. As I shall suggest in the next section, to put the debate in these terms catches it up in the very problems an abandonment of epistemology is supposed to address. If we change the way we describe what we are doing, have we merely redefined the same thing or changed to something else altogether? Armstrong's desire to hold onto the word *epistemology* seems to be based on an interest (which I share) in being able to adjudicate critical claims. But I think that can be done in terms consistent with Rorty's position. What I call the abandonment of epistemology, Armstrong might call the revision of post-Cartesian empiricism. The distinction matters little. What matters is the claims we make for our accounts and the kind of accounts our claims incline us to produce.

Part 4

1. Even some of the most recent theoretically informed revisionist scholarship in American literature leaves traditional assumptions about the integrity of the field unquestioned. See Donald E. Pease, ed., *The New Americanists: Revisionist Interventions into the Canon*, a special issue of *boundary 2* 17, 1 (Spring 1990).

2. See Dominick LaCapra, *Rethinking Intellectual History* (Ithaca: Cornell University Press, 1983), pp. 63–65. On the difficulties of formulating contexts, see Steven Mailloux, "Convention and Context," *New Literary History* 14, 2 (Spring 1983).

3. Dominick LaCapra, *History and Criticism* (Ithaca: Cornell University Press, 1985). p. 126.

4. Edward Pechter, "The New Historicism and Its Discontents: Politicizing Renaissance Drama," *PMLA* 102, 3 (1987): 292. See Stephen Greenblatt, *Renaissance Self-Fashioning: From More to Shakespeare* (Chicago: University of Chicago Press, 1980); Richard Helgerson, *Self-Crowned Laureates: Spenser, Jonson, Milton, and the Literary System* (Berkeley: University of California Press, 1983); Louis Montrose, " 'Shaping Fantasies': Figurations of Gender and Power in Elizabethan Culture," *Representations* 1 (1983); Jerome McGann, *The Romantic Ideology: A Critical Investigation* (Chicago: University of Chicago Press, 1983); Marjorie Levinson, "Wordsworth's Intimations Ode: A Timely Utterance," in *Historical Studies and Literary Criticism,* ed. Jerome McGann (Madison: University of Wisconsin Press, 1985); John Turner, *Wordsworth: Play and Politics: A Study of Wordsworth's Poetry, 1787–1800* (New York: St. Martin's Press, 1986).

5. Richard Rorty, *Philosophy and the Mirror of Nature,* (Princeton: Princeton University Press, 1979), p. 58.

6. For a sensible discussion of the motives behind the New Criticism and the distinctions between its practice and its polemic, see LaCapra, *Rethinking,* pp. 14–15.

7. Matthiessen has been the favorite target of critics who would enforce this rigid distinction as a feature of American literary scholarship. Tompkins's claim that her work and F. O. Matthiessen's represent "competing attempts to constitute American literature" (*Sensational Designs: The Cultural Work of American Fiction, 1790–1860* [New York: Oxford University Press, 1985], p. 200) puts her in heady company, but her insistence on their differences obscures their fundamental kinship. If one looks more deeply into Matthiessen's work than the "universal truths" against which Tompkins protests, his views of the relationship between literature and culture appear more complex, and more like her own, than Tompkins admits. On one hand, as Tompkins alleges, he values works as "great art" when they explore the full range of human experience that he considers "eternal and universal," but on the other hand, works of art have value because they do social and/or political work that he thinks is desirable for the culture. When Matthiessen proposes to examine "a literature for our democracy," he is insisting that literature and criticism must be measured by a populist political standard. "Are you," he asks through Louis Sullivan, "using such gifts as you possess for or against the people?" And, like Tompkins, he is imagining the debate over the interpretation of American writing as a "struggle among contending factions for the right to be represented in the picture America

draws of itself.'' To slight Matthiessen's political motives oversimplifies his work and obscures the elements that made that work influential.

Cain's more balanced view of Matthiessen's formalist bias does greater justice to his political convictions. But the fact that the apparent discrepancy between Matthiessen's politics and his criticism so persistently troubles Matthiessen's readers seems to me an example of our continuing uncertainty about the connections between texts and life, as well as an example of Matthiessen's unsuccessful attempt to make that connection. This treatment of Matthiessen raises in the context of our reading of the critical tradition the issues I bring up below regarding our scholarly impulse to master literary works. Do scholars like Matthiessen, arguably great scholars, have to conform to our scholarly ideals, or could they be offering ways of questioning them?

8. The idea of cultural context replies to our vestigial need for mimesis, our desire to believe that our understandings are understandings *of* something. But in their polemical intensity, revisionists too often overlook the daunting task of accounting for their ability to constitute and read a particular cultural con-''text'' and rely instead on a hypostatization of culture that begs all the questions that trouble historical understanding. Cain says of Lentriccia, but I say of ideological historicists in general, that their position ''is founded less on logic and reasonable exposition than on a desire for a certain, preferred state of affairs.'' William Cain, *The Crisis in Criticism: Theory, Literature, and Reform in English Studies* (Baltimore: Johns Hopkins University Press, 1984), p. 244.

9. LaCapra, *History*, p. 46.

10. I use this traditional term to balance the traditionalist reference of *New Historicism*. Ideally, the term *textualism* might replace both.

11. This same point could, of course, be made about American Literary Scholarship itself. I would argue that its roots do not go so deep in our language as those that anchor some version of formalism. Giving up foundations means giving up certain *elements* of formalism, particularly its claims to universality, but it means giving up the American Ideal entirely.

12. Steven Mailloux, ''Rhetorical Hermeneutics,'' *Critical Inquiry* (June 1985): 632–37.

13. Richard Rorty, *Consequences of Pragmatism: Essays, 1972–1980* (Minneapolis: University of Minnesota Press, 1982), p. xx.

14. On the contrary, the traditional dualism leads to conceptual relativity, making the truth relative to the scheme that supplies it. Without that dualism, relativity goes by the boards. Truth remains relative to language, but that's as objective as can be. See the discussion of Donald Davidson's work in Rorty, *Philosophy*, p. 310.

15. Nor is this emphasis on a re-viewed formalism necessarily apolitical in its implications for either teaching or scholarship. While it is obvious that language can be mobilized for domination, that does not mean such language must be effective, and it may be argued that the attention to textual details that is being

condemned along with formalism can be just as effective in disarming such language as a criticism that makes disguised hegemonic motives explicit.

16. On the history of this debate, see Rorty, *Philosophy*, p. 173. Jameson asserts:

> In the declining years of the model's history, a proportionately greater amount of time has to be spent in readjusting the model itself, in bringing it back into line with its object of study. Now research tends to become theoretical rather than practical, and to turn back upon its own presuppositions (the structure of the model itself), finding itself vexed by the false problems and dilemmas into which the inadequacy of the model seems increasingly to lead it. One thinks, for example, of the ether or of collective consciousness. (Frederic Jameson, *The Prison House of Language: A Critical Account of Structuralism and Russian Formalism* [Princeton: Princeton University Press, 1972], p. v)

17. For valuable reinterpretations of these debates, see Steven Mailloux, *Rhetorical Power* (Ithaca: Cornell University Press, 1989), pp. 19–53, and Paul Armstrong, *Conflicting Readings* (Chapel Hill: University of North Carolina Press, 1990), pp. 1–19.

18. Much of the difficulty that criticism has had figuring out how meaning is constituted depends on what I take to be a confusion, preserved from Lockean epistemology, between seeing and understanding. As N. R. Hansen argues, following Wittgenstein (and, as in Part 3, Thoreau), the point about human observation is not the mere recording of physical impressions on the retina, which then must be "constituted" by some process that depends, in turn, on assumptions and conditions. "The paradigm observer is not the man who sees and reports what all normal observers see and report, but the man who sees in familiar objects what no one else has seen before." Quoted in *Modernism, Criticism, Realism*, ed. Charles Harrison and Fred Orton (New York: Harper & Row, 1984), p. 83. See also pp. 77–78, and Barry Barnes, *Interests and the Growth of Knowledge* (London: Routledge & Kegan Paul, 1977), p. 10.

19. Needless to say, Goddard was not alone in this sentiment. Bliss Perry virtually abandoned the effort to discover the intellectual coherence of American literature and culture and turned to "sentiment" as an alternative, though without much greater success. "One feels," he said, "somehow that the net is not holding." Quoted in Gerald Graff, *Professing Literature: An Institutional History* (Chicago: University of Chicago Press, 1987), p. 131.

20. I do not mean to claim by this (perhaps overly dramatic) talk that language is God and that we bask in its all constituting glory. I only want to suggest that we cannot get beyond language to some prior explanatory ground, that our *understanding* of the world depends on it, and that our understanding is pretty important.

21. Ludwig Wittgenstein, *Culture and Value,* ed. G. H. Von Wright in collaboration with Heikki Nyman, trans. Peter Winch (Chicago: University of Chicago Press, 1980), p. 16e.

22. Nelson Goodman, *Fact, Fiction, and Forecast* (Cambridge: Harvard University Press, 1955), p. 67.

23. For a discussion of the idea of ''going on'' as applied to literature, see Charles Altieri, ''Going On and Going Nowhere: Wittgenstein and the Question of Criteria in Literary Criticism,'' in *Philosophical Approaches to Literature,* ed. William E. Cain (Lewisburg: Bucknell University Press, 1984), pp. 202–26.

As Niels Bohr said, ''The opposite of a correct statement is a false statement. But the opposite of a profound truth may well be another profound truth.'' Quoted in Robert Heisenberg, *Physics and Philosophy: The Revolution in Modern Science* (New York: Harper, 1958), p. 102. Coming from a somewhat different direction, Nietzsche too argues that the ''validity'' of a judgment is of less importance than its use. ''The question,'' he says,

is to what extent it is life-promoting, life-preserving, species-preserving, perhaps even species-cultivating. And we are fundamentally inclined to claim that the falsest judgments . . . are the most indispensable for us; that without accepting the fictions of logic, without measuring reality against the purely invented world of the unconditional and self identical, without a constant falsification of the world by means of numbers, man could not live—that renouncing false judgments would mean renouncing life and a denial of life. (*Beyond Good and Evil,* ed. Walter Kaufmann [New York: Random House, 1966], p. 12)

On the idea of coherence as a way of measuring conditional validity, Fredric Jameson says, ''Ultimately, if the process of thought bears not so much on adequation to a real object or referent, but rather on the adjustment of the signified to the signifier . . . then the traditional notion of 'truth' itself becomes outmoded. Barthes does not hesitate to propose a replacement of it by the notion of a proof 'by internal coherence': 'if the rhetorical signified, in its unitary form, is nothing more that a construction, this construction must be coherent.''' *Prison-House,* pp. 133–34.

24. That sort of inquiry has not characterized debate about canonical revision in American literature. Despite their centrality to revisionist discourse, it is not self-evident that works like those by Douglass or Stowe (much less those by Warner, or Fern, or Tuckerman, or Sedgewick) are central either to American literature or American culture, or even that they tell us something about American culture that we cannot learn (or have not learned) from other sources. Like the belief in America itself, to date the assumption of their centrality has been what amounts to an act of faith—more a matter of assertion than of argument. Despite our ethico-political inclinations, the status of these works ought to be a matter of critical debate and depend on the ability of those who write about them to make

a case that justifies that status. For most of these texts, this case is still to be made.

It is not enough simply to say that recent moves to open up the canon have made American literary studies more inclusive and pluralistic. The desire to make American literature more capacious, pluralistic, and inclusive could be seen, after all, not only as too-long-delayed recognition for minority writers but as a sort of institutional imperialism that extends the power of the traditional perspective over an ever-widening textual territory. In that respect, gestures to expand the canon mirror the critical impulses that promoted canonical exclusivity in the first place. A more desirable pluralism would open the borders of the field altogether and suffer the contents to emigrate out into the larger textual world from which they have for so long been isolated.

25. Jameson, *Prison-House*, p. vii.

26. Walter Michaels comes close to this notion when he asserts that a particular text "shows us exactly what it would mean to think that [writing is representation of the self]." Texts work out possible forms of life. They ask "what if" and project the results with a "validity" that is limited only by the complexity and coherence of their own terms. Roland Barthes seems to be making a similar point, if somewhat reluctantly, in *Systeme de la mode* (Paris: Seuil, 1967), p. 237.

27. For Robert Nozick, *Philosophical Explanations* (Cambridge: Harvard University Press, 1981), this ability to project possibilities for life distinguishes analysis from explanation.

28. Dominick LaCapra offers an admirably balanced view. "Certain artifacts," he points out,

> are exceptional products of cultural activity, and it is ill-advised, even self-defeating, to deny their critical power or uncanny ability to play uncommon variations on commonplace themes. It would, however, be equally misleading to promote them to a detached, transcendent plane or to espouse an elitist aesthetics of genius. A careful and, in certain respects, noncanonical reading of canonical texts, open to their contestatory dimensions and alert to the problem of how to relate them to artifacts and issues excluded from established canons, is in no sense a full answer to the transferential problem in the study of culture; it is, however, a part of any acceptable answer. (History and Criticism, p. 93)

29. Rorty, *Philosophy,* p. 360.

30. George Steiner, *Martin Heidegger* (New York: Penguin, 1962), p. 11.

31. Rorty, *Philosophy,* p. 346.

32. Emerson warns, "I think we cannot safely argue. I think it needs a saint to dispute. If we set out to contend, almost St. Paul will lie, almost St. John will hate. . . . Shuffle they will & crow, crook & hide, feign to confess here, only that they may brag & conquer there; & not a thought has enriched either party."

The Journals and Miscellaneous Notebooks of Ralph Waldo Emerson, ed. William H. Gilman et al., vol. 7, ed. A. W. Plumstead and Harrison Hayford (Cambridge: Harvard University Press, 1969), p. 25.

33. What I want to suggest is that recognizing the limitations of scholarly narratives could turn scholarship in more productive directions even within conventional narrative forms. In his "Divinity School" address, Emerson urged his audience to "breathe new life through forms already existing." Although this has often been taken for a conservative gesture, it seems to me quite radical, requiring, in the case of academic literary history, a reordering of values and practices far more wide-ranging than additions to the canon or revisions in the curriculum. It would be a fundamental step in the right direction if the fact of what Stanley Cavell calls the "unspeakable" superiority of writing like Emerson's and Thoreau's to our own should really go without saying among literary critics. I mean by that not just that it is obvious, though it is, but that, without having to say it, this assumption should be an active and shaping force in our work, informing our stance toward the texts we study and toward the students with whom we study them. That it so rarely plays such a role says much, I think, about the insecurities of professional literary scholarship. Scholarly writing still cherishes positivist vestiges, though it no longer is willing to embrace overtly the assumptions that once made those forms vital. The challenge facing historical narrative is to invent what analogs it can to the risky improvisation and continuous self-reflection and re-vision that characterizes the texts we study. We need to consider what steps we can take to refute Thoreau's accusation that "we do not learn much from learned books" (100).

34. I do not believe that ideological accounts achieve the complexity and nuance required to make them adequate accounts of these exceptional texts. If that is so, the question becomes, why do them at all? Since all texts, from this ideological point of view, reflect the workings of power, there would seem to be no particular reason that canonical works are getting so much attention, especially in light of the straitened accounts of them that ideological readings tend to generate. As producers of scholarly accounts, we might wonder about the circularity of formulating contexts to let us use texts to know the context. To explain this process away as simply an inevitable turn of the hermeneutic circle is to ignore the regularity with which the original contextual formula and the final conclusions coincide, as if the textual middle-term had no substantial influence on the outcome. That being the case, one wonders, why bother with the text, which seems to be making a guest appearance merely to lend a certain vestigial authority to cultural analysis. The prominence of exceptional texts in ideological criticism looks, finally, like a bow to professional tradition and disciplinary identity. If professors of literature do not profess *literature,* what do they do? Thus, ideological critics incongruously use the legitimizing authority of exceptional literature to bolster their project.

35. "It is clear that allegiance to the new ideas will have to be brought about by means other than arguments. . . . We need the 'irrational means' in order to uphold what is nothing but a blind faith until we have found the auxiliary sciences, the facts, the arguments that turn the faith into sound 'knowledge.'" Feyerabend, *Against Method*, pp. 153–54.

36. Walter Whitman, "Song of Myself," *Leaves of Grass (1855)*, ed. Malcolm Cowley (New York: Viking, 1967), 1. 1242.

37. As Paul Feyerabend says, "We need a set of alternative assumptions or, as these assumptions will be quite general, constituting, as it were, an entire alternative world, *we need a dream-world in order to discover the features of the real world we think we inhabit* (and which may actually be just another dream-world)." *Against Method: Outline of an Anarchistic Theory of Knowledge* (London: NLB, 1975), p. 32.

38. This has not, however, been the characteristic posture of professional literary scholarship. One of the real contributions of the historicist perspective on criticism has been to remind critics of the conditionality of their interpretations. But if one of the points of historicism for art is that there is no clinching argument, that there is only a series of arguments making claims and counterclaims, then there is no reason that one interpretation *must* prevail. Arguments will persuade some and not others, and possibly even change some minds. It is not a matter of proof (see Paul Armstrong, "The Multiple Existence of a Literary Work," *Journal of Aesthetics and Art Criticism* 44 (1986): 321–30). And that fact only emphasizes the importance of continuous and detailed discussion, a critical give-and-take in which arguments are called upon to justify themselves. But in contemporary criticism, even the process of debate by which critical positions can be tested for their coherence and usefulness has been short-circuited by professional circumstances.

One alternative explanation for the common observation that one could never get consensus about critical interpretations is that they are put under so little pressure. They appear in print amidst too many others, like opposed spokespersons on television talk shows, and to the same trivializing effect. Interpretations that are offered are seldom examined closely enough to determine their adequacy. That is, they are treated as analogues of art rather than as useful examinations of a literary object, accounts that deal more or less adequately with the features of that object. A more desirable posture would be to take what other critics say seriously enough to pay close attention to it, to assess its adequacy by readily available criteria, what Kuhn calls the "good reasons" for accepting propositions, and then to engage it seriously by incorporating it by appropriation or reaction, into one's own work (Frederick Crews, *Skeptical Engagements* [New York: Oxford University Press, 1986], p. 174).

As Crews has pointed out in a different context, critical positions—interpretations of texts, critiques of American literature—are not treated as a series of propositions that need justification and testing. And William Spengemann has observed that substantial critiques are sometimes not even included in the recognized bibliographical reference guides such as *American Literary Scholarship (Mirror for Americanists: Reflections on the Idea of American Literature* (Hanover, N.H.: University Press of New England), p. 3). This phenomenon suggests that criticism may have ceased to be a productive conversation about ideas, and has become a matter simply of publishing one's self. Though politically committed critics have taken the notion of "conversation" as it is used by Richard Rorty and others to entail a certain political quietism, it can more usefully be viewed simply as an effort to describe the results of living in history. In such a world, it is true, conversants would be interested in keeping the talk flowing. But that activity is closer to what Wittgenstein means by "going on" than to the monotonous buzz of voices, or to polite (and hence trivial) cocktail-party chatter. The continuance of such conversation, in the absence of absolute standards of measuring progress, is evidence that we are "going on." It is an activity the continuance of which is synonymous with Western culture, not a standard of behavior, like good manners, we have to measure up to, but an activity, like breathing, a sign we are still alive. Such a notion does not deny the role of motives or of power in individual bits of discourse, but I think it does deny the notion of a will to power as a foundation that explains discourse, as at the root of discourse.

The loss of this conversation, and of the intellectual community that makes it possible, is a more serious blow than has been acknowledged. In effect, collective professional advancement has been purchased at the cost of the substantial activity that justified the profession in the first place. Moreover, political change, in fact, any deliberate political discussion, seems to be more effectively muffled by the immersion of individual political inquiries in a vast and trivializing sea of undifferentiated and only superficially examined discourse. No one can be heard above the din. No one has time to listen and respond.

39. Quoted in Steiner, *Heidegger,* p. 85.

Index

Ahlstrom, Sydney, 46
Altieri, Charles, "going on," 201 n
    23
American Literary Scholarship
    accepts conforming discourses,
        17
    "America" as transcendent signi-
        fier, 16
    and the American Ideal, 8
    Brooks's innovation in, 124
    as case study, 5
    central project of, 14
    conservative revision of, 13, 16–
        17
    founding motives of, 41, 150
    fragmentation of, 12, 149
    historicism in, 16–17, 25, 148, 155
    history of, 149
    and idealism, 75, 122
    as idealist historiography, 39
    incomplete revisionist history of,
        13–14
    and institutional change, 8
    institutionalization of, 55
    institutionalizes American Ideal,
        3
    key conflict in, 18
    and literary history, 150–51
    as moribund debate, 5
    and "National Character," 14
    and nationalism, 98
    and the new, 17, 21–22

New Orthodoxy in, 14
Pease's innovation in, 201
and philology, 57
as professional discourse, 41–42,
    65
radical scholarship in, 148
and realism/idealism debate, 100
as repressive discourse, 8
revisionist anti-formalism in, 16,
    27
subordinates texts to culture, 34
and textual change, 122
and theory, 10, 15
and traditional rhetoric, 4, 11, 17–
    18, 44, 147
unjustifiable claims of, 27
American Studies, model for revi-
    sionist rhetoric, 174–75 n 18
Armstrong, Paul, on espistemology,
    180 n 47, 197 n 52

Barfield, Owen, on polar unities,
    191 n 16
Bercovitch, Sacvan
    American diversity, 27
    American Ideal, 293
    conservative rhetoric, 51, 172 n
        11
    and ideology, 34, 177 n 28
    and professional prominence, 186
        n 26
    revisionist ethic of, 175 n 20

207